SMOLDERING EMBERS

SMOLDERING EMBERS

*The True Story Of A Serial Murderer
and Three Courageous Women*

By
Joy Wellman,
Lisa McVey
and
Susan Replogle

New Horizon Press   Far Hills, NJ

Wellman, Joy, McVey, Lisa, and Replogle, Susan

Smoldering Embers: The True Story of a Serial Murderer and Three Courageous Women.

Library of Congress Catalog Card Number: Pending

ISBN: 0-88282-154-7

Interior Design: Darrell Goza

New Horizon Press

Manufactured in the U.S.A.

2000 1999 1998 1997 / 5 4 3 2 1

Authors' Note

This book is based on the experiences of Joy Wellman, Lisa McVey and Susan Replogle and reflects our perceptions of the past, present and future. The personalities, events, action, and conversation portrayed within the story have been taken from our memories, extensive interviews, research, court documents, letters, personal papers, press accounts, and the memories of participants.

In an effort to safeguard the privacy of certain people, the authors have changed their names and the names of certain places and, in some cases, altered otherwise identifying characteristics. Events involving the characters happened as described. Only minor details have been changed.

Acknowledgements

Our thanks go to *The Tampa Tribune* for their extensive coverage of the Bobby Joe Long case and their permission to integrate some of the pertinent articles into our true story.

We also want to thank *The St. Petersburg Times* and *The Ocala Star Banner* for their photographs and cooperation.

Our gratitude to Corporal Lee D. Baker of the Hillsborough Sheriff's Office for his information and cooperation.

Thanks also to Lt. Larry Pinkerton of the Tampa Police Department for his long time interest in and attention to Lisa McVey. His insights, information and cooperation have enriched this story.

TABLE OF CONTENTS

Introduction

The public and the media are fickle lovers. They feed each other's momentary desires and create a voracious flame that dies quickly, but is all consuming for the short time it lasts.

In November 1984, the white heat of the media focused on a growing number of dead females in the Tampa Bay area. Photos of four of the murdered women, raped and strangled, as well as other details of their ghastly deaths engrossed readers of *The Tampa Tribune* and the newspapers across America which picked up the terrifying story.

Meanwhile, as the police searched for the killer, more and more victims were added to the list. The media speculated on what kind of maniac would perpetrate the horrors and then, when every avenue of this discussion had been pursued and produced the titillation desired, a new subject was introduced: what kind of woman made herself the target of such pursuit?

1

While the faceless killer was frantically hunted, the stories continued circulating. When he was apprehended and later brought to trial, an even larger fire was built as stories of his family, friends and childhood adventures added color and depth. Finally, the fire dwindled down.

However, even when it dies, every fire leaves glowing coals, blackened debris and ruins. The bodies, which had so quickly consumed headlines, were interred and interest in these women disappeared, turning to dust. Those for whom their stories were once fiery kindling forgot. Only the families and living victims could not extinguish their memories.

They are the smoldering embers fanned into new flames each time the killer, fighting in the courts and availing himself of every right and opportunity not accorded to his victims, battles to stay alive. It is a battle his living victims, their relatives, and friends have vowed they, not he, will win.

This is the gripping story of three women who bonded together, vowing that justice for one killer rapist, Bobby Joe Long, will finally and irrevocably be done.

Little did I know, in 1975, reaping the rewards of being the host of a popular cable television show in New York, that I would be one of those women.

Chapter 1

A Killer is Spawned

Standing next to her fiancé Dan, Susan flipped her long chestnut hair as she swayed to the beat of the music. Disco blasted from the amplifier. When the slow dance they waited for didn't materialize, Dan retreated to the edge of the room leaving Susan stepping to the beat herself. She frowned, they hadn't been getting along well lately. An old high school girlfriend grabbed Susan's hand, and they rocked together as they had at their high school dances.

"Where is John Travolta now that we need him?" Susan quipped to her partner. They both giggled as they had at fifteen.

"My boyfriend is a real nice guy, but he won't learn anything but the foxtrot," Betty Lou enjoined.

"Mine either." Susan smiled at her high school friend, and they began to move again. Susan loved the beat and the rhythm. Her body swayed as she spun around in time to the music. She threw her head about her proudly, and her hair flowed gently around her shoulders. The pulsing cadence of

the dance freed her spirit. Her skirt opened like a flower as she whirled to the melody.

Finally, Susan managed to tear herself away and go to her boyfriend. Dan wrapped his arm around her in a familiar way. "See that guy over there? He's moving to Tampa. He's a friend of Tony's." Tony was one of Dan's best friends. "We should invite him to stop in and visit us," Dan added. She looked in the direction he pointed. A tall man was smiling shyly.

Susan followed Dan through the crowded room, which felt stuffy and warm. Smoke hung in twirling wisps and made her throat constrict. Her heart was still beating rapidly from the dancing.

Dan held his hand out to the dark-haired, handsome stranger. "I'm Dan Walker and this is my girlfriend, Susan Replogle."

"I'm Bobby Joe Long," the brown-eyed man replied sheepishly.

"Tony told me you're moving to Tampa near where we live," Dan said in his relaxed way.

Bobby Joe nodded. "I need to find a new job as an X-ray technician. I've lost mine."

"Well, you be sure to call us when you get there. I'm in the medical equipment business. Maybe I'll hear of something for you."

The drive back to her apartment complex only took a few minutes. Susan touched the back of Dan's neck lovingly. His profile was almost Roman. His large nose and full lips made his face more masculine. He wasn't Adonis or arrogant like so many of the handsome men to whom she'd once been attracted. In fact, she no longer saw Dan's thinning

blond hair and pockmarked complexion. His kindly blue eyes flooded her with warmth each time he'd flash her a smile, and the gentle way he treated Andrea, her 5-year-old daughter, warmed Susan's heart.

"I'm so happy I met you. You were right about us. We should get married."

Dan kept his attention on the road. "You've always said no."

"I just needed time. I didn't want to make another mistake."

"And now you think it's a great idea."

"I've been thinking about the two years that we've been friends. You make me feel loved and comfortable."

"I have to think about it. I was so in love when we met, marriage was all I wanted. But when you wouldn't, I had to get used to the idea of just dating. Now I need time. I can't change again so fast. Look, I have an idea. Give up your apartment. You and Andrea can move in with me."

She shook her head. "I am not sure I want to do that to myself or my child. And if we don't get married, the relationship won't grow."

Dan chuckled. "That was my line, remember?"

"Oh Dan, you're just teasing me. You always said you wanted to be married. All those sweet words about your love being enough for both of us. Now I know I love you that much too."

"Let's talk about it after we see how we get along just living together."

"Okay, Andrea and I will move in. My lease is almost up."

At first, things went along better than she could have

dreamed. She told herself she would worry about marriage later. Dan just needed to know how much she loved him. Susan made extra efforts to please him. She cooked Dan his favorite dinners and when Andrea was visiting her father, Susan used her lace tablecloths and lit candles to make the meal more festive. She did his clothes and ironed them herself. It was an enormous effort, because she also was working and taking college classes at night.

When Dan was transferred to Tampa, they moved together into a house. Finally, they were both interested in their future wedding at the same time. Making plans monopolized their free time. Only a few days after they'd moved in, Susan was surprised when the phone rang. "It's Bobby Joe." Susan handed Dan the phone.

Susan and Dan met Bobby Joe at a local club. He asked Dan to help him get another job like the one he lost at a hospital in North Miami Beach. Not long afterwards, Bobby Joe moved into a furnished room close to their house. He was polite and always stood up when Susan entered a room. He pulled out her chair for her whenever they sat down to chat. He never talked much, but always stared worshipfully at Susan. She often made efforts at conversation and learned he was recently separated from his wife and two children. At first, Susan enjoyed their new friend. She, Dan, and Bobby Joe went out often. It was nice to have an admiring man around. He was shyly flirtatious, but Dan didn't appear to notice.

Each time they were together, Bobby Joe talked endlessly to Dan about his finding a job in a hospital. He resented working as an attendant in a funeral parlor. Dan and Bobby Joe grew closer and closer. They practically always   left

Susan out of their conversations. Even when they were out dancing, Bobby Joe monopolized Dan's time, telling him every detail about his X-ray work as though Dan understood it. As Susan sat there night after night, she silently began to fear she was losing her best friend, confidant and lover. After a particularly frustrating evening, Susan presented Dan with an ultimatum. "If we don't schedule our wedding, I'm moving out."

"If that's what you want," Dan answered diffidently.

"I want you to be the same loving man you were. I need to know you still love me like you used to."

Dan embraced her and told her how important she was to him, but he stopped short of setting a marriage date. His words didn't console her. She hoped he would see how much he needed her once she found an apartment and he realized she was really leaving. Susan believed all she had to do was show Dan the deposit, and he would beg her to stay. As she packed her things, Susan expected him to stop her. He didn't. With a heavy heart, she moved into a new apartment in Lutz.

The first night there Susan closed her eyes and blinked back tears. Had she waited too long to give Dan an ultimatum? Should she not have given him one at all? The man she had learned to trust enough to be the beneficiary of her insurance policy, her best friend – steady, dependable, kind, easy going, stable Dan – did not ask her to come back.

In the beginning, she continued to talk to him by phone, but he seemed distant, aloof. For Susan, leaving the relationship was more difficult than she could have imagined. As months passed, she grew more and more lonely. It wasn't Dan who called to console her. It was Bobby Joe Long. Finally, she accepted his offer to take her out to dinner.

When he arrived, she couldn't help noticing he was even better looking than she remembered. His curly brown hair, impeccable clothes and his mustache added an element of maturity to his boy-next-door appearance. He stared at her longingly.

But it was an awkward evening, with immense pauses and little conversation. "Goodnight," she said softly when he brought her back to her door and kissed him on the cheek.

The best she could hope for was to make Dan jealous.

Chapter 2

Jilted

The only thing worse than being possessed by unrequited desire is trying to recapture the illusion of a lost love. Susan's emotions were in turmoil.

She spent days, weeks, and months trying to get Dan back. She tried to see him in any way she could and suffered the indignity of meeting him with his new girlfriend, Julie. It was devastating because once Susan had tried to fix up Julie, her co-worker, with Dan. At the time, Julie had told her she was repulsed by Dan's appearance. Who would have guessed she would someday see Dan's superior attributes. Susan resented seeing Dan under such strange circumstances, but she tried to make the best of it. Soon she prayed he'd come to his senses and again realize how much he loved her, not Julie.

Then Susan had a car accident and injured her back. Everything seemed to be going wrong. She continued to date Bobby Joe, who seemed congenial and kept his distance. His occasional lewd comments about waitresses and other

women were annoying, but she ignored them. The guy really didn't like women. Under the surface, Susan thought, lots of men felt that way.

During the next few weeks, while she had to have physical therapy, Susan concentrated on her daughter, Andrea, and on furnishing their apartment so it would be nice for her little girl. Since Susan was a decorator, she got big discounts on the furniture they both admired. She even managed to buy Andrea, on the installment plan, of course, the canopy bed Susan had for so long promised the child.

One day, while waiting in the long line of cars at Andrea's school, Susan watched joyful children jump into their mothers' cars, and wondered if any of those mothers lived such an empty life. "Happily ever after" seemed an elusive dream for her. Suddenly Andrea bounded into the front seat next to Susan and handed her the precious, crumpled papers containing all her work for the day.

"Andrea, I'm so proud to see all those happy faces on your papers." Susan hugged and kissed her little girl, hoping the child could always be as full of happiness. Susan's mood lifted.

At night, the clock on the dresser ticked through two bedtime stories, a trip to the bathroom, and the usual kisses and hugs, followed by extra drinks of water, until Andrea finally began to nod off to sleep. Then Susan felt utterly alone. Her back ached and her heart ached more. She ran to her bedroom and cried.

Trying to escape her depression, she began seeing someone new only to find he had a volatile temper. Her feelings of inadequacy increased. So did her depression. Then the man threatened her! Who could help her? Her brother? No,

he was occupied with his wife and children. Dan? No, he didn't care. He had a new girlfriend. She picked up her phone and dialed a familiar number. "Hello, Bobby Joe."

Chapter 3

A Living Arrangement

When Bobby Joe arrived at her apartment, Susan felt grateful. "It really was very nice of you to come. First, my problem with Dan and now this. How can I ever thank you for coming to my aid?"

"I'd like it if you could make some dinner," he said wistfully.

"Definitely, I will." She smiled.

While they sat eating dinner, she slowly began to draw Bobby Joe out. He talked of how he missed his two children. Susan felt badly for him.

"The worse part is when I do see them I have no home to bring them to." Suddenly his face brightened as he looked around.

"Susan, you've plenty of room here. Have you ever thought of taking in a roommate? It would be a lot safer for you and Andrea. And you wouldn't have to spend so much money."

"A roommate? Well, no I hadn't thought of it, but you know, you're right, it would be cheaper and safer."

He broke in, his face reddening. "I was thinking of me."

"I thought you were." She smiled again and paused. Then she added, "Remember though, this isn't a romantic relationship. This is just a living arrangement. We can try sharing the apartment and see if we get in each other's way."

"Yeah, but when my kids come tomorrow could you cook?"

"Kids like hamburgers. You can take them to McDonald's. You're the daddy." His face was so downcast, Susan relented.

"One weekend won't hurt. I do cook for my daughter."

"I'd appreciate it."

"Anyway, I do owe you one," Susan said.

"Well, thanks. Where can my kids sleep?"

Susan pondered the space. "There are two twin beds that make a corner arrangement. You can take one and your daughter the other. I ordered a canopy bed for Andrea, but I'll have to cancel it until we have more room. If we can be roommates, we can get a larger place. Until then, Andrea will sleep with me."

"If you say so. What about my son, Tony?"

"He can have that sleeping bag."

"I guess it will do. It's a lot better than the three of us staying in the cramped tiny room I have."

"Your share of the rent will be about the same as you were paying," Susan told him.

He nodded. "Well, we have a deal then, roomie. Is it alright if I stay here tonight?"

"Suit yourself."

"I'll just run back to my place and get my things." She left him at the door and retired to read a book. The day had been hectic, and she nodded off after the first few pages. She

awoke, startled, to find Bobby Joe sitting on the side of the bed beginning to remove his shirt. He was casual, like a long time husband.

"No, Bobby. I told you this will only work if we just share the apartment. I don't go with this deal. You've got your own room."

"The kids aren't here." He bent over and removed his shoes.

"You don't get it. We're not going to sleep together! Go in your room. If you're going to live here, it's the only way!"

His face reddened. His voice was angry. "I don't think it will work. I'm leaving as soon as my kids are gone."

Susan breathed a sigh of relief, as the door slammed. He was annoyed, but he'd get over it.

But she was wrong. The next morning, Bobby Joe was still mumbling about getting out, throwing things into his suitcase and telling her, "This is a promise, I'm going to move to Dan's and soon."

However, Dan must have put him off because Bobby Joe stayed on after his kids had come and gone. For several weeks, they lived under an unspoken armistice. Then one night, after she'd finished work and dropped Andrea at her Dad's, Susan came home to find an empty house. Bobby Joe had made good on his promise. He moved to Dan's. Never had she been so confused. On the one hand, she was very relieved to find Bobby Joe gone, but on the other, she knew that his living with Dan made her chance of getting the man she loved back even less likely.

Susan tried not to drive by their house or to call, but finally one weekend when Andrea was with her father, Susan could resist no longer. She left a message on Dan's answering machine.

"Dan, this is Susan. I have to see you please."

Chapter 4

Surviving

Knocking, Susan heard Bobby Joe's voice calling something about the door being unlocked. She entered. Embarrassed, but determined, she sat down on the couch.

"I'm waiting for Dan."

"Make yourself comfortable. Do you want a drink?"

"I like C and C or a screwdriver. I probably shouldn't drink. The doctor has me on Valium for my back injuries, but I'm a little nervous coming here to see Dan."

"I don't think he wants to see you just now. He's in his room with Julie, his new girlfriend. You're surviving without my protection?" Bobby Joe asked.

"Yeah, thanks," she said. Her face reddened. "I need to make a phone call. Can I use your phone?"

"Suit yourself."

Susan couldn't believe Dan wouldn't even talk to her. She expected him to come out of his room if he heard her voice. She made some phone calls to everyone she could think of. She even called her ex-neighbor trying to buy time. Bobby Joe refreshed her drink.

"God my back is killing me." He walked over and began to rub it.

"That feels good, Bobby Joe. I have to go to the chiropractor to get my back injuries massaged. The Valium relaxes it a bit, but it doesn't relieve the pain."

"Does this feel good?" Bobby Joe said, moving his hand close to her breast.

"Stop it. The massage is over."

"Okay, but I'm driving you home. You can't even walk."

The screwdrivers and Valium had dulled Susan's senses. She imagined that Bobby Joe had some fatherly concern for her welfare. *He must have*, she told herself. *He wouldn't let me drive home.* True, she could get in trouble driving in her condition. "I want to stay until I talk to Dan. If I stay here awhile, I'll be okay to drive," she protested meekly.

"No, you won't. Get in my car," Bobby Joe commanded.

Susan followed Bobby Joe submissively out to his car. He drove the two miles to Lutz without speaking. She laid her head back and closed her eyes. "We're here," she heard him say from a distance.

"Thanks for the ride," she managed to say, as she fumbled to get the car door open.

Bobby Joe, the gentleman, ran around the car. He opened the door and took her arm. Susan let him guide her to her apartment. As she stumbled up the walk, she tried to get the keys out of her purse.

"Give me those." Bobby Joe took the keys out of her hand and opened the door.

"Thanks," Susan said stepping inside and reaching her hand out for her keys.

"You think I'm a taxi driver? Give your old friend a kiss and get in that bedroom of yours."

Susan fell backwards as the door he pushed hit her. "No, Bobby. Just give me my keys and go home."

"Hell no!" His angry voice penetrated her befuddled senses. She felt his arms lifting her. She went limp trying to cooperate. Her head whirled as she felt her body land on the bed. She tried to push him away. The weight of his body was on top of her. She closed her eyes and again tried to push him off. He knocked her head back on the bed. She passed out.

The sunlight flooding the bedroom hurt her eyes. Susan's head throbbed. For a few minutes she didn't know where she was. What happened? Was it a nightmare? She felt her body. She was naked. She had a fuzzy recollection of Bobby Joe being on top of her. She managed to sit up and look around. Her clothes were strewn about her. "Oh God, he raped me!" Susan slumped back on the bed. Remorse filled her. She trusted that man. How stupid. She lay there feeling used. Self loathing consumed her. She fell back and curled her body in a fetal position. If only she could close her eyes and never wake up. Life had become so ugly. Why? All she wanted was to be happy with Dan. She cried and tried to retreat into sleep.

The phone rang...once...twice. It was Dan's neighbor. "Kay, I'm so glad it's you. I let Bobby Joe drive me home last night and he raped me. I was so drunk, I couldn't protect myself."

"Call the police and report the rape," Kay responded with concern in her voice.

"I can't do that. They'd laugh at me. Woozy on Valium. Drinking. I knew the guy. I let him drive me home. For God sakes he even stayed here a few weeks."

"I never trusted him."

"That's why I'm telling you. I wanted to let you know you were right. I shouldn't have trusted him either."

"Your car is in front of Dan's house. I thought you stayed with Dan all night. I saw his car there."

"I'll pick it up tomorrow. I need to get my head together before I see Dan."

"You should stay away from both of them."

"Maybe you're right. I'll think about it."

Susan thought and thought some more. But she couldn't seem to help herself and called Dan. "Dan, Bobby Joe raped me when he brought me home...Why don't you believe me?...I have to see you please." He hung up.

Susan put back the phone in total frustration. She couldn't believe her friend and lover couldn't understand and didn't care about what had happened to her. Their relationship was ruined the day they met Bobby Joe. Obsession captured her mind. Dan would realize how much he meant to her if she died. She grabbed a handful of Valium and swallowed them with some water.

Within minutes everything went black.

Having one's stomach pumped is a sobering experience. Susan couldn't believe she had tried to kill herself. She was out of her mind to forget Andrea. Andrea was the most important thing in her life. Susan vowed never to be that foolish again. But she couldn't forget Dan. Now she needed more than ever to redeem herself to him.

Nothing worked. Despite the messages she left, he never called back. Rage consumed Susan when she heard from some of her friends that Bobby Joe bragged about their sexual encounter. Since when was rape a sexual encounter?

Dan was hearing that too. She needed to defend herself. For days, Susan planned what she would say when she saw Dan. She'd tell him what Bobby Joe did to her. She'd explain how dizzy and sick she'd been and how Bobby Joe had taken advantage of her. This time she'd talk to him. He'd have to listen to her.

One day Susan could stand it no longer. She went to visit her friend, Kay, who lived across the street from Dan. She handed Kay the coffee cake she'd brought. "I miss seeing you a lot." It was true, but it paled in comparison to her need to talk to Dan. Susan had fantasized that he would see her entering Kay's house and run across the street to beg her to come back. She would hesitate and then run laughing into his arms and feel that soft cuddly body again. They would languish in his nice comfortable bed in the morning, making wedding plans like they once had.

Susan made small talk, waiting and hoping Dan would come over. "Your son must be almost grown. And how's Kate? She must be a big girl now. Andrea's almost six."

"Oh, if she was only little again. She's a handful. I guess everyone is at thirteen." Kay said, "Come sit down. I've missed you since you moved out. I'll get us some coffee, and we'll have a piece of this delicious looking cake."

From the window, Susan watched Dan's house and noticed his car wasn't in the driveway. Disappointment flooded her, recognizing Bobby Joe's car past the hedge.

Thoughts of Dan saying "I love you" flashed before her. Hope began to creep into her mind. Kay came back with a tray. She poured the coffee into the two porcelain tea cups and cut two slices of cake. "I hope you reported the rape. I hate to see him get away with it. Your being woozy doesn't give him the right."

Susan gulped the coffee faster than she should have. Maybe the caffeine would give her more energy. "I reported it, but I don't know what good it will do. Anyway, at least there's a record in case Bobby Joe ever comes after me again." She didn't wait for Kay to refill her cup, but poured in some more coffee.

"Well, I'm glad you did it."

Susan inclined her head. "I see Bobby Joe's car across the street. Is Julie living there?"

"I don't know. I haven't seen her lately, but I've seen more than enough of Bobby Joe. He's there all the time watching television. I guess he lost that job Dan helped him get at the hospital."

"He's had a couple of those losses now," Susan snapped.

Kay nodded. "I think he's the loser. I found my daughter in the street the other night. She said Bobby Joe came over to borrow the phone. For some reason she ran away from him. I don't know what it was about, but she's been moody ever since. I don't trust him."

"I don't trust him either. Why would he need to use yours? He has a phone over there."

"My husband, Jim, thinks Bobby Joe used it as an excuse to talk to Kate."

"I hate him because I used to trust him. I'm such a fool. He was good to his kids though. Kate isn't much older than his daughter."

"The girl across the street, who used to cut Dan's hedge, won't go near the house anymore. I think the girls are afraid of Bobby Joe. They have good instincts, I'd say."

"I used to think he was a big bluff. Now I wonder if he hasn't a much more serious problem." Susan stared across

the street hoping to see Dan's car arriving. The lights were on in the house.

"Dan seemed to be a nice guy. The girls weren't afraid of him when he lived there by himself."

"Oh, Kay, he is. If only I hadn't been so foolish. If only I could get Dan back, I'd appreciate him. Remember how happy I was?" Susan drained her cup.

"What happened? I thought you two were going to get married."

Susan shook her head. "I gave him an ultimatum. Marriage or I'd move out. I was so disappointed he let me."

"You were probably lucky. His friendship with Bobby Joe isn't too healthy."

"Dan is such a softy, he must think Bobby Joe is a macho man. I know differently now." Tears welled up in Susan's eyes.

"I don't even know how Dan can stand him," Kay said.

"He knows how to be pleasant, when it suits him." Susan began to cry and tried to stifle her sobs. "Dan doesn't believe that Bobby Joe raped me. The worst is I feel so stupid."

"Susan, you have to keep telling yourself it wasn't your fault, because it wasn't."

"I've been so upset since the rape that I can't concentrate. I'm so in need of money for Andrea and me, that despite the pain from my back injuries, I've taken a job dancing in a club as well as working days. Luckily, I've found an elderly woman whom I can trust to babysit. I made my mother and brother come to the club to watch, so they'd be convinced it's not a degrading thing to do. They both hate the image people have of dancers. It was me who needed

convincing. I wish I could go back, marry Dan and live happily ever after."

"Susan, I'm so sorry. Sometimes we can't have what we want." Kay paused. "I'm surprised you are able to dance with your injuries."

"It's hard, Kay. I haven't been feeling well. The doctor prescribed Valium after that automobile accident. It's supposed to relax my muscles, but it doesn't. I can dance because I have to for Andrea and myself." Susan got up from the couch. "The Valium doesn't help my depression either. Kay, I'm pulling you down with me. I'd better go home. I'll come back some other time." She didn't add what she was thinking, when Dan's home.

"Susan, you're welcome to stay."

"No, I'm not much company, and I have to get ready for my job anyway."

That night Susan entered the ladies' room of the Sly Fox Lounge to transform herself from a domestic 30-year-old mother into a go-go dancer. Finally, she was ready. She stepped out of the stall and moved closer to the mirror to critically examine her new costume. The chiffon float with the silver sequins was eye-catching and hid her less than firm stomach. As Susan stood twisting her head to try and see how she looked from the back, the door blasted open. Loud music and billows of smoke invaded the room. The door banged shut.

"The ladies' room is a hell of a place to have to get dressed," Rhonda, one of the other dancers, complained, throwing her pocketbook and small traveling bag next to the others on the floor. "Nobody gives a damn if we get robbed.

It's no skin off the manager's nose." She entered a stall to change her clothes.

"I leave my wallet and money in the trunk of my car. Of course, someone could steal my keys, but it hasn't happened," Susan confided.

"You better not pass that information around," Rhonda called from the stall as she threw garments over the top of the door.

"Some of the heads are pretty desperate for money. This business is a magnet for them. They're attracted to the money, but it's never enough."

"Most of the dancers are just kids. Some of these guys take advantage of them. I've seen them try and slip cocaine in their hands. Heck, they even try that junk with me. I'm lucky to have a daughter I have to stay straight for. I never even learned to smoke." Susan shook her head.

"The nose habit costs more than the girls make. It's not an accident that it's so available," Rhonda observed, rushing out of the stall.

"Shush," Susan said, putting her finger to her mouth while she furtively looked around. "It's better not to say some things out loud. This place could be bugged."

"Come off it. The guys who run these places don't worry about us. They have the run of Tampa. If they first get some girl busted for showing too much ass or some other misdemeanor, then anything the girl could say about them giving her coke is meaningless. The cops must know what's going on."

"It's best to keep your nose clean and not notice. I just dance and leave as soon as I can." Susan applied the last touches of makeup.

Susan and Rhonda left their makeshift dressing room to

take their places at each end of the stage and began to move to the music. Susan looked down at the predominantly male audience and forced a smile. A few clapped like they noticed the exchange of dancers. The majority talked, drank and ignored the stage.

Susan caught a glimpse of the tired, wilted girl she replaced going off stage. Then Susan gave Rhonda the signal that she was ready to do her special routine. She began the Sly Cat Strut.

The smoke, as it filtered up through the spotlight, became wispy, white summer clouds. They blanked out the black lacquer and red plush decorations of the nightclub. Nothing and no one existed but the beat and rhythm of the music. Even her back stopped hurting. A euphoric feeling engulfed Susan, as she strutted and danced gracefully. Her three numbers were quickly over, and she stepped back in the shadows and watched Rhonda take her place.

As Susan walked to the ladies' room her mind drifted to happier times with Dan. She castigated herself for not appreciating those comfortable days and nights. She imagined herself married to Dan, feeling the daily comfort of his loving embraces. *What is he doing right now,* she wondered. She would have to visit Kay again to find out. As soon as Andrea went to her Dad's, she would go back. *Andrea,* she thought and bit her lower lip. She had to better their life before Andrea grew older and became ashamed of her.

The following week, Susan started to go to school on a night she didn't dance. She wanted to prepare herself for a better job at more pay. Time passed. She felt better about herself. She was sure Dan would be interested in her new efforts. She had made a lot of changes. She called Dan. His

voice was friendly. Susan was thrilled when he invited her to come over. "It will only take me twenty minutes to get there." Happiness and relief flowed through her during the short drive.

She knocked on the door. No one answered. The door wasn't locked. Susan entered and called to Dan. Just as the last time she'd gone to his house, it seemed empty. So she sat down on the couch to wait for him. He couldn't have gone far. He was expecting her.

She must have dozed off. Suddenly, a tall, dark form stood before her. "It's you. Get out of here!" Bobby Joe yelled, as he stomped into the living room. His hair was wet from the shower.

"Dan told me to come. Where is he?"

"None of your damn business. Get the hell out."

"You're not going to bully me. This is his house."

Bobby Joe thrust his fist at Susan and hit her nose. Blood spurted out. He landed a second punch to her right eye. She tried to get up and run out. He grabbed her, opened the front door and threw her out on the porch. Following her, he slammed her again and she fell. She started screaming. He grabbed her and threw her off the porch onto the grass.

Dan came running from Kay's house across the street. Kay yelled, "Susan, I'm coming." She stopped and shouted to her husband who was working in the yard. "Susan's been hurt. Get a towel. She's covered in blood."

Dan reached Susan first. "Please take me to a hospital," Susan managed to beg through her hands, which she held up to her nose. Blood ran down her clothes.

Dan helped Susan up from the ground.

"I called the police," Kay's husband yelled, arriving with the towel.

"I need to get her to the nearest hospital," Kay cried.

"No, no, I want Dan to take me," Susan protested frantically.

"Come back to my house and lie down," Kay ordered.

Susan leaned against Kay, who helped the shaking Susan across the street.

Dan ran after them. Once inside the house, Susan called the police. Dan stood by listening to her describe what happened to her. Before Dan could drive Susan to the hospital, Julie arrived with words of concern.

"Julie will go with us," Dan said.

"No!" Susan cried not only from the pain, but the sight of her past love embracing his new girlfriend. "Kay, will you drive me?" Dan and Julie stood hand in hand watching Susan being driven off.

In the emergency room, after the doctor stitched her cheek and packed her nose, Susan turned to Kay. "Bobby Joe Long isn't going to get away with this attack."

And it seemed she was right. Soon after, Long was arrested and brought to trial. Despite a vicious court battle in which he vilified Susan, he was given six months probation. Susan had little time to feel vindicated, however. The sentence was appealed, and Susan had to face her attacker once again.

Chapter 5

Further Trials

Susan paced in front of Judge Bonanno's courtroom. Anger and frustration made her fidgety. She found it impossible to sit still and wait. How many appeals could Bobby Joe Long get from one battery charge? It was bad enough last year before Judge Hinson when Long bragged about raping her, then laughed and denied it. After that a Public Defender decided to represent Long right after the judge found him guilty. This was even worse. A jury trial! At least Bobby Joe couldn't trash her for her occupation as a dancer anymore. She had become a full time interior decorator. Susan replayed in her mind over and over the three years since Long's attack. Being in court again was like having a repeating nightmare. Rage consumed her as she threw herself on the long bench outside the courtroom only a few feet away from Dan. He avoided her eyes by looking down at his hands as he waited to testify.

Kay and Jim walked in. "Susan, I'm so happy to see you."

Susan ran toward her old neighbor. "You too, Jim. Thanks for coming. I can't even go in the courtroom to hear what's being said about me because I have to testify later."

Kay held out her arms. Jim scowled at his neighbor, Dan.

"Jim and I are here to tell the truth. We saw you right after he hit you. When I saw all the blood, I thought you were in serious trouble. He won't get off. He brutalized you."

Tears ran down Susan's cheeks. "I thought Dan was my friend for life. I loved him so much," Susan said in a hushed tone.

"You were so convinced Dan was a nice guy. There must be something wrong with him if he continues to be Bobby Joe's friend. He saw how beaten up you were."

"I even asked him to be a witness. I believed he'd take my side. Julie used to be my friend. You know, I introduced her to Dan. She thought he was such an ugly frog that I bribed her with ten dollars to go out with him. The joke's on me. Last year she married Dan!"

Kay nodded. "Consider yourself lucky. They obviously both think it's all right for a man to beat a woman."

"In Texas, where I grew up, real men don't hit women" Susan complained.

The bailiff appeared. "They don't in Florida or anywhere else either," Kay managed to say, running after her husband and the bailiff into the courtroom.

Susan looked at Dan beseechingly. He turned away. It was evident he didn't want to converse. The man she had wanted to marry so much, the man she put herself in jeopardy to see. She yearned to have him look at her as he once had.

If only she could see into his mind and learn why his love for her had died. He avoided even looking in her direction. It hurt. Tears ran down her cheeks.

By the time the bailiff came to get Susan so she could testify, she had managed to compose herself. Slowly, she followed him into the courtroom.

"Do you, Susan Replogle, swear to tell the truth, and nothing but the truth, so help you God?"

"I do."

Once she was seated and arranged her full navy blue skirt, her eyes scanned the spectators, and she saw Julie. Susan winced.

State Attorney Ron Ficarotta questioned her. "Point out the man who assaulted you."

"He's right there. Bobby Joe Long."

Susan described the attack. Her words flowed as if she was reading a script, having given the same testimony so many times since the battery. In the past three years, she had told her story to police, judges, in numerous hearings and the other trial. Nevertheless, the hurt and anger she felt were apparent.

"Your witness."

Dan Kirkwood, Bobby Joe's Public Defender, stood before her stern-faced. "Is it true on November 16, 1981, you no longer resided at 1516 Meadowbrook Road?"

"Yes." Susan glanced at the jury and hoped that the women would be sympathetic. They outnumbered the men.

"Were you aware that Mr. Long resided at that address?"

"It was Dan's house."

"You didn't answer the question."

"I knew Bobby Joe lived there."

Kirkwood looked up at the judge. "Judge, my client has a right to remove anyone from his property."

"Objection. He doesn't have the right to use bodily harm to a person to remove them. We need to define property. Does renting a room qualify as ownership?" the assistant district attorney asked.

"In this case, is he allowed to use reasonable force to remove this woman?" Kirkwood interjected.

Judge Bonanno called both attorneys for a conference before the bench. Susan could hear irate voices in the arguments, but the words were jumbled together.

"The witness is excused," Attorney Kirkwood said when he came back.

Susan left the courtroom with as much dignity as she could. She held her head even higher, when she walked past Bobby Joe, and he sneered. But the emotional ordeal was exhausting. Why had they asked her so few questions? What had happened between the judge and lawyers?

Outside, she sat on the bench. An hour passed. Then two. Suddenly, Kay and Jim emerged from the courtroom and ran up to her.

"What's happened?" Susan asked.

Their eyes spoke volumes. "I guess he has to kill someone!" Kay said bitterly.

"You mean the jury voted in his favor?"

"Yes."

"Oh my God," Susan wailed.

During the days that followed, the feeling of triumph Bobby Joe expected after beating Susan Replogle in court evaded him. He vented his still simmering anger again very soon.

Chapter 6

Bobby Joe

Thoughts of Susan overpowered him. *The cunt told everyone he raped her. If only he had degraded her as he had done the others.* Rape had served his purpose for longer than he could remember. The "Classified Rapist" stories about him in the Miami papers brought pleasure. He dug through his mementos to savor the headlines again.

Reading his treasured clipping, he remembered the rape he'd committed near Orlando on January 26th, a week before the trial. When he discarded the woman's pocketbook on Route 4, headed back to Tampa, the idea struck him that maybe some reporter would realize there was another "Classified Rapist." But, no. He was just too good. His excitement level was building. He needed to discharge it.

He ran out to his Dodge Magnum to cool off. New Port Richey was far enough away from home to be safe. He stopped on a quiet street, attracted by a "For Sale" sign with a car in the driveway. Bobby Joe reached for his gun from under the seat and carefully placed it in the back of his pants

where the bulge wouldn't show. He concealed his knife and bindings under his sport jacket. Quickly, he glanced on either side of the house to see if any nosy neighbors could be watching before he knocked on the door. If a man answered, he could ask to see the house. If it was a woman, rape, his one great release, filled his mind.

A girl in a McDonald's uniform opened the door, and while she babbled something about calling the owner, he forced her back into the house. He pushed her towards the bedroom and onto the bed, where he bound her like the others.

Driving back to Tampa, his mind centered on Susan again. He felt cheated. Damn Susan! She always entered his thoughts and stole his pleasure.

On the 27th, he had a day off from his job at Humana Hospital. The cops in New Port Richey might be looking for his car. South would make a good drive. Before driving very far on one of the less traveled roads leaving Tampa, he spotted a thin, blond girl walking along a narrow path hugging the edge of the road.

Bobby Joe stopped and smiled. "Get in. A pretty girl like you could get in trouble walking in this desolate place."

"I just came from the convenience store back there. I was out of cigarettes. I don't have far to go. No thanks," the girl said as she continued her walk.

Bobby Joe cruised next to her slowly. "Seriously, I'd feel bad if I didn't offer to give you a ride. Look at all that palmetto brush. You couldn't run away if you tried. I look like a nice guy, don't I?"

"Well, yes," the girl stammered, as she got in the car.

Bobby drove along a few minutes, looking for some place to drive the car off the road.

"What's your name?"

"Artis Wick, but it won't be for long. I'm getting married next week."

"You look too young."

"I'm seventeen."

Bobby drove the car off the road into a field. A scared look came into her eyes. "Where are you taking me?" She tried to jump out, but he grabbed her.

"Take your clothes off."

"Please don't hurt me," she screamed. She tried once again to get away, but Bobby jumped on top of her as he cut her clothes off with a knife. He wrestled her to the ground and continued slashing her clothes off. He smacked her face hard to get her under control. Then he squeezed her throat until he could feel her stop struggling and go limp. Afterward, he dragged her lifeless body to a dry creek bed near Ponderosa Street, close to the border of Manatee County, and left it there.

Fear gripped him, when he realized how close the body was to Humana Hospital. Then he rationalized that his job sucked anyway. He quit Humana on March 30th, three days after the murder.

The following month, on April 3rd, Bobby Joe entered Tampa General for his first day on his new job, feeling safe and confident. It was a bigger, better place to work anyway, he reasoned. Within two days, he felt frustrated. Death had come too easily to his last victim. To the bargain no one had found the body. If he killed Susan, it would be long and slow he promised himself.

On April 5th, he spotted an attractive woman in the busy Carrollwood Shopping Center trying to put a load of packages

in her Jaguar. Bobby Joe, the gentleman, offered to help. If
something happened to a rich bitch, surely she would be
missed. Finally, he would get the notoriety and respect of
which he dreamed. Despite the woman's protests, he managed to get in the car beside her. Once inside, he flashed his
gun and ordered her to ease the car into the traffic on Dale
Mabry Highway. She did as she was told, and Bobby Joe
relaxed, savoring the images of raping her and then squeezing the life out of her. The same way he would do to Susan
someday.

Before he realized what was happening, the car hit a pole
and flipped over. He struggled to get out. He was stunned,
but not enough to stop him from trying to get away. He
threw away the gun. He was four blocks away when he saw
the flashing blue lights on his tail. Damn!

The policeman ordered Bobby Joe to stop and frisked
him. Bobby Joe felt pleased with himself that he had the
presence of mind to ditch the gun en route. It would be her
word against his, unless someone turned in the gun with his
prints. Her word prevailed. After she identified Bobby Joe,
he was taken to jail, where he immediately called his public
defender. Within hours, Bobby Joe Long was back on the
street.

From the newspaper accounts he read the next morning,
he learned that the woman's name was Gail Neale. He
cringed reading his own name, realizing he'd have to find
another job. Damn that cunt, Susan. She was the one who
was the cause of all of his trouble.

Less than a month later, he found a job at Gulf Bay
Electric. Within ten days, he chose his next conquest. The
victim looked like the woman he really wanted to destroy.

She had full, long dark hair and danced at the Sly Fox Lounge, where Susan had once danced. He took great pleasure in raping and killing her. This time he didn't risk leaving the body where it would not be found. He draped her clothes on a tree and spread her legs wide. This posture was the one he would use as his signature on future victims. The body of Nguen Thi 'Lana' Long was discovered on Mother's Day, which added to his pleasure. He was disappointed at the small notice in the papers.

When he lost his job again on the 23rd, Bobby was angry. What was the matter with his bosses? No matter where he went, they kept complaining about his attitude. What attitude? He was one of the good ole boys. A great guy. If only they knew how good.

May 27th was Long's best day in a long time. Michelle Denise Simms, the victim he chose this time, was the image of Susan. A brunette with high cheek bones, she also danced at the Sly Fox. Beating her, smashing her face, strangling her out of breath and seeing her beg when he allowed her to breathe for a short time was all empowering. Finally, he decided to end it with his knife. In his rage, he almost took her head off. It was almost as if he orchestrated Susan's death in his mind. During the next few days, the articles in the newspapers were small, but at least they found the body. Yeah, the feelings were a little like he imagined, but nothing would feel as good as squeezing the real bitch's neck.

After reading *The Tampa Tribune's* small article about his deed, Bobby Joe scanned the classified ads in *The Clearwater Sun*. Without his job, he needed to get money to pay rent on his new apartment. Rape no longer held the pleasure it once had, but murder gave him a rush. And robbery

had a nice ring. He concentrated on Palm Harbor, where there were expensive homes, and found a bedroom set advertised for sale. When the man of the house answered the phone, Bobby Joe learned he would be at work, but his wife would be home to show him the furniture. It sounded promising.

On the 29th, Bobby Joe drove to the Continental Inn on U.S. 1, nineteen miles south of Palm Harbor. He called ahead from the Inn and asked the woman who answered to give him directions or ask her husband to do it. The husband was at work. A gardener's truck in the driveway almost made Long turn around, but he needed the money badly. It was the end of the month. *Working people don't pay attenion to callers,* Long told himself. He rang the bell.

Chapter 7

Lisa

Working at Krispy Kreme was the only happy time of 17-year-old Lisa Rhodes' day. She loved being there. Her boss, Leo George, was easy to work for and the atmosphere was pleasant. When Lisa arrived, she'd take a deep breath of relief, glad she was away from the tension at her home. The wonderful aroma of vanilla, spices, pungent coffee and the delicious smell of donuts cooking always perked up her sad and enduring mood.

The people who ate at the counter were always polite, and she looked forward to the regulars, whom she knew by name. They complimented her all the time for her fast service and pleasant smile. It felt good to be appreciated. Because of the warm atmosphere and kindness she received at work, in contrast to the abuse she experienced at home, Lisa offered to work any hours. The longer the better. That night they were busier than usual. It was almost 2 a.m. when Lisa finished her work. The night was warm and breezy for early November. She mounted her bicycle and rolled up the

right leg of her white workpants so she wouldn't have to worry about catching it in the bicycle chain.

The wind blowing on her face felt refreshing. With so few cars on the road, Lisa was able to look up and enjoy the stars. The moonlight illuminated bright objects, making them seem brighter and the shadows darker. As she rode, the past came flooding back into her mind.

Lisa thought her prayers had come true when her grandmother invited her to come live with her. Life in the projects with her mother, two brothers and twin sister crammed into a tiny apartment was hard. She felt she had been chosen as special over the other four children in the family. She adored her C.B. radio-addicted grandmother. She was fun. Lisa would get to have her own room. The first night she moved in she felt like a princess seeing her big new bed. She had a dresser all to herself, too. Best of all, it had a mirror! She didn't have to share. On that first night she put her clothes away and carefully arranged the comb and brush her grandma gave her on the dresser. Then, she ran downstairs to help.

After Lisa finished the dishes and taking care of her grandmother's needs, she went back to her room. It was such a luxury to be able to get in bed and read. She didn't even want to watch television. The next morning, Lisa started school. Everything seemed to be wonderful.

Then about a week later, one evening after dinner, Marce, Grandma's boyfriend, smiled at Lisa while he fixed himself a drink. "How come you never sit in the living room and keep me company while I watch television?"

"I have a lot of homework," Lisa said. She started to go to her room.

Marce blocked her way. "Your grandmother needs her rest. I'll sleep in your room." He looked at her with bleary eyes, staggered slightly toward her and put his arms out to embrace her.

Lisa felt threatened. She stepped back and looked at him strangely. "Did Grandma say that was okay?"

"Sure she did."

"Well then, I'll sleep on the couch."

"Now sweetheart, I wouldn't want you to sleep on that old uncomfortable thing. Look, see it's kind of lumpy. Here have some of this." He pushed a bottle labeled Sprite in her hand.

"Sleeping on the couch is fine with me." She took a sip of the soda. "It tastes strange." Then she began coughing. Her throat felt like it was on fire. "Aah, it's terrible."

He laughed. "You're young. Don't you like Vodka?"

"No."

"Drink it, baby. You'll like me better. I like you. You have such beautiful brown eyes."

"Get out of here. I'll tell my grandmother."

"Ha Ha. What's she gunna do? Do you want her out in the street? This is my house."

Lisa threw the bottle at him and stepped back. It gave her time to get to her grandmother's bedroom, where her grandmother cowered under the covers. Only her gray-streaked pony tail was visible. Lisa slammed the cracked old door and went to lock it. There was no lock.

"He's after me." She flung herself on the bed, embraced the old woman, held tight, and nestled her head in the soft, plump flesh.

Marce pushed the door open and grabbed Lisa's shoulder.

Grandma patted her. "Now, now, it's all right. Go out Marce. I'll talk to Lisa."

He turned and slammed the door. "You'd better," sounded loud and clear through the thin door.

"Lisa, my little sunshine, Marce is a nice man. He'll be good to you if you're just nice to him. He has lots of money. He can buy you things."

"I don't want him to. I just want to be here with you, Grandma."

"Lisa, I wish I had the money to live somewhere with you, but Marce is my only source of decent shelter."

"I think he's an old fat pig. Those tattoos...he's disgusting."

"I talked with Pathfinder - that was his nickname - for hours on the C.B. before I met him. I think he's kinda attractive, and he's safe. Marce had a vasectomy."

"A what?"

"He just wants you to be nice and affectionate to him. He's lonely."

"That's not all he wants."

Her grandmother turned her face away.

Lisa released the old woman and recoiled in horror. "I'll go back to Mom."

"Marce will throw me out."

"I can't help it." Lisa crept toward the door. She was in luck. Marce was in the kitchen pouring another drink. She tiptoed to the back door and fled.

Lisa's mother opened the door yawning. Her brown hair hung limply around her face. "What are you doing running out in the middle of the night? You in some kind of trouble?"

"Marce, Grandma's boyfriend, wants me to sleep with him. He's a fat old pig," Lisa cried desperately.

"Shush," her mother hissed with her finger up to her lips. "You'll wake everyone."

"I don't care. You don't understand. She wants me to sleep with him so she and I can live there."

Her mother shrugged. "I had sex with my stepfather at your age." Her mother turned from Lisa, so the girl wouldn't see the tears falling down her cheeks.

"Well, I won't do it."

Still sniffling, Lisa's mother said in a hushed, desperate voice, "Keep the family secrets private or our family will be destroyed. The Welfare Department will jail us all for fraud."

"I'd rather die. I want to come home. I don't want to be there."

"Just pray to Jesus for strength. He'll help you."

"That means you won't let me come home, doesn't it?"

"I can't. I signed you over to your grandmother legally. The Welfare Department contributes to your grandmother as guardian. They won't give me money if you return home."

"So I'm a meal ticket! Why didn't you tell me?"

Her mother just continued to sniffle. Lisa looked at her weak mother. She wanted to reach out to her and beg, but she didn't. What was the use? She was the same woman who long ago put her twin toddlers in foster care for two years. Lisa had blocked that nightmare out of her mind. It returned with a vengeance. Being left at the police station and then the children's home. For all she knew, the welfare money could have been the reason her mother had taken them back. When they were back together, Lisa stuffed her

resentment toward her mother into a little place in her heart.
Her mother tore it open now.

Reluctantly, Lisa started walking back to her grandmother's. Maybe her grandmother had reconsidered and
would stop Marce from attacking her. She had always said
her prayers faithfully. Now she prayed fervently for deliver-
ance for her and her grandmother. She heard no answer. Her
mother's words about social workers destroying the family
rang in her ears. They were both the enemy and the source
of the family's existence.

As she got closer to her grandmother's house, her fear
mounted. Just then, a police car slowed down as it passed.
The police terrified her even more than Marce and her grandmother. Blue uniforms, badges and flashing colored lights
meant trouble. Lisa quickened her pace to get to the little
house.

Chapter 8

Nightmares

School became a nightmare for Lisa. Everyday she'd bathe and try to wash away the memory of the night before. The new dresses Grandma bought from the money Marce gave her didn't help the disgust Lisa felt. She imagined the kids knew she was different. Lisa sat silently when the girls giggled over the boys in school and wondered what it would be like to really kiss a boy. When they complained about their parents making them come home early, or other trivial things, Lisa felt jealous and depressed. She didn't say a word, afraid she might reveal her dirty secret.

"It must be my fault that this awful thing is happening," she began to think. It was difficult to concentrate. Her marks began slipping. Just staying awake in class was an effort because she had so little sleep at night. One day she skipped class altogether.

That day, when she got home, Grandma was in the living room. "The school called to ask if you were sick."

"I went walking. I needed to think."

"What do you mean, you went walking? With your
poor grades, you need every day of school you can get. Your
sister gets A's."

"She doesn't have Marce in her bed. If he'd leave me
alone, I'd do my homework."

"He has given us a place to live and buys your clothes."

"He does not. The money you get for having me here
pays for them."

"You're a disobedient girl. I'll not have it."

"I'm tired of all this. I hate it."

"We'll see about that." Grandma lumbered into the bedroom where Marce was resting. His legs, the blood supply
compromised by arthritis and diabetes, were giving him
trouble.

A few minutes later, Marce appeared in the living room.
"So, young lady, you think you can skip school. Your father
will not have it." He struck Lisa with his closed fist.

She reeled backwards. "You're not my father."

He used an open hand on her face. "Don't ever say that
again. As long as you are in this house, I'm your father.
You'll do as I say. You'll go to school until the law says you
don't have to. We're not having any truant officers here. If
that ever happens, you'll know what trouble is. I'll kill you."

Not long afterwards, Marce went to the hospital to have
his legs amputated. Lisa prayed he wouldn't come back, but
he did. Lisa had to care for him. The days and nights that
followed were one big blur.

She longed for school to start again after Christmas vacation so she'd have an excuse to get out of the house. But
when it did, more problems arose. As the year progressed,
the homework increased. Some nights Lisa was able to

sneak a little time to do her school work, but many times she had to attend school without it being finished. She'd try to get the homework done in homeroom in the few minutes before each class started, but the task was overwhelming. She couldn't keep up. Since she wouldn't give an excuse or explain, the teachers called her insolent. Soon Lisa became the focus of the teachers' anger. Counselors harassed her and took up precious time she needed in the classroom. Their questions terrorized her.

Marce began to recover and use a wheelchair. He ignored his diabetes and started drinking heavily again. Every night Lisa had to get in the same bed with him. He always wanted oral sex, and then he'd get on his stumps and have intercourse. She would grit her teeth and close her eyes until it was over. Then, she would run into the bathroom and scream. One night, the long days and nights of holding her emotions in gave way. She kept screaming. No one cared. Hoarse and red-eyed, she went to school the next morning.

When she got home, Marce was in the bedroom. Her grandmother was talking to a strange woman with shoulder length brown hair dressed in a police uniform. "This nice lady would like to talk to you Lisa."

Grandma went into the bedroom with Marce. Lisa could see the intercom was on. They were listening. The woman explained, "The neighbors heard someone screaming. They thought it was you. Is someone hurting you?"

"No." Lisa looked down at her hands.

"Did you scream?"

"I had a bad dream."

The woman studied Lisa, but couldn't see any signs of abuse. She put a card in Lisa's hand. Grandma entered the

room and walked the woman outside. They talked quietly together on the porch steps.

As soon as she was out the door, Marce wheeled into the kitchen and grabbed the card from Lisa's hand. "You have to learn to control your epilepsy. Here, take two pills this time." He used a loud voice so the woman could hear him.

"I don't have epilepsy," Lisa spoke quietly, remembering her mother's words about the welfare and jail.

Lisa began to check off the days until her sixteenth birthday. Until then, she went to work and asked for overtime. The thought that March was only a month away gave her hope and made each day bearable.

One night, while Marce and Grandma were having drinks in the kitchen, she slipped into bed hoping they'd drink so much that she'd be able to sleep. She heard their voices droning on as she nodded off.

Suddenly the door opened, and the light from the living room woke her. Marce was all red-faced and puffing. "Get out here, you stupid moron," Marce shouted.

"No, Marce, let the girl sleep."

"I told you, and I'll show you why I can't stand her."

Lisa almost sleepwalked into the living room, rubbing her eyes.

"Take your night shirt off." Marce didn't wait, but rolled his wheelchair toward the quivering Lisa and lifted the shirt.

"See that, you fat cow! Now that's not a human body. Who would want to have sex with anyone like you?"

Lisa's grandmother sat crying. In spite of her own agony, Lisa wanted to hug her and make her feel better, but Marce was even more threatening than usual. She ran back to bed and cried herself to sleep, while the sounds of angry voices ebbed and flowed.

Marce and Grandma were still fighting while Lisa dressed for school. They didn't even notice her slip out to catch the school bus. When Lisa returned, Grandma called her into the kitchen. Lisa could hear Marce on the C.B.

"Lisa, Marce keeps a gun under the bed you sleep in. I want you to crawl under and find it. You can shoot him," Grandma whispered.

Lisa couldn't believe her grandmother's words. The woman who told Marce everything. The woman who insisted she sleep with Marce to keep a roof over their heads. "I can't shoot anyone."

"Do you like sleeping with him?" Grandma hissed through her teeth. She frowned at Lisa.

"Of course not." Lisa paused and then added, "I plan to leave as soon as I get a job." Her grandmother's eyes widened.

Realizing, she had said too much, Lisa immediately felt fear. She covered her mouth. Would her grandmother tell her secret? Lisa watched her grandmother turn quickly and leave the kitchen. Lisa put her school books on the kitchen table and held her breath. For some reason, her grandmother seemed angry at her too.

She could hear Grandma and Marce fighting again. She winced at the banging noises.

A furious Marce wheeled into the kitchen. "Sit down there, young lady." Lisa sat down without question. His voice was harsh.

Marce handed her a blank sheet of paper. "Write every word I tell you exactly as I say them. I, Lisa Rhodes, admit that I planned to shoot my father, Marce Rhodes."

"But I didn't."

"Shut up and write, you imbecile. You can write, can't you?" He shouted and hit her on the jaw.

Shaking, Lisa tried to write the words he said.

"I further admit that I am responsible for him losing his legs. I put alcohol in his insulin."

"No, I can't. I didn't."

"You wanted to find my gun. Do you like the way it looks?" He pulled the gun from underneath the coverlet on his stumps. Cocking it, he clicked the trigger. He put another paper down and made her copy it over. "Sign your confession. I'm going to have it notarized. If you ever think of leaving, you'll go to jail." He placed handcuffs on the trembling girl and hooked one side to the chair.

"You and your grandmother will both go to jail when the Welfare Department finds out about your fraud. And you, young lady, will be charged with attempted murder. Keep your eyes on that paper and don't move."

He wheeled his chair back to the bedroom. For what seemed like hours, Lisa sat staring at the paper on the table and listening to Marce and Grandma fight. She laid her head on her free arm to relieve her cramped position. She felt stiff from sitting in one place so long.

Finally, Marce came back and released her. "Go help that old bitch get her stuff together."

Lisa cried, watching her grandmother pack.

"At least you'll have somewhere to stay. Maybe you'll start to like him."

"No, Grandma," Lisa sobbed. "I did what you made me do."

"You have to stay here. I have nowhere to bring you."

"No, no. I don't want to be here with Marce. You must know that."

"There's nowhere else for you."

"Take me with you, Grandma. Please! I can't stand it here."

"You have to stay and I have to go. Call me a cab, Lisa."

They had not heard Marce come to the bedroom door. "I'll call you a cab, you fat slob. Good riddance." Marce grabbed Grandma's suitcase, wheeled it to the door and tossed it out. "Get out! You can wait outside. Lisa and I don't need you. Stay with your friend in Land-O-Lakes. You should know better than to give me any ultimatums."

Lisa's fear of Marce grew even greater after her grandmother left. Yet she was afraid to leave. Afraid of Marce and the paper she'd signed. Lisa's added tasks opened greater opportunity for criticism. Marce was relentless in his demands. School became impossible. She felt tired and hung over every day. Her failing marks added to her feeling of desperation. The medications Marce forced her to take made her nauseous and dizzy, but didn't dull her emotional pain.

March 24th, her sixteenth birthday, was one of her worst days. Marce relented and let Lisa speak to her grandmother when she called. Hearing Grandma's voice trying to sound cheerful sent Lisa into a crying fit, and she was unable to talk. When Marce presented her with a cake and presents, she hated him even more. He seemed to think the gifts made up for the abuse he was heaping on her. She wanted to throw the presents in his face, but knew better. He grew angry because she couldn't act happy. But her birthday counted for something. He didn't hit her.

Two days after her birthday, Marce ordered Lisa to quit school. The little child who had happily run to school every

morning trying to beat her twin sister didn't exist anymore.
Who would have thought that, one day, quitting school
would be a reprieve? Yet every time she thought of leaving
the house, she remembered the paper he'd made her sign.
She was trapped.

Lisa found a job three miles from home, in the
Krispy Kreme Shop. To get there and return, she had to
ride her bicycle late at night. Many times, Lisa would see
Marce driving by the shop. The nights he didn't drive past,
he called several times. He made sure Lisa knew he was
checking to see that she was working.

Chapter 9

Terror Strikes

Lisa's mind suddenly returned to the present. Her muscles were cramping from working all evening and biking so many miles. Her eyes momentarily blurred. She must have closed them. Lisa swerved to avoid a white parked car. Suddenly, not knowing what happened, she was off the bike, laying in the street. The donuts she was bringing home flew helter-skelter all over. It took her a few seconds to realize she hadn't fallen; she had been yanked off the bike. A man's hand was on the back of her neck.

"Get up! That's a gun you feel. Walk straight ahead or I'll blow your head off," he said. The pressure of the gun pressing against her skull felt like it was bruising her head. She dared not turn for fear the gun would explode. The man slipped something over her eyes. The gun bumped against her as he tied the blindfold so tight it hurt. Her hair caught as he pulled the knot tighter.

"Ow!" she involuntary called out.

"Don't make a sound or you're dead," he whispered harshly.

A car door opened, and he forced her through the driver's side. She clumsily fell into the passenger seat which was reclined almost flat. Her head hit the window. Grabbing her roughly by her hair, he pulled her head toward his erect penis.

"Suck it for all your worth, you whore!" he seethed.

She did as she was told. Terror filled her body. The blindfold had come askew, and she noticed the words "Dodge Magnum" on the dashboard in the dim light. Although she was shaking from fear, she tried to remain calm and record the details in her memory. *You have to stop trembling*, she told herself, as he pulled her head away.

"Take your clothes off and sit on me," he ordered.

Lisa struggled to get off her blouse and slacks in the confined space. She didn't protest, fearing if she didn't comply he would kill her immediately. It wasn't easy to get on top of him, but she awkwardly straddled him. Clinging to his neck, he pushed her up and down.

"Speed up bitch!" the man said with frustration.

She increased the momentum. Her muscles were aching, but she never slowed.

"Put you clothes back on!" he coldly ordered when he had enough.

Oh God, where is he taking me? Lisa thought as he turned on the car. Sitting on the edge of the reclining seat, she felt around on the floor of the car for her clothing. She only had sight from the tiny spaces at each side of her nose. She felt for her panties, but only found her white pants and struggled to get them on while he drove. With the loud motor echoing in her ears, she felt around for her white shirt. The car halted as she finally located the blouse and pulled it on. The man reached over and began to tie her hands with more sheeting. She noticed a flower pattern on the material as it passed below her line of vision.

"If you don't do what I tell you, I'll blow your brains out," he growled.

Lisa sat still and prayed silently. The man stepped out of the car.

"My eyes are on you. Don't think of running or you'll be dead," he warned.

Maybe if I compliment him instead of screaming I'll have a chance to get away, she thought.

"I think you sound nice," she said.

There was no response, just an echo in the darkness. She wondered if he would kill her. Immersed in the terror of her nightmare, she wondered what she could do to survive.

Suddenly, she heard steps close to the passenger door. Violently, he yanked open the door and pulled her out. Grabbing the back of her shirt in his fist, he guided her. Blind Man's Bluff had once been a fun game in the projects where she lived, turning around and around and being pointed in the right direction. This was no game. Trembling with fright and surrounded by darkness, she became disoriented. He pushed her up some stairs, bruising her shin. She moaned.

"I told you to be quiet or you're dead," the man spoke in an angry, harsh whisper. "There are seventeen steps. Don't touch the walls."

Lisa raised her feet carefully, fearing she might stumble again. *If I live,* she promised herself, *I won't forget one detail that could help the police find him.* If she squinted one eye, she could see the edge of the steps. She could not see sideways, he had such a tight hold on her. He reached past her and opened a door. Once inside, he turned on a light. The room smelled like disinfectant. They continued through the apartment and stopped at a bathroom.

Pulling off her clothes, he pushed her into the shower and

turned on the water. The cold water raised goosebumps on her flesh. When the water warmed, he got in too. Lisa felt shampoo being poured on her head. Slowly at first, then roughly, her captor began washing her hair. Liquid dripped down behind the cloth and stung her eyes. He removed her wet clothes and began to wash her body with strong strokes. Afraid of falling, she leaned back slightly against the shower stall. He turned off the water and opened the shower door. Lisa heard a door open and close. Standing alone in the steaming fog, she wondered where he had gone.

Jerking, when she felt the soft cotton touch her left breast, she realized he must have opened a cabinet to get a towel. He turned her back to him while he dried her hair. Suddenly, he pushed himself against her back and tried to enter her from the rear. The force of his body almost knocked her down. She steadied herself by putting her hands on the toilet seat and shrieked out in pain. "I really like you," she said, praying she sounded convincing. He climaxed.

Then he grabbed her and pushed her across the tile floor. With a forceful shove, she fell onto a bed. He mounted her. Entering her with tremendous force, his body slammed against her. "I'm going to kill you," he said again and again. The rough, repeated battering made her short of breath. Then suddenly, he stopped almost as quickly as he had mounted her. Sprawled out on the bed, Lisa lay silently crying, fearing what he would do next. She soon found out. The terror went on and on.

Chapter 10

Missing

Around 8 a.m. on the morning of November 3, Marce Rhodes called the Tampa Police Department to notify them that his daughter, Lisa Marie Rhodes, was missing. Like many child abusers, he tried to appear to be a caring father by answering obvious questions before they could be asked. He explained that his daughter had to ride a bicycle, rather than drive a car, because she was epileptic and unable to drive. "She needs to take her medicine three times a day to prevent seizures," he lamented. He also told them that they lived alone and he was so disabled he couldn't get in and out of the car himself. "So I can't even go out to look for her," he said in a tearful voice.

Later that day, a terrified, trembling Lisa was let out of the car by her abductor after twenty-seven grueling hours of captivity. While she was still blindfolded, her kidnapper kissed her and reminded her again, "Tell everyone that I'm black, have long greasy hair, and a pockmarked face. And you'd better count to thirty before you dare to move.

"Say it. I want to hear you say it," Bobby Joe demanded gruffly.

"My kidnapper was black, had long greasy hair and a pock-marked face." She began to count slowly, "1-2-3-4-5-6-7-8-9." *Thank you God. He still trusts me,* Lisa prayed silently.

She peeked under her blindfold when she heard his car motor start and pull away. It was maroon and white. She ran towards the road. A car approached from the direction into which he had disappeared. Lisa jumped into the ditch by the side of the road and lay in the dirt, shaking until the car passed. She couldn't believe her good fortune. Her kidnapper had believed her bluff about liking him and allowed her to live. She started to walk, then run. Suddenly, she saw headlights from the opposite direction. Once again fear overcame her. He could have turned around. When the car passed, she half ran, half crawled the two blocks to her house, all the time hoping her grandmother had returned. Lisa yearned for the plump comfortable woman who held her as a toddler, stroked her hair and called her "Sunshine." Lisa crawled up the steps of the old frame house and looked both ways before knocking on the door. The door opened and Lisa stepped in. Marce sat in his wheelchair, his red puffy face frowned at her. Grandma stood wide-eyed beside him. "Marce called me to come and look for you. We called the police after I found your bike in the street."

Lisa stepped towards her grandmother to get the comfort she needed. Marce grabbed Lisa with his strong arms. As she cowered in her shocked condition, he wheeled over and hit her so hard in the mouth that her head hit a low table as she fell to the floor.

Blood ran through her fingers as she held her face.

Marce screamed at her in a jealous rage. "You whore, you slut...you were out screwing some boy all night."

Lisa tried to tell Marce and her grandmother what had happened, but Marce kept yelling insults. It took five hours for Lisa's grandmother to convince Marce to call the police and let them know that Lisa was home.

Within minutes, Detective B.D. Black arrived. He gathered Lisa's clothes, as well as taking the flowered blindfold and explained, "I have to take her to the hospital to be examined and meet our rape expert, Polly Goethe."

"My poor daughter has been raped and just got home. If I could get the bastard, POW! That's what I'd do to him." Marce smacked his hands together to demonstrate what he'd do to the rapist. "She's my only daughter and means the world to me." He wiped a tear from his eye. "I'm devastated that such a terrible thing happened to her."

Grandma stood by, shaking her head affirmatively.

Lisa left with the policeman. In the car on the way to the hospital, Lisa reaffirmed what Marce Rhodes had said about their close father and daughter relationship. "Like that," she said, showing them her crossed fingers.

She followed the dictates of her family conditioning: cover up all personal things. Along with abuse and intimidation, she had been conditioned to believe she was a person who got exactly the treatment she deserved. The paper that Marce made her write was in the house, and he claimed that he had her signature notarized. He had shown her an embossed, official-looking symbol to prove it. *I'll be jailed too.*

She did tell the police officer that, coming home from the Krispy Kreme Shop, she was kidnapped off her bicycle at

2:30 a.m. by a man who threatened her by placing a brown and silver revolver at the back of her head. "He covered my eyes with a blindfold made of a torn flowered bedsheet, and told me if I peeked to see him I'd be killed. He dragged me into the car, and when he forced my head down to give him oral sex, I could see the word Magnum, like my favorite show, on the dashboard. I swore if I got away, I'd remember every detail."

"Good girl," the officer said. "Can you describe him?" Lisa wasn't about to lie despite her abductor's instructions. She described her abductor as a white male in his thirties with brown hair and a mustache. After the examination and questioning by Polly, the officers returned Lisa to her house.

Marce insisted that Lisa go to work Tuesday morning in spite of her swollen face. He told the girl she was strong and working would be good for her. "Daytime hours will be safer," he insisted.

Lisa's boss, Mr. George, was shocked to see the girl after her long ordeal. "I'm going to see you home," he said. "You're not well enough to work this soon."

"Please don't," Lisa pleaded trembling. But her boss insisted. He had no idea that he was bringing her home to be beaten and further abused. "Come on, dear. I'm concerned for your welfare."

Chapter 11

Danger, Danger

The person in the mirror with hazel eyes hadn't changed, Bobby Joe Long reassured himself, as he brushed his teeth. He rinsed his mouth and spit. Raking his fingers through his thick, wavy brown hair, he grinned. He was a man - powerful! Next he removed two days of stubble and ran his hand over his prominent jaw. He looked into the mirror. It felt smooth and handsome. Satisfied, he grabbed the towel he had just dried himself with, wiped the flecks of toothpaste off the glass and removed his whiskers from the sink.

His mind turned to the last few days and his latest victim. *It was an act of genius...letting that frightened little girl go. She was so scared, she'd tell the cops exactly what he had ordered her to. She'd tell the cops her kidnapper was a black man. That would throw them off. He could trust her; she never told anyone else about her abusive stepfather.* He chuckled aloud. *She wasn't like the whores who did it for money. She'd really liked him. And no wonder,* he thought. *He was damn good.*

Long punched on the television. Maybe he'd hear some-thing about the story he'd told Lisa to repeat about the greasy-haired black man with pockmarks, raping young girls. He looked at the watch on his wrist. "Damn, it's too late to catch the news," Bobby Joe complained to himself, pushing the T.V.'s off button. He could still get the weekend papers he thought, swaggering down the hall. His anticipation and excitement showed, but no one saw him.

The paper dispensers on Fowler would still have *The Tampa Tribune*. He walked there and shoved a quarter in the slot, grasped all the papers and rushed back to his apartment. Sitting down in the blue striped easy chair, his eyes hungrily scanned the words looking for news of his latest conquest. He was annoyed it wasn't front page, but found the story on page three...MISSING GIRL SUBJECT OF POLICE SEARCH.

Bobby Joe read that Marce Rhodes had reported his daughter Lisa missing. Her bicycle and the donuts she was bringing her father were found in the street. Bobby Joe started to feel uneasy when he saw her name under her picture. The reporter must have made an error. The girl he'd held captive for twenty-six hours was named Carol, but under the picture was the name, Lisa Marie Rhodes. Had she lied about her name? Annoyed, he turned the page to continue reading. Then he saw the headline: MURDERED WOMEN OF TAMPA. Above the story were the pictures of four women killed and a map showing the locations and dates the bodies were found. His heart began to pound. The rush was so high, it was almost better than the feeling he got killing the bitches. *The Tampa Tribune* story went on:

Karen Beth Dinsfriend, 28, found October 14th.

The body was partially clothed and bound. It was found in an orange grove on the west side of Lake Thonotosassa. Death by asphyxiation.

Chanel Devon Williams, 18, found October 7th. The nude corpse was found alongside Morris Bridge Road, just north of Branchton Road near Hillsborough State Park. Death by gunshot.

Seeing the word "gunshot" triggered a savored memory in Bobby Joe of how the black bitch struggled and refused to die. She was so strong he needed to shoot her, so she couldn't overpower him. Dismissing his annoyance, he read on.

Michelle Denise Simms, 22, found May 27th, nude and bound in the woods north of Plant City near Interstate 4 overpass at Park Road. Death by stabbing.

Nguen Thi Long, 19, found May 13th, nude and bound, in a field where Interstate 75 bypass stops south of Gibsonton. Death by strangulation.

He concentrated on the picture of Michelle Denise Simms. She was so much like Susan; high cheek bones and big brown eyes. She had to have Indian blood. The oriental he'd killed recently was a good substitute too. His feelings of euphoria grew. He read on.

The bodies of two other women were discovered last week, but so far have not been linked to these four.

Only he, Bobby Joe Long, knew they were his victims. He could make women tremble and the police appear idiots and fools.

He looked for more information about the girl he'd grabbed off the bicycle. Quickly he scanned the page for more news of Lisa or whatever the hell her name was. He read the description of her kidnapper.

White Male, Brown Wavy Hair, Mustache, Stocky Build. F.B.I. steps in...

For a moment he couldn't believe his eyes. Then he cursed out loud. "That rotten, lying little bitch." He paced back and forth like a caged tiger. The stupid little cunt had lied to him. She'd ruined his plan. He could stay, but it would be stupid. His parole officer might see his description and recognize it.

Running outside, Bobby Joe got into his car. He drove around hour after hour looking for the bitch. She was responsible for his description being splashed through all the papers. His anger grew when he realized there was a task force after him. They'd even called in the F.B.I. As he pushed the accelerator down, his fear gave way and began to feed another feeling: excitement. All his attention fixed on it. He felt a power surge. Look at all the people looking for the killer. He wondered how some of his friends would feel if they knew how important he was. His feelings of power felt good, but he needed to feel even more stimulation, and he knew just how and where to get it.

Bobby Joe headed for the Sly Fox Lounge on Nebraska Avenue, where he had gotten the oriental chick. It was busy and there were always new girls, but he had to be careful. He parked in the back between two other cars. Once inside, he checked out the women sitting in the red plush seats that surrounded the bar. Some were regulars. The sound of music pounding and the sight of the two dancers writhing on the stage stimulated him. He went into the men's room to try and calm down. Checking his reflection in the mirror, he smoothed his hair and took a few deep breaths before reentering the bar. He had to be careful. Even sluts could read the papers.

Suddenly, Bobby saw a new face. "Can I sit down?" he asked. He'd learned early in life that being polite paid off with women — even whores. The girl was pretty, brunette and young. "How about taking a little ride?" Bobby Joe asked, holding out a twenty dollar bill.

"I'm a dancer," she snapped and jumped up from the table. *Damn,* Bobby Joe thought, *that Vietnamese gook thought she was a dancer too...inflated ideas for two bit whores.* He wanted to tell this one to go to hell. All he needed to do was get her in the car. Then he'd get even. He watched the girl with long dark hair get up on the stage.

Calling over a waitress, Bobby Joe ordered a seven and seven. He stared at the woman on the stage while she gyrated just above his head. He sipped his drink and focused his eyes on her face. She smiled and kept looking down in his direction. The fact that she wasn't eager to go with him presented a challenge. It made the sport even better.

When she returned to a table, he walked over and explained that he just wanted to buy her a drink. She seemed to warm up. The bitch was pretending she wasn't a hooker. Two could play that game.

"You have beautiful brown eyes," Bobby Joe said as he sat next to her. She accepted his offer and began to sip the drink he paid for. His compliment paid off. She relaxed and giggled. He ordered another round of drinks.

The girl excused herself and went to the ladies' room. When she returned she informed Bobby, "I called my boyfriend, and he's coming to pick me up."

Furious, Bobby Joe jumped to his feet and headed toward the back door. He jumped into his car, turned the key on, floored the accelerator, and headed south on Nebraska. A

girl with dark blond hair driving the Toyota in front of him drew his attention. He pulled up next to her and pointed for her to pull over. She smiled and sped up. Bobby Joe got on her tail, then fell back and followed her from a distance. She turned west on Busch Boulevard. He increased speed and kept her in his sight when she went south on Dale Mabry. Again, he drove over next to her and signalled for her to pull over. She turned into a parking lot just west of Dale Mabry on Humphrey.

As Bobby Joe pulled his car up next to her, the girl stepped out of her car. He was surprised. She was big... almost as tall as he was. He noticed her cowboy boots; they added to her height. He pointed his gun at her. "Get in the car." She started yelling. He grabbed her and forced her into the car. His adrenaline pumped. His plan was to tie her up and then see her squirming, helpless, begging. He removed two pieces of rope from the glove compartment.

"I don't like kinky stuff," she protested, staring at his gun. He put the gun in his waistband.

"Strip, you two-bit whore and shut up," Bobby said, hitting her with his fist across the bridge of her nose. Her eyes opened wide. She cried out in pain. He perceived fear in her eyes and felt pleasure. Then he flashed his knife and cut her heavy, velour flowered shirt off. "Hurry up you bitch. I haven't got all night."

"Don't hurt me. I'll do anything you say," she pleaded, wiggling out of her jeans. "Don't hit me again. I'm terrified of being hurt."

He grabbed the girl by her blond hair. "Suck my cock, you no good whore!" he ordered and hit her with his fist before she could comply. She struggled to open the car door.

He grabbed her by the throat and began to squeeze. She started to beat him on the chest. He drew his knee up and slammed it against her crotch as hard as he could. She had managed to get the car door open. Her head hung out the passenger's side. With two hands around her throat, he pressed against her windpipe. She strained to breathe. She pushed her arms against his chest and dug her nails in. He kneed her again. Her bowels exploded all over the car. "You stinking whore! You think you can get even with me by shitting in my car?" He pounded her body and face until she stopped straining and collapsed. He reached over her inert body and managed to close the car door.

Panic seized him. He was in a populated area. The sign, LaPetite Academy, came into his consciousness. His car was right under it. He needed to get to a deserted place. He'd chased her for miles. It was too far to go north, so he pulled back onto Dale Mabry and followed it to Kennedy. The naked woman laying on his reclining seat rolled toward him as he turned east. Fear possessed him as he looked out for police cars. He slowed down trying not to attract attention. The task force was looking for him. He had to be careful. He took Adamo Drive north towards the railroad yards, an area he hoped would be isolated enough to discard the body. At the overpass by Orient Road, he slammed on his brakes and drove his car as close as he could to the tracks.

The smell of fecal matter assaulted his senses. Repulsed, he opened the door on the driver's side and got out.

He tied one rope around the girl's throat and used the leash to pull her out of the car onto the ground. Afterward, he wrapped the long end around her elbows and jerked it tighter and tighter until he heard snapping noises. The bitch

groaned! Bobby Joe felt pleasure knowing she was in pain and he caused it. An adrenaline high increased his sensation of power realizing she was still alive. It was the satisfaction he was seeking. She would rob him of it by dying too quickly. With renewed enthusiasm, he tied her wrists together. His rage was just building. He began to kick her all over.

Once life went from her body, there was no more sport. He turned her body face down, and spread her legs apart like he'd set up the others he'd killed. The cops would appreciate his technique, he thought. Satisfied, he drove his car to the nearest car wash to remove the filth.

Chapter 12

On A Rampage

Fear of a mad killer striking spread through Tampa. Public pressure mounted rapidly as bodies continued to be discovered. The strange link between them were mysterious red fibers found on each one. An unidentified body was unearthed on Wednesday, November 1st, on U.S. 301, and the nude body of Margaret M. Slayton, age twenty-six, was stumbled upon Friday, November 3rd, in a clearing on MacDill Avenue and Osborne Street. Florida newspapers included long stories about the women and Lisa's kidnapping. Wire services picked up the gruesome news. More reporters trooped into the state ready to pounce on new developments. They started bombarding the Hillsborough County Sheriff's Office and the Tampa Police Department with questions to fill their papers with titillating new copy. Speculation about who was to be the next victim reached a high.

The Tampa Police Department exploded into action. Some police detectives filed reports, others checked records,

and still others milled about collecting data. The din of
voices intermingling with ringing phones created it's own
level of tension. The pressure to solve the crimes increased
each day. But despite the intense investigation, the police
still did not have a suspect.

Polly Goethe, who was working under Sgt. Pinkerton,
entered his office carrying some old files on Lisa Rhodes.
Since her examination of the girl, she hadn't been able to get
Lisa out of her mind.

"Larry, that girl who was kidnapped, Lisa Rhodes, I
remember that one of her neighbors called about a year ago
with suspicions that she was being abused, so I went out to
see Lisa and asked if she was being mistreated. Lisa denied
it, and I could see no signs of abuse. I dismissed the accusations as false, but now I think that was premature. I'd like
to bring her in here and question her without her father and
grandmother present."

"You want to investigate those charges now?" He looked
perplexed. "Do you think her information about the rapist
isn't true either?"

"On the contrary, she was very open and informative. In
fact, even though she was blindfolded, she peeked through a
small space where light got in. She was able to describe the
man, the surrounding environment. She is alert and a fine witness. Lisa has powers of observation that are far better than I
have ever experienced with any rape victim. Lisa remembered
the digital clock on the dashboard and that Q105 was on the
radio. She even noticed the door locks didn't have a knob on
the top, the motor was noisy and the muffler vibrated." Polly
paused and looked thoughtful. "When I questioned her previously, she didn't look at me and gave one syllable answers. It
doesn't fit. Besides, I think the rapist could be the killer."

"Well forget it! There's nothing to connect the rape to the murders. The fact that she is alive is testimony to that."

"Please, let's call her in. See if she can tell us anything else. Then you can question her about her father."

"You did that and got nothing." He shook his head. "What makes you think we'll get more now?"

"If we had her hypnotized, I think we could. She might even give us a fuller description of the rapist and be able to pinpoint his location."

Finally, Pinkerton agreed. "Okay, let's follow your gut instincts." She smiled.

When Lisa got to the police station, she felt uncomfortable. This time the police rape expert with the short cropped, mannish hair and no makeup seemed threatening and nosy. Except that the other woman had long hair, this officer looked like the one who came to Lisa's house a year earlier. How could Lisa have admitted the truth the year before when Marce was listening to everything she said on a two-way radio he had set up? Since Lisa had to lie then, how could she now tell the truth? Frightened, Lisa thought she had better remain silent about the terrible things Marce did to her. The same terrible things that Bobby Joe did.

"Lisa, we're going over your testimony to see if we have all the facts about your kidnapper." Polly looked at her closely. "And there's something else." She paused and tried to put her ideas sensitively, so as not to further scare the girl.

"I'm concerned that something is going on in your house. I talked to you last year. You said no. Remember?"

Lisa looked away. All she could think was, *if they know, I will go to jail.* She kept seeing in her mind the signed paper that Marce kept locked up.

"You can tell me, Lisa."

Sgt. Larry Pinkerton sat down with Polly and Lisa. He smiled as he drew his chair close to her. He showed Lisa pictures of his daughter. He said gently, "My daughter means everything to me. Young girls should be protected and cared for. They shouldn't ever have to go through the terrible things that rapist did to you." He reached out to Lisa in a fatherly way. "I'm going to ask your father if we can hypnotize you so we can get a better idea of what the rapist looked like."

Tears flooded down Lisa's cheeks...tears for herself. The loving words the policeman spoke about his daughter overwhelmed her. Why couldn't she have a father like him? But she didn't. She had none. "No, no," she cried. "Don't call Marce. He will never let you do that."

"I'm sure he'll want to catch the rapist." Sgt. Pinkerton went to call Lisa's father and left Lisa with Polly. Lisa was obviously traumatized by her family so much that even her abduction was easier for her to talk about.

Polly went back to the subject of the kidnapping. "You were a very good witness about your abductor. You said you peeked under the blindfold and saw a bank when he let you go. Were there other landmarks to let us know the neighborhood he lived in?"

Lisa thought for a moment. "He stopped at a gas station."

"When you're hypnotized, you'll be able to remember everything and tell us."

Lisa shivered. She grew more afraid. Maybe she would tell them about Marce, too, and go to jail. She heard about hypnosis making people tell things they didn't want to. "No, I can't, and Marce won't let me."

There it was again. The girl's visible agitation about her

family. "Are you afraid of your father, Lisa? At school, your counselors thought you might be abused. So did your neighbors. I can help you."

Lisa said nothing.

Sgt. Pinkerton, a frustrated look on his face, returned from his telephone conversation with Marce. "Your father refuses to give his permission for us to question you under hypnosis. I'd think he would want to do anything to help find the man who kidnapped and raped you. If you were my daughter I would. The guy is out there. What secrets is he trying to hide?" He paused. She still was silent. Polly flashed him a look telling him to get off the subject. "It's all right, Lisa. Can you go over the testimony you've given us?"

Lisa blinked back tears, as she went over her testimony again, trying to remember everything she could about her kidnapper. "The apartment smelled clean. The kidnapper led me into a shower, scrubbed me down, washed my hair. He told me that he grabbed me because women dumped on him all the time and were pigs. He was a clean freak. He wanted sex over and over. He was painfully rough like he was using a broom stick." As Lisa talked, she self-consciously covered her bruises on her face. "Sometimes he would threaten me with his gun, and sometimes he'd act like I was his girlfriend. Over and over he said he would kill me."

"When did he hit you?" Sgt. Pinkerton asked, brushing aside her hand that covered the swelling.

"Hit me? He threatened to, but I just did everything he said. I must have hurt my face when I dove into the ditch at the side of the road after he left me off. Every car I saw, I thought was him coming back."

He looked towards Polly, who nodded knowingly. "Was there anything about the apartment that you could identify?"

Lisa sat quietly. "I took my barrette off and pushed it under the side of the water bed closest to the bathroom. So when the police got him, they'd find it." She looked down shyly. Then, she almost whispered, "Well there was something. When I had to go to the bathroom, he wanted to watch. I pleaded with him to leave and he stepped outside the door. I put my finger prints under the toilet seat, so if he killed me the police would know I'd been there." Lisa didn't want to tell the police how he tried to enter her from the rear. She was too ashamed. How could she explain that when he did that, she bit down on the bed coverlet to keep from screaming.

"I hope we can find his apartment, before the clean freak cleans. That was so smart of you, Lisa. Anything else?"

"Only his sneakers. There was a rooster on them. They were in the bathroom, and I could seem them under the blindfold. The had blue lines of trim."

"You were with him a long time. Did he sleep?" Sgt. Pinkerton asked.

"Sometimes he lay still like he was sleeping, but I was sure he was testing me. I pretended to sleep too. He said over and over, 'I'll blow your brains out if you're not quiet.' It kept going around in my head. I took deep breaths and lay as still as possible."

"I think he may be the man who's killed all those women around Tampa. Did he say anything about other women?" Polly leaned forward and looked directly into Lisa's brown eyes.

Lisa's eyes widened, her mouth opened and she expelled air like she was hit in the stomach. "Oh, my God, it may be him, but I don't know. He kept threatening to kill me. I tried

to make him realize I was a person — a person with feelings
and a life. I told him a little bit about myself. He thinks my
name is Carol. Oh God! My real name was in the paper.
He'll try to get me again. The neighborhood! My address!
Everything! I'm dead meat."

Sgt. Pinkerton frowned at Polly. "Now why did you tell
her that? You know that the detectives don't think there's
any connection. The guy who killed those women goes after
dancers and housewives, not little girls." But he was beginning to wonder, could it be the same man? Was he widening
his attacks? He looked at the trembling Lisa. "You're just
like my daughter, and we'll protect you. I tell my daughter
she's like *The Wind Beneath My Wings*. You know, like the
song. So are you, Lisa." Sgt. Pinkerton soothingly patted
Lisa's hand.

Lisa had steeled herself from hurt. She was rigid in protecting her emotions, but she had no protection from kindness, especially from a man. The song he'd mentioned
played in her head. Suddenly, she burst into tears. It was the
first time she felt free to cry. Her body shook uncontrollably.
It seemed like forever before she was able to talk.

The detectives silently stared at her. Hoarsely, she finally
said, "He did say he raped other girls; but he was going to
kill me. He repeated it while he was screwing me. He said
he kidnapped other girls; he didn't say he killed them," she
managed to say. "He said he had problems with women."

"Did he use the term girl and women interchangeably, or
do you think he thought of women as different?" Pinkerton
asked.

"Yes, girls and women were all bitches. He broke up with
some woman who lied about him. I looked like her. He said

that's why he grabbed me. So I tried to pretend to be his girl-friend. So he'd forget about killing me. It was hours since I ate anything. He ate, but I couldn't even pretend to swallow. More time went by, and then he made me a ham sandwich. I tried to pretend I was having a good time, but I was terrified. I couldn't eat. My mouth was so dry. I felt the couch. It was covered with velour. Once I peeked under my blindfold and saw a picture of an owl on the wall."

"He held the gun against you all that time?"

She shook her head no. "But I felt he was going to kill me. I was so afraid. Sometimes he put the gun at the head of the bed. Other times he picked it up and brushed the gun across my body. He would ask if I could feel it. Then he said he was emptying the gun. I heard thumps in the drawer next to him. He said there were no more bullets in the gun, but he could've been lying and just tapping the drawer."

"How were you able to see that the gun had a brown handle?"

"When he kidnapped me, before the blindfold. When he was telling me I was going to die. After I said I liked him, he changed from being threatening and acted like I was his girlfriend. I tried to remain calm so he would stay calm. I pretended to like him and what he was doing. I told him that if he let me go, I wouldn't tell a living soul about him. He gave me a black sweater to wear. He said my white one was too dirty. Lying in the bottom of the car, I peeked at him when he went over to the teller machine. I almost thought he saw me peeking. But he didn't. On the way home, he said we were on Himes Avenue. I told him he had gone too far and he cursed. I believed he was going to kill me until he let me out. When I heard the car driving away, I removed the

blindfold so I could see it. It was maroon with a white top. The light flashed off the spokes like wire wheels."

"That's the same description of a car given by the rape victim in New Port Richey. A Dodge Magnum, maroon with a white top. You did great, Lisa! We've got something now that connects your case to another case." Polly squeezed Lisa's hand. For a minute she lost her professional reserve and appeared almost girlish. She composed herself. "Anything else?"

Lisa felt less threatened. Polly seemed more human, almost like a sister sharing experiences. "He told me again and again to say he was black and smelled bad, with greasy hair and pockmarks. I think he believed I would."

"He probably did," laughed Polly. "You fooled him."

"You said you got banged up hiding in a ditch?" Sgt. Pinkerton looked intently at Lisa.

Lisa appeared confused. She soberly and minutely described her time with the kidnapper, but when asked about the bruises, she appeared agitated and upset. The two detectives stared at one another. Polly made a gesture with her hand to Sgt. Pinkerton...one that said leave us alone.

"I think you need our help, Lisa. If someone is hurting you, Sgt. Pinkerton and I can see that it stops."

Lisa stood up unsteadily. "I have to go home."

"All right, Lisa, but remember we're here for you." As Polly drove Lisa home, she talked about other girls she had helped who were being abused at home. Lisa just listened silently.

Once inside the house, Lisa leaned against the closed door. Before she could think of what to do, Marce held out his arms to her. "Come make your daddy happy."

"Leave me alone, I don't want you to touch me."

"I know you didn't mean to say that. Here, I've got something for you." He touched the fly of his loose, old wrinkled pants.

Ignoring his gesture, she talked as if thinking out loud. "The policewoman thinks that my kidnapper is the man who killed all those women, and I got away from him."

"Don't get any smart ideas about getting away from me. I can use my gun if I have to."

Lisa looked at the old man without legs sitting in the wheelchair.

"Your gun. Aren't you going to tell me how I'm going to jail?" Marce wheeled the chair closer to her. "Just keep your distance." Lisa's body trembled with fear after her words. She turned and ran to the kitchen to make dinner, hoping Marce would forget her insolence. He wheeled himself into the kitchen. She held her breath and put on a happy face, calling out, "I'll make your favorite pork chops." She tiptoed around the kitchen trying not to let him grab her. The old man ate dinner without incident.

When she came out of the bathroom, ready for bed, he was sitting in his chair with the gun in his lap.

"Get in that bedroom. And no more thinkin' you're Miss High and Mighty."

Chapter 13

Stakeout

Sgt. Pinkerton stared into space thinking after Polly left with Lisa. Then, distracted by animated conversation outside his office, he went to investigate.

Officer Trent, with a telephone receiver in his hand, announced, "Another body of a woman was found two miles north of Hillsborough County line."

A stampede of detectives followed by reporters made a thundering noise galloping out of police headquarters. They wanted to view the body. The office was left comparatively quiet. Sgt. Pinkerton returned and sat at his desk, writing his report on the interview with Lisa. Polly Goethe, the police-woman in charge of her case, thought Lisa McVey was detained and raped by the killer. Pinkerton tapped his pen on the paper, remembering the other detectives lack of interest in Lisa once she had been found alive. They were probably right that Lisa had been kidnapped by someone else. In fact, that was his opinion too. Why would the murderer let her live? Besides, red fibers were found on all the murder victims,

linking them to one murderer. As far as Pinkerton knew, Lisa didn't share that link. Still, he owed it to Polly to present her opinion to his captain. Let Martinez make the decision. He can take the flack. It's his job.

Getting up, Pinkerton went toward Captain Martinez's office and walked in. "Howard, I know you're busy but something's bothering me. One of my officers, Polly Goethe, thinks that Lisa Rhodes, the 17-year-old, was abducted by the killer everyone's looking for."

"What do you think, Sergeant?"

Pinkerton scratched his head and looked pensive. "Well, the detectives were all on the case until she returned home. Some even think she wasn't telling the truth. One even laughed when she described the rooster on her abductor's sneaker. But it was Lisa's testimony that the guy was driving a two door, maroon Dodge Magnum with wire wheels which Polly immediately connected with a rape in New Port Richey. If Polly is right, the girl is in terrible danger. We should search for the car and him right now."

"It's been a waste of thirty-six hours even if he's not the murderer. The hell with what the other detectives think. Polly is the rape expert. Let's go with it. In the meantime, put out a bulletin about the car. Time is our enemy."

"I'd like to get the bastard. Lisa's such a good kid. I've got a daughter almost her age."

There was some commotion outside. Some of the detectives had returned with the grisly details of the body found off Morris Bridge Road. "The putrid remains were strewn all over. The woman had been bound like all the other bodies," Detective Trent reported. Pinkerton thought uneasily, *Lisa was bound in a similar way.* He was beginning to think

Polly was right. *Why*, he wondered, *had the abductor let Lisa go?*

During the next few hours, the Tampa Police Department began to search for a two-door, maroon Dodge Magnum with a white top. Word was out that another woman had disappeared from the Sly Fox Lounge: Kim Marie Swann, 21 years old, a dancer. The case was similar to that of Ngeun Thi Long, whose body had been found in May. The killer defied understanding. Taking two women from the same place, Pinkerton mused, shaking his head.

Two days passed. On November 12th, Kim Marie Swann's body was found face down on the side of Orient Road overpass, just north of Adamo Drive. Her naked body had marks on the wrists and arms as if she had been bound. She had been strangled.

Next, reports came in that red fibers had been found on Lisa's panties. The discovery shocked most of the detectives. This directly linked her abductor to the killer. The detectives and a new task force now theorized that Lisa was the one witness who could identify the man. Polly, working with the task force decided to become Lisa's constant companion. She telephoned Lisa and told her of their discovery. "I'm coming to get you," she said firmly.

Lisa looked out of the living room window, anxiously waiting to see the Sheriff's car before telling Marce she was leaving.

"The policewoman asked me to help them find the killer," Lisa called and ran out the door. She didn't wait to see Marce's reaction. The door slammed, shutting off his shouted response.

Breathlessly, Lisa entered the back seat, as Polly stood holding the car door open.

"You didn't give us a chance to knock on the door. I wish every witness was so cooperative," Polly said, getting back in the car next to Lisa.

"Lisa, we want to find the exact spot the kidnapper left you off. We'll time the different routes the man could have driven that night. I'm going to tie a blindfold around your head exactly the way he did." The material was torn from a flowered bed sheet. Lisa nodded to Polly, and the detective put the blindfold on her. It was a few minutes before the car started to move.

"If you hear anything that triggers your memory, tell us immediately even if you don't think it's important," Polly directed.

Lisa tensed with concentration. Street noises were more numerous in the daytime. "I didn't hear any other cars that night," she said. "Now they're confusing me."

"Put all your attention on that time. The time you were in the car. Think back."

Lisa tried to put her mind on the task Polly set for her, but she kept thinking of Marce. "He threatens me with his gun."

Polly looked at the girl quizzically.

"Did he stop the car and threaten you?"

Lisa shook her head.

"He threatens me every night with his shiny gun."

"Who does? The kidnapper?" Polly asked. "You said the gun had a brown handle."

"No. Marce, my grandmother's boyfriend."

Polly put her arm around Lisa. "You *are* being abused at home. I knew you were. Thank goodness you've told me. You can't go back there."

"I don't want to," Lisa wailed.

Polly directed the detectives "We have to find a safe place right away for this girl."

Lisa pulled off the blindfold and sat back relieved. Whatever was going to happen, her admission couldn't be changed now. Maybe she'd finally be safe. She listened while Polly and the detectives talked about options for her. One of the detectives in the front seat offered his place. "My family and I have a spare room."

"Is that all right, Lisa?" The girl nodded.

"You're too upset today. We'll try this tomorrow after you're settled in your temporary new home," Polly told Lisa.

"I can do it now. As long as I know I don't have to go back to Marce, I can do anything. Let's go on."

"Lisa, you're one brave girl."

Lisa refocused on the kidnapping. "The time," Lisa estimated, "that I was with the kidnapper, before he dropped me off, was less than twenty minutes."

They made some trial runs, with Lisa blindfolded again. Finally, they determined the approximate location of the killer's apartment. It was close to Marce's house.

Polly then took Lisa to her temporary new home. "Lisa, if you have to leave for any reason, I'll accompany you. Detective, tell your wife and kids they're not to talk about their house guest."

Polly and Sgt. Pinkerton were relieved to know that Lisa was out of her home. "She'll be safe. The kidnapper won't know where she is, so he won't be able to snatch her again," Polly said.

Meanwhile, the hunt for the fugitive continued. The police were inundated by newspaper reporters and calls from

higher ups asking what was being done on the killings in the Tampa area. The Hillsborough County Sheriff's office in Ybor City called a press conference on November 14th. They announced that the F.B.I. was now working closely with the sheriff's office, and a task force had been formed to find the killer. They publicly linked four deaths and said five others were being examined closely.

Meanwhile, the task force, made up of homicide and sex crime detectives, was divided into teams and given specific areas. They were to search for both the vehicle and possible residence of the kidnapper. Nothing turned up.

The search continued. Since Lisa had said her abductor cashed a check, nearby banks were canvassed, and one detective was dispatched to Tallahassee got information about all Dodge Magnum vehicles in the surrounding area. No detective, as yet, had any luck in identifying the apartment complex.

Then, officers David Wolf and Carson Helms spotted a maroon and white car with wire wheels on Nebraska Avenue. Stopping the car, they asked to see the driver's license and registration. A man with brown curly hair and a mustache handed them over politely. His name was Robert Joe Long, age 31. He appeared calm and confident, but fit the description Lisa gave. The police noted the time as 10 a.m., November 15, 1984.

Although they allowed Long to return to his apartment, he was under constant surveillance. They watched as he left the apartment several times. He was observed taking things out to a dumpster and throwing them inside. Later, the police took the items back to headquarters. Some were pictures of nude women having sex. Others were articles of clothing and papers. To the police, it looked like Long was ready to get out of town.

The following day, two F.B.I. experts flew to Tampa to examine the red fibers that connected all the murders, as well as the kidnapping and rape of Lisa. Meanwhile, more information poured in about the man they suspected. Long had used a credit card at a First National Bank automatic teller on November 4th, the day Lisa was abducted. Moreover, he was on probation for aggravated assault of a woman who had fled him in her Jaguar. Even earlier, he'd been arrested for rape in Dade County, Florida. The charges had been reduced, and he'd been placed on probation.

Assistant State Attorney Michael Benito reviewed the evidence with the detective. An arrest warrant was issued for Robert Joe Long, charging him with kidnapping and sexual battery in the abduction of Lisa Rhodes.

Long had left his apartment and was watching a Chuck Norris movie in Carrollwood Plaza at 2:30 p.m. on November 16th, just twelve days after he had released Lisa. Although Long wasn't aware of it, Detective Turner followed him inside.

Outside, the task force teams were surrounding the theater. The movie ended — it was now about 4 p.m. As Long walked out to his car, Detectives Radford and Davis came up behind him.

"Robert Joe Long?" Davis asked. Bobby Joe nodded.

"You're under arrest." He handed Long the warrant and Detective Cribb, who had joined them, read off the specific charges. It had been thirty-six hours since the formation of the task force. Long was then taken by several detectives to his apartment to witness the search. Afterward, he was brought to headquarters to be interrogated. A cooperative Long signed a Consent to Interview Form.

The detectives began questioning him. Slowly, friendly,

at first, the detectives began bringing out their knowledge of Long's past, including his arrest for rape in Miami in 1974.

Their questions turned to Lisa, and Long admitted he'd abducted her. He seemed reluctant to discuss details, telling them only he'd had sex with Lisa. When asked why he hadn't killed her, Long indicated that he'd taken the bullets from his gun and dumped them into the trash so he wouldn't be tempted.

The detectives moved on to the subject of Long's other abductions, telling him they had hair and fiber evidence. "You need to tell us your side," one said convincingly. Eventually, Long admitted to murdering nine young women between May 4 and November 11, 1984. He even directed police to a body they hadn't yet found. "When you find that body, you'll also find a pair of scissors." At the end of the interview, Long returned to the subject of Lisa McVey.

"You guys know that the only reason you caught me is because I let Lisa go. But the truth is, letting Lisa go makes it worth getting caught for killing the others."

After he returned Long to the holding cell, the detectives searched recent missing persons reports. They spotted one for Vickie Marie Elliott, a waitress at the Ramada Inn. She had been missing since September 6, 1984. Noted in the description was that she always carried scissors for protection.

The police called a news conference. They announced Bobby Joe Long's arrest and confession, adding that he'd committed another murder.

Lora Elliott wasn't prepared to learn of her daughter's death when she answered the phone. "I'm not relieved. I was hoping she'd still be alive," she told the excited reporter trying to get his own unique news angle.

Police next found the body of Kim Marie Swann, dropped in the open inside the city limits. Bobby Joe had claimed to detectives that he lost interest in having sex with her because she had defecated in his car. He didn't talk about the fecal matter that remained on the body and covered her clothes. He did say he went directly to a car wash after dumping the body.

Detectives viewing the body weren't spared the stench of it rotting in the Florida sun. Nor the sight of orifices and open wounds writhing and pulsating with live maggots, while red ants teamed over the putrid flesh. Meanwhile, the directions Bobby Joe Long had given led detectives to the body of Vickie Marie Elliott. Just as he said, the petite strawberry blond 21- year - old waitress, had a pair of scissors protruding from the area that remained of her vagina.

Reporters fixated on information about the man in jail. Searched records of crime dated back to 1970. They found evidence of arrests in 1971 for lewd and lascivious assault; in 1974 for battery against a woman; in 1981 for assault against a neighbor in Kenova, West Virginia; and in 1982 an aggravated assault for pulling a gun on a woman, for which Long was placed on three years probation.

They discovered more trouble in his work records in hospitals in West Virginia and Tampa. The records contained complaints by women whom he'd X-rayed. Embarrassed hospital directors where he had worked instructed employees not to talk to reporters.

New headlines now revealed these early crimes, and speculation arose about the young man who committed them. Pictures of Long appeared in every Bay area newspaper and on national television programs. Telephones rang constantly at the Tampa Police Station and Sheriff's Department.

Bobby Joe Long's first hearing was scheduled before
Judge Perry Little. He was formally charged with eight
counts of first degree murder, eight counts of sexual battery
and nine counts of kidnapping.

Meanwhile, the newspaper stories, now nationwide,
continued with vignettes of Bobby Joe from childhood as
supplied by neighbors and relatives:

     *** At 6, he was hit by a car crossing the street.

     *** At 7, he began elementary school.

     *** At 12, he moved to Hialeah with his mother.

     *** At 17, he was arrested for stolen property.

     ***** At 18, he dropped out of school and enlisted
in the U.S. Army.**

     ***** At 21, he was married, had a son and a
motorcycle accident.**

     *** At 22, he had a daughter.

     *** At 24, he became an electrician.

     *** At 26, his wife filed for divorce.

     ***** At 27, he moved to Tampa and began
working at Asturiano Village Hospital.**

     ***** At 28, he served two days in jail for displaying
obscene material to a young girl and went to California
for an intensive course in commercial diving.**

     *** At 29, he returned to Tampa.

     ***** At 30, he produced $4,000 in back child sup-
port and got a job at Tampa General Hospital and lost
it the same year.**

Police were able to add another fact to the timeline:

     *** At 31, he murdered ten young women.

The media attention gave Bobby Joe Long celebrity status.
More friends and neighbors from Kenova, West Virginia

(Long's birthplace), Miami, California and Tampa were asked for their opinions of the "Serial Killer." His mother spoke from her West Virginia home: "Everywhere he turned his life has been a dead end. It's been torture." Garland Wilson, a city judge in Kenova, who tried Long for an assault in 1982, said, "He was a handsome looking fellow, just a gentleman."

Two women who worked with him in the Veterans Hospital in Huntington, West Virginia had positive things to tell reporters and expressed shock after being informed Bobby Joe Long was a serial killer. Both women knew, however, he had been fired after working less than a month in the radiology department for complaints of improper behavior lodged by women.

One of Long's Miami neighbors voiced a discordant note. "We visited his wife Cindy, but me and my sister would never stay if he was alone. He talked dirty." In contrast, another Miami neighbor said, "He was a good kid. Never caused trouble."

Most of the reports were positive, but some gave insight into the real Long. An Indian Rocks Beach resident, who was in Long's driving school class in California, remembered, "Long boasted about dating a 13-year-old. He said he tied her up, and she was kinky."

Susan Replogle told a CBS news reporter in a taped interview that Bobby Joe had raped her and was granted two appeals for a battery crime against her. "The charge was dismissed on February 6, 1984 — two months before his killing spree started." She went on to speak of his abusive characteristics. The final program only showed Susan's form and didn't identify her. When she watched the dark shadow

on the broadcast, she heard her words cut to one line: "He
had the boy next door kind of good looks." She was grateful
to be hidden from the public.

Chapter 14

Who's The Victim?

Once Bobby Joe Long was in jail, Lisa had to give up being in protective custody at the home of the police officer and his lovely family. Polly drove Lisa to a new residence, Beach Place. It sounded like a condo on the gulf, but in reality, it was a home for delinquent teenagers.

Lisa cried all night lying on the hard, lumpy bed. How could life be so unfair? All she ever wanted was to be a good girl. Why had her life been so terrible? Did she really deserve this? In the project in Pennsylvania, the day her mother had Lisa and her brothers and sister give away their toys, choose their best outfits and get into the car, Lisa had given her childhood away. No, it was stolen by Marce. No, she had never had one.

She tried to feel comfort in the fact that she didn't have to see him again. That made her feel better, but her surroundings made her feel as though she was being punished. Neither Polly nor Sgt. Pinkerton seemed to blame Lisa. They blamed Marce, but he wasn't in a home for wayward teens. She was!

Lisa spent her time thinking about the past. Damn, she didn't even know who her father was. Nevertheless, no father was better than one who beats and screws you. She'd never have to use the name Lisa Rhodes again. She was Lisa McVey. She shuddered and promised herself, "I'll never be afraid again. I survived a mass murderer."

Lisa began to realize she was not alone in having ghastly memories when she met two sisters who were sexually abused by their own father. The girls shared horror stories. It was the first time Lisa learned that there were other girls who had terrible secrets. They were in the institution for protection too. Being able to share experiences was liberating. At least Marce wasn't her own father. Her father would be like Sgt. Pinkerton, tall with dark hair like hers.

When they visited, he and Polly praised Lisa for the help she'd given them and told her they continued to be concerned about her welfare. Sgt. Pinkerton even called her a hero. Their praise made her feel so good that she wondered if it was like feeling loved. For the first time, she began to trust two adults. Sgt. Pinkerton took Lisa and his daughter out to lunch many times. The outings diminished the feeling of punishment the institution created.

During the time Lisa had been in protective custody with the policeman's family, she had been asked not to read any newspapers or watch any television news. Although she didn't know the reason, the police didn't want the news stories to scare her, or effect her testimony when the criminal was caught. Lisa had complied with their requests.

In the detention center, everyone watched. Sitting next to her new friends, Lisa was shocked to see a story on Bobby Joe Long mentioning her. It felt so strange to hear her own

name and the words of praise projected on television. She felt special and brave. She vowed that the shy, scared little girl she'd been was gone. She would never let horrible secrets control her again.

Later that day, Sgt. Pinkerton walked across the living room at Beach Place toward Lisa. He was smiling. The other kids glanced at him and directed their attention back to the television. They had become used to his visits to Lisa. Lisa jumped up and ran to him. "Why are you here? You weren't supposed to come today. Is something wrong?"

"I had to come to let you know, I had the pleasure of putting Marce Rhodes in jail for his abuse of you." Sgt. Pinkerton touched her shoulder compassionately. "I know this isn't the best place for you, but someday things will be better. You won't be here forever."

"I'm glad. I've been feeling like I was the one being punished."

"There should be better places for kids who need temporary homes, but the staff is nice to you aren't they?"

"Yes, but it's not like having a home. You've made me feel so much better. You and your daughter have treated me like family. Without you and Polly I would've never been able to take it."

"Lisa, as a policeman, I meet a lot of people. One shining star like you makes up for the bad ones. I wanted my daughter to meet such an inspiration to young women everywhere."

Lisa bounded back to her two friends to tell them about Marce being arrested. She couldn't tell them the policeman told her she was a shining star, but Pinkerton's words boosted her morale so high, her surroundings were more bearable.

During the next few weeks, stories about Bobby Joe

Long appeared almost daily in the papers. Lisa managed to
get copies to read to her new friends. Many of the stories had
references to the seventeen-year old girl who worked in the
donut shop, the girl whose testimony helped catch the murderer. The Beach Place kids laughed at depictions of Bobby
Joe Long as a boy.

"Look at the picture of him in his Boy Scout uniform.
He was a scout all right."

"Poor little Bobby Joe fell off his tricycle and bumped
his head."

All the kids agreed Bobby Joe's childhood had been a
bed of roses compared to the lives of the residents at Beach
Place. The kids said that despite the turmoil in their lives
they hadn't turned into mass murderers.

When Sgt. Pinkerton came back to tell her Marce had
been released despite all his effort, Lisa shared with the kids
the experience of having her grandmother ask her to kill
Marce. "I wished he was dead, but I couldn't kill him." Many
comforted her and each other having had the same feelings.

Time passed. Christmas at Beach Place was traumatic for
the teenagers. The cheerful decorations only confirmed their
isolation from family. Lisa longed to be with her brothers and
sister. However, her conditioning of always appearing happy
on the outside served her well through the holidays. She
spent the time trying to cheer up the other kids.

Trying to trace Lisa's relatives in the next weeks, the
social workers found that Lisa's oldest brother had established a home and was living with her twin sister. Finally,
Lisa was reunited with her brother and sister. The months
she'd spent at Beach Place were drawing to a close. Not long
afterwards, she went to live with her brother and sister.

When the new Lisa tried to share all the horrible things that had happened to her with her brother and sister, each of them would say, "Don't talk about it."

They refused to believe anything bad about Marce. Lisa was shocked that they wouldn't even believe he had been in the county jail for abusing her. "He was released after serving only a few days because the jail couldn't care for someone in a wheelchair." When Lisa tried to tell them about Sgt. Pinkerton coming to tell her of Marce's release and how frightened she'd felt, they looked at one another and laughed. They thought she was telling lies.

If Lisa tried to talk about her experience with the serial killer, they walked away. Her brother acted embarrassed and her sister wasn't interested. Lisa felt confused and lonely. She began to go back into her shell. Her nightmares of Marce and Bobby Joe Long returned. In the dreams, Marce became Bobby Joe Long and killed her. She'd wake up screaming, "no, no." In the morning, her brother and sister would never ask if she had a bad dream. Their own conditioning caused them to repress thoughts of what caused such nightmares.

When the bad feelings overwhelmed her, Lisa picked up the phone and called Sgt. Pinkerton. His encouragement continued to lift her spirits. Polly was busy with other cases. She was polite and listened, but she didn't invite more calls. Sgt. Pinkerton, on the other hand, continued to accept Lisa almost as a daughter. He was her lifeline and encouraged her to get out of the house and get a job. She did and felt better.

On her way to her job at the luncheonette one day, Lisa met Tom, a boy she'd known in high school. He asked about her experience with Bobby Joe Long. For Lisa, talking to

someone she'd known before her traumas with Marce and
Bobby Joe was wonderful. She made friends with his whole
family.

Tom's mother offered to let Lisa live with the family.
Lisa gratefully accepted and paid them the little rent she
could afford. However, since she was eighteen now, she
dreamed of living on her own. She wanted the total respon-
sibility of taking care of herself.

It was too painful to blame her mother and grandmother
for the anger she felt. They were weak and she had to for-
give them, she told herself. It was the weakness they taught
that had kept her a slave to Marce. Their lies were responsible.
Never again! And she would begin by telling the whole truth
to everyone about the horror she had faced and overcome at
the hands of Bobby Joe. She welcomed the idea of facing
Bobby Joe in court. Nevertheless, her nightmares didn't
stop.

There wasn't any compensation to help her recover from
years of abuse and her experience at the hands of a serial
killer. The rape counselors to whom she talked weren't helpful. They were used to conspiratorial counseling, of keeping
the women's confidences, of promising never to tell anyone,
and dealing out gobs of sympathy. Meanwhile, bits and
pieces of Lisa's life were being paraded in the newspapers.
For her there was no privacy and she had renounced secrets.

Like lies, secrecy to Lisa was now an enemy and the
counselors just didn't get it. The greatest relief she found
was being able to tell her own story in her words, but there
were few who wanted to listen.

Chapter 15

Another Open
Window

"Andrea Sue, please turn off the TV and start your homework," Susan called as she opened the door.

Susan looked into the eyes of a stranger. "I knew I didn't recognize that insistent knock." The man was handsome, with blue eyes and dark hair peppered with gray. The vitality in his unlined face didn't match his graying temples.

"I'm Corporal Lee Baker. If you're Susan Replogle, I have a few questions about Bobby Joe Long." He flashed his badge and handed Susan his card.

Susan read the word "Homicide" and gestured. "Come in."

The detective stepped into the little hall, but refused Susan's invitation to sit down.

"I understand you know Bobby Joe Long."

"I knew him."

"You were his girlfriend?"

"I'm so tired of telling people I wasn't his girlfriend. Once I thought we were friends; then he raped and battered me."

"I came to find out why he hates you so much. I guess it's because of your court case against him."

"The battery?"

"Exactly."

"Bobby Joe liked to be in charge. Especially with women. I wouldn't let him tell me what to do. When he raped me, I blamed myself, but my friend reported it. Then he beat me up and I reported it."

"You did live with him?"

"Briefly, I needed financial help and protection and he offered to be my roommate. How does everyone know that? Even the newspapers published it."

"His letters to the judges to get a retrial. They're a matter of record."

"I'd like to see them."

"A letter he wrote in jail concerns me more. It was confiscated. He isn't just angry with you. He hates you."

"Should I be concerned? Get a gun?"

"He's in tight security now. I can't tell you to get a gun, but he has planned to escape."

"Who was the letter to? Was it me?"

"I can't tell you that. Does he have a lot of friends?"

"He talked like he had friends everywhere, but I don't think it's true. Dan, my ex-boyfriend, is his friend. So is his wife. They testified for him and against me in court."

The detective looked at his watch, "I have to go but here's my card. Call if you ever need me." Susan wanted to ask more questions. The thought that Bobby Joe was writing about her in jail was electrifying. *Good God, who could his friends be? Other criminals like him?*

Terror gripped her. She ran into the living room and hugged her daughter. She held Andrea a long time, rocking back and forth. The worst thing that could ever happen to Susan would be something happening to her daughter.

"Mommy, what's the matter? You're crushing me."

"Nothing dear, Mommy's being silly. I watch too much TV, but I want you to come right home from school from now on. Don't talk to strangers."

"You still think I'm a baby or something. They tell us that in school."

"I know, dear, but you can't be too careful."

"Oh, mommy."

Susan went in the kitchen to make dinner. Her mind couldn't get away from the detective's words. Why does he hate you so? Who wouldn't be terrified? She had read about his torture of his victims, it was so cruel, so hideous. How could she have ever trusted that monster? Now she knew she would never be free while he was alive. Prisoners talk to other prisoners. They write to friends on the outside. "Ouch." She burned her hand. "Damn that frying pan is hot." She held her hand under the cold water faucet, while she felt on the shelf for the burn ointment.

A gun. I need a gun. Where do you hide a gun from an eight-year old? What good is having a gun if it isn't loaded and you don't know how to shoot it. "If I buy a gun, I'll have to take lessons," Susan said out loud. She couldn't sleep that night. The next day she went out and bought a small revolver. When she arrived home, Susan took the small hand gun out of her purse, and put it in the drawer next to her bed. *No, Andrea might go in there looking for a nail file. I'll put it under my pillow...*she pushed the little gun out of sight and walked out of the bedroom. She ran back. The child might get into bed. Andrea liked to lie there and watch television.

Susan took a shoe box out of the closet, wrapped the gun in the tissue paper and placed it inside. She got on her hands

and knees to look under the bed. It will have to do, she decided. She pushed the box arm's length toward the middle. *What if Andrea looks under the bed? God help me. What am I going to do with this gun?* She laid down on the floor and got it back. Finally, she she took the gun from the box and shoved it under her mattress.

Every night during the week that followed, Susan would take the gun out and lay in bed holding it. She wanted to get used to how it felt. Then she put it back. It was a ritual, like brushing her teeth. But afterwards, just to be sure, she'd slide her hand under the mattress. Knowing it was there was comforting. If she didn't feel it immediately, panic set in. Every time she heard a strange noise, she'd reach for it again.

Fear of the unknown kept her from sleeping. Fear of the gun took it's toll. When she was awake, Susan felt exhausted all the time.

By the second week her terror subsided. Before going to bed, she locked all the doors and windows. The windows in her room didn't lock and she left one slightly open for fresh air. She would hear if anyone tried to cut the screen. She got in bed and slept soundly. Suddenly, her eyes flew open. It wasn't morning. This wasn't a dream. The man on top of her was real. His knife at her throat was sharp and cold.

Her heart pounded. She tried to move her hand toward her gun. His knee was on her arm and he held one hand over her mouth. It was almost impossible to breathe.

"If you say a word, I'll cut your fuckin' throat."

The guy on top of her had a peaked hat on over wild dark hair. He smelled like gasoline or car grease.

"Suck my dick, you rotten whore. You ratted on Bobby."

He took his hand off her mouth.

Susan answered in her soft, southern drawl. "I'll do anything you want." *Just don't hurt my daughter,* she prayed.

"I want my come in your mouth. If you get smart ideas like biting me, I'll cut your throat from ear to ear."

"I won't hurt you. Don't hurt me."

He had soft blond pubic hair. Susan looked closer at the hair on his head. It was a wig. Susan took his penis in her mouth.

"Not like that. Take it all down your throat. If you gag, you're dead meat."

She felt like retching, but fought not to. *Bobby you've done me in again. If only I can get this guy to let me live.* What if he knew she had a little girl in the next room? What if he were to find her gun. If he starts to use his knife, she determined that she would get the gun somehow and kill him.

Susan prayed that when he climaxed he wouldn't make any noise. Andrea might walk in. She could imagine both their bodies like the corpses which were described in the newspaper. He was Bobby's friend. He might want to leave more dead bodies around Tampa.

"Give me your money and jewelry."

Susan emptied her purse and stripped the rings off her fingers giving them to him. Then she watched silently as he left through the front door.

The first thing she did was check on Andrea. Afterwards, she frantically searched for the detective's card while she dialed Kay. "I've been raped. Remember what I told you about the detective? Can you remember his name? Damn, neither do I. I need to get Andrea out of the house before I call the police."

Susan rustled through the catch-all drawer tossing everything

out on the kitchen counter. The phone rang and she answered it automatically.

"Hello."

The voice on the phone was strangely familiar. It was the rapist. Her body vibrated as she listened to him in disbelief. "I'm glad you had a good time." Somehow she managed to hang up. He had her unlisted phone number. Fear mounted. She dialed 911.

Kay arrived with her son, who soon left to search for the rapist. Susan aroused her sleeping child, who groaned and complained bitterly. There was no convincing Andrea it was an adventure to visit with their old neighbor before dawn.

When the police arrived, she told them about the rapist.

"The guy wore a black wig."

"How do you know that?"

"He had blond pubic hair."

"He smelled like he worked around engines or gasoline. I think he was a friend of Bobby Joe Long's who came here to kill me."

The policemen stopped writing and looked at Susan.

"A detective was here a few weeks ago and told me that Bobby Joe wrote a letter in jail saying how much he hated me. I lost his card. He's in homicide."

She described the homicide detective to them. "He had salt and pepper hair. He stood maybe an inch or so taller than me."

They wrote the information down, but shrugged when she asked them to find the detective to tell him.

"The guy's just a rapist. He saw your window open. It happens."

The phone's shrill ring stopped the discussion. Susan put her hand over her mouth as she listened to the rapist's voice

threatening her for calling the police. He was watching. "I'm coming back, " he said. "You won't know when." He hung up.

She was relieved to hear the policeman who walked into the house saying, "They just got the guy."

Disappointment took over when she found out it was Kay's son they'd caught. Andrea was involved in an adventure she couldn't have imagined. Susan took the opportunity to let Kay leave with Andrea. At least the child would be safe for the rest of the night. If she wasn't so frightened, Susan would have thought the incident with Kay's son funny.

The officer went back outside. He returned after going around the house. "There are bicycle tire tracks and a lot of cigarette butts by the bedroom window."

"I can't believe this is happening to me. It's a nightmare that won't end!" Susan began to cry.

The policemen went through the house thoroughly and determined that the rapist entered through the bedroom window, but hid in the utility room until Susan went to bed. They dusted for fingerprints and then took Susan to the hospital.

When Susan returned from the rape examination, she started packing. Ocala was her only refuge. The sooner she and Andrea Sue could get out of Tampa, the better. Then she realized that Ocala wouldn't be any safer. Bobby Joe had other friends besides her brother-in-law, who lived there, too. They'd have to go somewhere new. Suddenly she realized they were stuck where they were. For the first time, Susan regretted buying the house. She didn't have the luxury of leaving. No, she and Andrea had to tough it out, no matter what the outcome.

Chapter 16

Secrets, Lies and Confidences

Newspapers around the country screamed the stories many had picked up from *The Tampa Tribune:*

'ACCUSED KILLER LONG FACES TRIAL TODAY FOR RAPE' Accused in nine area murders, "Bobby Joe" Long must face rape charges in Pasco County. NEW PORT RICHEY - Long, who is accused in a string of brutal murders that terrorized the Tampa Bay area last year will finally come to trial today. Long's first trial, which begins with a jury selection, involves the rape of a twenty-one year old, New Port Richey woman who was going to work at McDonald's in New Port Richey.

Pasco Sheriff's Department, Major Tom Berringer, reported to the press that they were taking unusual steps to protect Bobby Joe Long, because there were reports that he had hatched an escape plan. A prosecutor told Circuit Judge Ray Ulmer, at a hearing on February 12th, Long planned to get

police to arrange a trip out of jail to look for a body. He would have a friend plant a gun near the search site. There were fears that family members of his victims might seek revenge also.

Circuit Judge Lawrence E. Keough asked area newspaper and television stations to edit out damaging information from stories run before jury selection. Over 200 were to be queried to pick twelve who could be open minded about Long. Assistant Public Defender Robert McClure asked for a change of venue and was refused.

Lisa was surprised, but relieved at all the protection they were giving Long. But she was still afraid he'd get out. She needed to know he'd be in jail forever. She called Sgt. Pinkerton hoping to be reassured.

"Lisa, he won't get out. They'll watch him closely during the trials. I knew about his escape plan. On the one hand, I wanted the detective to let him out and take him there, so when he went for the gun, I could shoot him, but my rational side prevailed."

"Will there be a trial for the rape against me?"

"There won't have to be. He's already confessed."

"Oh. No one tells me anything. If I couldn't talk to you, I'd have to get all my news in the papers. Thanks. It's good to hear your voice."

"It's good to hear yours."

She clipped the article from the paper. The rape victim's experience was so much like her own that she felt sick to her stomach. Long had threatened her with a gun and a knife just as he had Lisa. Lisa wished she could get up in court and face Long, just as the woman she read about. Instead all her anger and frustration stayed inside.

What if Pinkerton was wrong and he did escape? He knew her name and he knew that she was the reason he was caught. She shivered.

Two days later, Lisa breathed a sigh of relief when the jury found Bobby Joe Long guilty. But it was only the first step. The penalty for rape wouldn't keep him in jail forever. Only a conviction for murder would. That was the next crime with which Bobby Joe Long would be charged. Lisa thought of it night and day. She picked up *The Tampa Tribune*.

Long's first murder trial begins Monday, April 22, 1985 in Pasco County, Dade City Courthouse, Courtroom 1, for the murder of Virginia Lee Johnson, nineteen. To ensure a fair trial, with so much pretrial publicity, Judge Ray E. Ulmer ordered 400 jurors to be summoned.

Robert Norgard and Randall Granthham did not apply for an insanity plea, but subpoenaed five witnesses: Michael S. Maher, a Tampa Psychiatrist; Peter M. Dunn, a Tampa Neurologist; Long's ex-wife, Cynthia Levy, of Hollywood; Holly Dupree, a friend of Long and Levy; Helen Wandel of Miramar, a friend of the Longs. In summation, the attorneys asked that the Long's two children be able to testify on video tape on the separate trial for sentencing.

It shocked Lisa reading Bobby Joe had children. She thought of all the times she envied other girls and boys because they had two parents. What could it be like to have a father like Long? Much worse than having none.

Everyday there was a new report about Bobby Joe's life. It was as if the reporters were enamored by him. Lisa felt nauseous.

Long's mother, Louella Long of Kenova, West Virginia, told the jury how she, at the age of nineteen, and little Bobby Joe moved from place to place after she and her husband Joe Long divorced. They have since remarried.

She read the parts about his hard life...

Hit by a car and had facial injuries...Children made fun of him...Called him buck tooth... At four or five, he was pulled under a wave and almost drowned and blamed his mother...Said she was looking at men instead of him.

Try a foster home from two to six, Lisa thought, but she had to continue reading.

Bobby started developing breasts at the age of thirteen, and he was deeply humiliated. He had to have surgery and have several pounds of tissue removed.

Weird. Lisa tried to remember if she felt scars.

Mother and son drifted apart in his teens...He refused to accept her second marriage...One day he spanked her until her buttocks were blistered.

When the trial started reporters switched topics.

Assistant State Attorney called twenty-four witnesses to the stand. The medical examiner testified Virginia Johnson was strangled with a shoe lace and her hands were found nearby tied in like fashion. Many of the state's witnesses were police.

Lisa remembered how he tied her hands in a loose fashion so you could touch him. The thought revolted her. His body ramming into her loomed in her mind. The image returning again and again. If only she could tell that jury what it was like for the poor dead girl, but no one wanted to listen.

She read further.

**Police allege they were able to identify and cap-
ture Long only because he did not kill one of the
women abducted, a seventeen-year-old Tampa girl,
and the reason he didn't kill her is that when Long
held her captive she asked to stay with him instead of
going home. She didn't want to go home because her
guardian repeatedly abused her sexually.**

Lots of people saw the stories about her kidnapping. She
had told the murderer everything about Marce to gain his
sympathy. How could they print that?

Finally the verdict came. The jury had convicted Long
again! Lisa felt relief, but not peace. Finally, she prayed,
there might be an end to her own suffering.

**At Long's sentencing hearing for the murder of
Virginia Johnson, his attorney, Robert Norgard,
asked Judge Ulmer to consider Long a serial killer.
Long's attorneys didn't mention it during the trial to
avoid prejudicing the jury. "Serial murder," Norgard
said, "is a disease few people understand. Studies
done in other cases of serial killers like Ted Bundy
and John Gacey indicate the murderers' personalities
are similar." Looking at Long, Norgard said, "when
you look at Long, you see a normal, healthy, individual.
But when you talk to him, there's chaos, no internal
order at all." Long, he said "sought to put order in his
life by killing prostitutes, according to psychiatric
testimony. Mr. Long could flourish in jail, because
there is order there."**

Lisa thought the words a mirage: "flourish in jail." He
could flourish and indeed he was. Who the hell cares if he

flourishes? He ought to be in hell. That's where he belongs. Didn't they realized that he had cold-bloodedly killed all those women? How would they flourish? Dead, under the ground?

Assistant State Attorney Phillip Van Allen urged Judge Ulmer to disregard the other murders and judge Long only on the fact of Virginia Johnson's death. "Long," he said, "was guilty not only of murdering Virginia, but of subjecting her to a cruel death. She was slowly and agonizingly tortured when Long strangled her with a shoestring. The defense has yet to offer any justification for the killing, even any that Long may have felt." Assistant District Attorney Van Allen, a handsome young man, who leaned on a cane and sometimes held the podium, used it for emphasis. "I had somewhat expected that we would hear that Long was trying to clean up Tampa single-handedly by getting prostitutes off the street, a job which he cannot do legally. A job, which if he intended to do it in that fashion, would constitute a crime. But, at least there would have been on his part, justification." Van Allen waved his cane in the air and attacked the finding of the two psychiatrists who, testifying during the penalty phase of Long's case, found him mentally ill. They were confronted, by a result of an individual who committed a murder, and were working backward. They are trying to find a niche in the law that hasn't previously existed."

Lisa tried to picture Mr. Van Allen swinging his cane in the air and laughed. The reporter said he was handsome. Who cared about that? The important thing was he was telling them the truth.

Judge Ulmer accepted the jury's recommendation. Judge Ulmer read an order in legal language that Long be electrocuted until dead in Florida's electric chair after the Governor signs the death warrant. "Mr. Long, may God have mercy on your soul."

Lisa put the article from *The Tampa Tribune* in her scrap book. Thank God for Phillip Van Allen. His was a voice of reason, Long was going to pay for his crimes. Finally, she would be free of the fear of his finding her and this time making good on his threats.

It was an interval of peace. However, in September, Lisa found a small article in *The Tampa Tribune*, which made her tremble again.

Long's lawyers reached a plea bargain in Hillsborough County for twenty-six life sentences for the killing of eight Tampa women. The state kept the right to seek the death penalty against Long for one of the murder cases.

She was glad that Long had another murder trial to face.

December 10, 1985, the trial began for the murder of Michelle Denise Simms, who was strangled and stabbed 24 hours after she arrived in Tampa from Fort Pierce. Assistant Attorney Michael L. Benito and Long's attorney, Assistant Public Defender Charles O'Connor, took two days to pick a jury from a pool of one hundred and fifty. Many potential jurors were excused as a result of widespread publicity, and others for being opposed to the death penalty.

Long was already facing one death sentence for the murder in Pasco and six hundred and twenty-three years' prison time. One of the psychiatrists

hired from Chicago didn't come to testify in his sentencing trial on December 13th. She claimed she was
unpaid, but Long's attorney said she received
$3,900.00. Sentencing was postponed for a new trial.

Lisa couldn't believe her eyes.

Chapter 17

The Passage of Time

Living alone without a family had positive moments, but holidays were tough. Lisa was relieved when Mother's Day was over and the newspapers stopped running ads for chocolates and flowers. Her feelings about her mother were like an open wound. A headline on page eight of *The Tampa Tribune,* Thursday, May 22, 1986, attracted her attention.

'CONGRESS HEARS HOW CRIME SCENE LOOKED AND KILLER CAUGHT' WASHING-TON, D.C. It wasn't the murder itself that startled Hillsborough County Sheriff's officers two years ago on Mother's Day. It was, in the words of Detective Captain Gary Terry,..."the way the body was displayed."

Lisa scanned the words of the police captain as he described how crime scenes speak for themselves and realized he was talking of Bobby Joe Long. The first body found in Hillsborough County had a leash-like rope tied around the woman's neck. Because of the bizarre way the body of

Ngeun Thi Long was displayed, officers decided to take evidence from the crime scene to F.B.I. laboratories in Washington. There, Agent Michael Malone discovered the first red fibers eventually found on all the bodies and on the panties of Lisa McVey.

Her eyes skipped over the ghastly references to the second body, which was almost decapitated and stopped at another reference to her.

"Three more women were killed before Long made two critical mistakes. First, he chose Lisa McVey, who worked in a doughnut shop, as his next victim. His second mistake, ironically, proved to be his only act of mercy, he let Lisa live."

Lisa read the rest of the article, with her pulse racing. Terry went on to describe how Lisa, blindfolded, was able to tell police so much about her abductor. Captain Terry's words filled Lisa with pride. She imagined how they talked about her in front of Congress. The Tampa police gave her such a feeling of being a terrific person, she just had to be, she told herself.

Her confidence grew. She even asked for and got a raise at her job at the McDill Air Force Commissary. One day, she realized that a handsome young man was flirting with her. He worked for a number of companies that supplied the commissary with meat and other staples. His stature of 6'8" gave him the ability to keep Lisa in sight over the tall shelves. She stole glances at him only to notice he was smiling at her. "What is your sign?" he asked.

She laughed, "Aries. My birthday is the 24th of March."

"We share the same birth date." Lisa was sure he was lying. He came up to the counter and showed her his driver's

license. Sure enough, he had the same birth date and he was three years older than she was.

Jimmy and Lisa began dating. Like most couples falling in love, the fun of getting to know one another was all consuming. The hours they spent together were the happiest Lisa ever experienced and when he asked her to become his wife, she immediately said, "Of course." Not long after that they married. Lisa was so busy and in love, she didn't pay much attention to the trial for Bobby Joe Long that consumed so many headlines that July.

In the week long trial, high profile Miami attorneys, Mark and Ellis Rubin, acting as Public Defenders, defended Bobby Joe Long for the murder of Michelle Denise Simms. The father and son team had been successful presenting a defense of a young murderer in Miami, claiming that Twinkies and television violence had influenced their client.

In Bobby Joe Long's defense, they argued that the long-term effects of pornography and television violence played a role in Long's development. Ellis Rubin labeled his client a "special breed," who should be kept alive to provide more complete information on the increasing number of serial killers and help America put an end to an "epidemic."

"Bobby Joe Long deserves to die," Ellis Rubin told the jurors. "So does every other person who takes a life. Bobby Joe Long is vicious. Bobby Joe Long contains a flame of violence and (referring to the prosecuting attorney) Mr. Benito wants to extinguish it. And so do I." Rubin told the jury. "There are thirty to thirty five serial killers stalking prey in this country this very minute. I took this case because I want it stopped." The flamboyant Rubin continued his plea for not killing Long. "The question is to kill or not kill?

Revenge or research? Electrocution or prevention? When a jury kills, it is the same thing that Bobby Joe Long did."

Assistant State Attorney, Michael L. Benito, disagreed, reminding the jury, "Michelle Denise Simms is gone. She's gone and he killed her." Benito held the hunting knife used in front of a picture of her slashed throat. "The murder included attempts to strangle Miss Simms, beating her with a club and slashing her throat."

In his final argument, Benito said, "Long was not a psychotic out of touch with reality, but an antisocial sex maniac, who consciously planned his murders from the moment he stalked his victim until he stole her last breath. He left a trail of victims that would no longer make him feel inadequate."

Although, the Rubins' defense had been passionate, the Hillsborough jury didn't believe that Long should be spared and voted 11 to 1 that the confessed killer should die in the electric chair. Florida law provides the sentencing trial to be separate. Judge John P. Griffin, holding the power to accept or reject the recommendation, scheduled his sentencing trial.

Ellis Rubin expressed disappointment over the verdict, but said he thought Long had a fair trial and that he didn't expect to handle Long's appeal. "This is as far as I can afford to go." As a court appointed attorney, he was paid the fee of $3,500.00.

Jimmy and Lisa had a beautiful baby girl that January. Jimmy was busy working and Lisa adored caring for their beautiful daughter, Jennifer. The articles stopped appearing in the papers and Lisa began to live a normal life.

Not far away, in another Florida town, Susan Replogle had entered design school. She too was taking positive steps to recover and reclaim her life.

Chapter 18

Rape Case
88-037517

In the midst of a successful career, I had decided to become a sand bird, but trying to make the transition from my cable television show in New York to talk radio in Florida, wasn't as easy as I thought it would be. Nevertheless, after numerous interviews, WPLP Talk Radio, finally hired me. 'The Joy Wellman Show' followed Larry King's early morning repeat show at 5 a.m., on Saturdays and Sundays. I came to the studio after church service.

After a year of challenging encounters, read the ratings crunch, I was devastated when I was fired from the show. Sometimes life has a way of presenting obstacles that become opportunities. I launched a career in advertising, however, my experience with television paid off. People liked my commercials because they attracted customers. I knew many tricks about cutting productions costs. It surprised a lot of small business men that they could afford television advertising. It didn't hurt when I was on the cover of the Floridian section of *The St. Petersburg Times* twice the

year I started my business. I began to feel better about the future.

During the next few years, my self confidence bloomed. Business was so good that I was able to travel around the world, but on one violent night my new found sense of security was completely destroyed.

I woke to the hazy realization that my television was on. Suddenly, I was aware of someone standing in my bedroom. I got out of bed, to go toward the shadowy figure, thinking it was one of my sons. It was the only thought that came to mind. Within seconds, I realized I was mistaken.

"Lady, you left your door open and you're going to die for it."

The man lunged toward me, pushing me back on the bed. He was on top of me before I realized what was happening.

"This is a knife, and I'm going to kill you with it."

I was very aware of the knife as he pressed it against my throat. In spite of my dazed condition, my body began to tremble violently.

"How does it feel to know you're going to have your throat cut?"

He's going to kill me. How terrible to die this way. I hope he isn't going to take a long time to kill me. Pain terrifies me. The tension was almost unbearable. His whole body weight was on me, as he had one hand over my mouth and the other held the knife across my throat. If I could scream, no one would hear me. I knew if I tried, he'd stop me with his knife. I had to struggle to breathe.

"If you make a sound, you're dead."

It was impossible to let him know I wasn't going to

scream. I wished he'd move his hand so I could take a breath.
I was resigned to death. *I'm about to die because I forgot to
lock my door. How stupid! How horrible!* Briefly, I thought
about how terrible it was going to be for my children to find
my bloody remains.

He took his hand off my mouth and forced my arm over
my head. He leaned on that arm and with the knife wielding
hand, cut off my gown, and ripped it down.

"You don't need to do that, I'll help you."

"Shut up or I'll cut your throat. I've killed a lot of people,
and I like to cut people." He emphasized his statement by
smashing his fist into the bed.

"I'll do anything you want. Just don't cut me. What do
you want me to do?"

"Lay there, you bitch, and open your legs. I want sex."

I was shocked, when I drew my legs apart, that his penis
immediately entered me. I hadn't been aware that it was
exposed. I wondered, if he had removed his pants before I
woke up. How long had he stood in my bedroom watching
me?

He began to thrust with all his might, and I pulled my
knees up to try to relieve the hard battering. He pushed even
harder. The tension increased from fear and trying to resist
the blows. The muscles on the inside of my thighs started
twitching uncontrollably.

"Do you believe I will cut your throat?"

He held the knife's point at the soft center of my throat.

"I do. I do, but I can't understand why anyone would
want to kill anyone. You must have had some terrible things
happen to you."

He looked down at me in surprise. It was then that I

noticed his face. He was white, young, with a square jaw, a prominent nose and regular features. Just as if he was reading my mind, he reached over and touched the remote control of the television set, and it went off. I hadn't realized until the set went off that the only light was coming from the television. In the darkness I could still make out the outlines of his face, and see a light mustache. He smelled of Old Spice or Jovan. His hair was wavy and stylishly trimmed about mid ear level. I noticed it was thick, brunette, and clean, as though he had recently been at a barber's. The hand holding my arm was huge. It felt like a tree trunk, it was so hard and muscular. His size and strength added to my terror. I tried to talk to him in an effort to buy time and perhaps dissuade him from harming me.

"You're a body builder."

"You can tell that in the dark?"

"Yes, I can feel you have a beautiful body. You're a very handsome man. Lots of young girls must want to make love to you. Why are you doing this? Who are you trying to get even with?"

Although his penis was still inside me, his intense thrusting seemed to lessen slightly. It seemed as though he might be losing his erection, but he kept up his rhythmic thrusts.

"They don't, they want guys with money."

A small glimmer of hope came to me. He responded to my questions, and he was pleased when I paid him a compliment. I made up my mind to keep talking. I felt if he realized I was a person, and not an anonymous piece of meat, I might be able to keep him from killing me. It was a faint hope, but it was all I had. The fear, that I might say something to trigger a violent reaction, was a risk I needed to take.

"Have you ever looked down the barrel of a gun? Have you ever seen your friends blown away? Do you know what it looks like to see their brains splattered all over. Are you afraid of me?"

"I'm terrified."

"Does it feel good to be terrified?"

"No, it's horrible."

"I've felt that many times."

"How? Why? You're so young."

"How old do you think I am?"

"In your twenties. Are you working now?"

"Shut up, stop talking. What do you know anyway? I've been beaten bloody by four cops. I'm a strong guy, but they beat me until they thought I died. I'll die killing one before I ever go to jail again."

"Was that what made you so angry?"

"You want to know what I'm angry about. Just the whole fucking society, that's all. And you're one of the ones responsible. I went through your purse, and I know you're in politics."

"If you went through my pocketbook, you know I sell advertising and real estate." Good God, how did he know. I just became secretary of the club. I couldn't remember anything saying so. Of course, I had a voting registration card.

"Are you Italian?"

"I'm just a Southern boy."

"I can hear your accent. I didn't think people in Florida had one."

"You ask too many questions."

His statement and his increased momentum made me realize that I was on dangerous territory. If I learned too much about him, he might feel he had to kill me, or be discovered.

What else is there? It was so difficult to think. "When you looked down the barrel of a gun, was it a policeman's?"

He didn't answer. I began to get desperate.

"Take the knife away from my throat. If you put the knife down, I'll do anything you want. Put it down. Please put it down."

"Are you afraid that I'll stab you with it when I climax?"

The horror of his words, and the pleasure in his voice terrorized me. He had just said out loud what I had thought earlier. The talking must be prolonging his ability to climax.

"Please put it down, I'll do anything you want. What time is it?" I tried to turn my head a little so I could see the clock. It was three something.

"Time shouldn't mean anything to you if you want to see the sun come up."

Finally he climaxed and then moving away from me, sat at the foot of the bed like an alert tiger.

"Turn on the light," I said. I tried to stay as calm as possible. I felt he was trying to decide what to do with me.

He chose not to. "Get out of bed," he ordered in a commanding tone.

"Can't I just lay here? I won't move. I won't tell anyone. I don't want anyone to know I forgot to lock my door."

Since he didn't answer I continued to lie there.

I watched him get dressed with his back to me. His body was trim, but thick in the middle. His shirt seemed loose and stylishly casual, as he slipped into it. He picked up something and put it on his foot and stood staring at me. It looked like a black, high top sneaker without laces.

Fear gripped me again. Was he going to leave, or was he going to spring back and try to kill me? I decided if he did,

I would roll away from him, and fall on the floor. I managed to say, "Would you do me a favor? You said you went through my pocketbook. On your way out, take one of my cards. If you get arrested, call me, I'll get you a lawyer."

He turned towards me. "I can't believe this. I'd be damned mad if someone threatened to cut my throat."

As he said that, he took the sheet and covered me with it. He walked toward the side of the bed I had decided to roll to, and picked up a pillow. I was sure he was going to use it to muffle my screams.

"Do you have any money?"

"You know what was in my pocketbook."

"Lift your head, you might as well be comfortable. Don't do anything wild or crazy for five minutes. Have a good life, and lock your door."

I lay there, hardly breathing, while I listened for his footsteps on the stairs. There was only silence and the pounding of my own heart. At first, I thought it was his. I imagined him standing out of sight waiting to pounce on me if I picked up the phone. If he wasn't a psychopath, he might need a reason to attack me again and kill me. As I lay there, I prayed that the rapist would really change, that God would help him. Carefully, I got out of bed, trying not to make a sound. Cautiously and quietly, I crept down the stairs expecting him to jump out of the shadows at me. I saw my front door open. I locked it, and sat down on my couch to gather my thoughts. Euphoria came over me that I was alive and uninjured.

I made myself get up, and look at my bed. Seeing my cut and bloody gown shocked me. My euphoria was gone.

Later I reported the rape to the police, but the rapist was not caught. Fear and anxiety accompanied my every move. I sought counseling. It helped, but I couldn't forget. I was beginning to realize it wasn't easy to dismiss my rape and go on.

Slowly I began to rebuild my life. Meanwhile, the Florida newspapers were filled with stories of a serial killer/rapist terrorizing women. Once I got over my own needs to be secretive, I decided to go public so I could help other victims. I called my friend, Ted Gordon, who was a radio and television personality in Florida, but whom I knew from our old days at the same station in New York.

Seeing an old friend across the microphone brought a sense of déjà vu. It was many years since Ted had taught me how to watch the producer in the booth for cues and follow the radio log to know when to introduce a commercial. The panel of lights indicating callers displayed one blinking. The producer answered it, while Ted presented his program for the day.

Ted talked to his audience like they were old friends. He romanced them with the deep timbre of his radio voice. He was a pro. I learned the mechanics, but I never learned to tease the listeners. Radio patter, the station manager used to call it.

I felt surprisingly calm waiting to be a guest. The sense of nervousness I suffered when I was the host had vanished. I still remember that Cleveland was in financial default and Nixon recognized Red China in the first morning I soloed. I thought I was making a joke when I said we could sell the Red Chinese Coca Cola. The joke was on me. We did!

At the end of his commercial message, Ted began to introduce me. The sound of my name brought me back to reality. I needed to tell my story with some sense of dignity, but I wanted everyone to understand my fear, the fear every woman feels, when they think they're going to be killed.

"Joy Wellman was a talk show host on this station, when it was W.P.L.P. She's my guest today to talk about a serious subject, which is making the headlines right now in Florida because of the serial crimes in our area, rape. We are not two people discussing it in the abstract sense. Joy was raped, and I asked her to tell us her experience since it's similar to that of one young girl I'm writing an article about. She was raped by the serial killer, Bobby Joe Long. That girl got away from a killer. Joy, you're also a survivor; have the police found your rapist?"

"No, but a rapist was found less than a mile from my house. I wish I could say it was the same man. It's terrifying to think there were two in the same neighborhood. The Pinellas County Sheriff's Department didn't know the Clearwater Police arrested a man so close to my house. It's even more terrifying to know they don't share that information. Traffic information yes, rapists - no"

"Women in Florida can have their names withheld to protect their identities. Why don't you feel you need to do that?"

"When it happened, I thought I would be able to go on with my life without telling anyone. During the rape I prayed to God and right after I did the rapist became less threatening. I believed God saved me and was going to change the rapist."

"You don't believe that now?"

"A part of me does. I don't know why I said the things I

did. Maybe God was helping me. It was one of the reasons, at first, I didn't want to tell about the rape. I made a pact with God. I was also afraid. I thought the killer would come back and get me if he knew I told the police. But as I recovered, I realized that I wanted him caught. I also don't think I have anything to hide, but he does."

"Give the audience a description."

"White, six feet, 200 pounds, medium complexion, very muscular, body builder type, wavy brown hair, cut mid ear level, about twenty years old. He was wearing black high tops with no laces."

"I guess it's fairly common for women not to want to tell about their rapists or even to have feelings about them. Someone told me they call it Stockholm Syndrome."

"Yes," I replied. "People are so relieved when they are not killed, sometimes they try to protect the criminal. It has helped me to learn about how victims react, but I think I really felt that the law and courts wouldn't protect me. Now I'm feeling more trusting."

The lights between Ted and I were blinking. I began to wonder if he was ever going to take a call. When I was a host, I was so grateful to see a light, I'd pounce on it. It was probably the reason he still was the host and I wasn't. He pushed the blinking light. A caller said hello.

"Do you have a question for Joy?" Ted asked.

"Where were you when it happened?"

"At home, in my own bed, and before you ask, I left my door unlocked. In my defense, I don't usually. I came home and my phone was ringing. I forgot to go back and lock it. Now I have an automatic lock and an alarm system." I thought about lying and saying I had gotten a gun too, just in case the rapist was listening to the show, but couldn't.

"Let's take another call."

"Was the man black?" The man asked.

"No, he was white and young. He had a Southern accent."

"You must live in a terrible neighborhood to have a rapist so close." The caller observed.

"I was told by a counselor that last year in Pinellas County, there were three hundred reported rapes. They think one in ten is reported."

"Are you sure? That would be three thousand." Ted said cutting the man off.

"I don't know where my counselor got her statistics, but the one she told me that bowled me over most was that only three rapists went to court, and of them there was only one conviction. It's the reason they don't try to convince women to press charges. Women have to be very motivated to take the kind of punishment the courts allow defendants' lawyers to dole out especially when so few rapists are found guilty. Most return to the streets and know who fingered them. So women who testify increase their jeopardy."

"Do you think the rapist was stalking you?"

"It's one of my greatest fears. I told the counselor from S.A.F.E. that more than a year before my rape, I turned on my answering machine and heard a young male voice telling me that someday, when I least expect it, he was going to rape me, cut me and kill me. I called the police immediately. An officer listened to the voice and told me to call if anything else happened. The counselor assured me that it was probably some guy getting his jollies."

"Do you think so?"

"I told the detective. He just took the information, but never called me back. I can only hope the counselor knows her business."

"So do I." Ted intervened. "Let's take the next call."

"Couldn't you stop him from invading your body? I'd rather die than be raped." The woman caller asked in a quavering voice.

"Well, I couldn't stop him from stabbing me. That's pretty invasive. I might add that I was so terrified, I didn't even know I was stabbed until after he left."

The callers kept up a continuous barrage of criticism, from the fact that I was shameless to even discuss my rape on the radio, to all the things I could have done to protect myself. One woman also fantasized about what she would do. "If a man ever entered my bedroom, he'd get a bullet right between the eyes. I keep a loaded gun under my pillow." I hoped she'd never have the need to try that.

During the last few moments on the program, Ted Gordon spoke again of the rape story he was reporting on. "The woman detective, Polly Goethe was the real hero. She had to convince all the male detectives that the rapist was really the murderer. Once the young girl returned alive, the other cops lost interest, they were so sure he was only a rapist. Joy, what do you think about this? One of the police officers was quoted in the paper as saying the girl asked to live with Long rather than return home where she was being abused?"

"Women will say anything to keep from dying. She could have said it. I said a lot of things to keep my rapist from using the knife he often had pointed at my throat. I don't think it means anything. I would hope a policeman would understand that."

"I'll introduce you to Lisa someday. She's a beautiful, forgiving young woman."

Chapter 19

Unending Fears

Susan Replogle and Lisa McVey each felt their ordeal was finally over. However, they were both wrong. It was not even close to ending. On November 5, 1988, Lisa was subpoenaed to testify in court against Bobby Joe Long. In a way, she felt elated finally facing him in court for the first time. Conversely, she resented that he was still trying to gain his freedom and that the courts seemed to be supporting his efforts. The murder trial for Virginia Johnson in Pasco County had been overturned by the Florida Supreme Court and Bobby Joe Long had been granted a change of venue to Fort Myers.

For Lisa, the idea that the higher court could throw out all of the efforts of four hundred plus jurors, prosecuting attorneys, twenty-eight witnesses (including police and doctors) was horrifying. She angrily shoved the subpoena back in the envelope. Round and round in her head went the question, *will this ever stop?*

Fort Myers is a four hour drive from Tampa and the

effort to go such a distance for Lisa to testify was time consuming, expensive and heartrending. The young couple needed every penny Jimmy made to take care of their little family. Lisa couldn't find a sitter for the child, so Jimmy had to stay home to take care of her. Jennifer was fifteen months old. It was the first separation between mother and baby. It was a trauma for each of them. To make matters worse, Lisa had to face the trial alone, without Jimmy's support.

At the courthouse, Lisa wasn't allowed to go inside the room where Long was being tried, but had to wait outside for ten hours, only to be told she had to stay another day. She learned the case was being held up waiting for the New York CBS News Attorney, Tom Julin. CBS was objecting to providing Long's defense attorneys with the "outtakes" of the CBS News report on "serial killers."

"It's a big fuss about the First Amendment Rights," Assistant State Attorney Phillip Van Allen tried to explain when he came out of the courtroom and spoke to Lisa. She couldn't grasp what he was saying about the Williams Rule and viewing a whole tape instead of part of one, but she appreciated his efforts. Van Allen was concerned about her reaction and he talked to her for a long time. The conversation relieved some of her anxiety in the impersonal atmosphere. It made waiting almost tolerable.

Jimmy wasn't happy when she called to tell him about the day. He was a loyal employee and had already missed two days' pay. Lisa walked the halls of the courthouse waiting to testify and worried about Jimmy at home minding the baby. She was determined to be strong and not cry. The hours made her more nervous as every minute ticked by.

The second day of waiting was almost over when she met

Bobby Joe Long's mother in the ladies room. The two women looked at one another while washing their hands. Lisa had been watching her go into the courtroom that day and the one before. Nobody had to point her out, because there was such a resemblance. In spite of her hatred of Long, Lisa couldn't help but feel sorrow for his mother. Could he hate her so much that he would kill ten women and rape so many more? Lisa hadn't forgiven her own mother for not protecting her as a child. Lisa was even given to other people to raise. Did this woman know the monster she created, or did she believe everyone told lies about him? How could even a mother love such a man?

On the third day of sitting on the hard bench outside the courtroom waiting, the bailiff came for Lisa. She walked, head down, with him toward the witness chair, but the judge told the bailiff to stop. The attorneys were called to the bench for a conference. She was standing next to Long. He was close enough to touch. The reality of the twenty-seven hours she spent with him came over her in waves. She felt unsteady. Panic seized her and she wanted to turn and run. She told herself to be strong. *Don't let that brute have the pleasure of seeing my inner fear.* She reminded herself he couldn't get her now. This was her moment to reveal the horror she'd been through. She had to talk for all those women in their graves who couldn't. The jury had to realize that a monster sat before them in a well tailored navy blue suit. She noticed he had shaved his mustache and had some gray hairs now.

It seemed like hours, but it was only minutes before she was asked to be seated in the witness stand to take an oath. She did so willingly. At first, she was disappointed that she was told to give only yes and no answers, but her mouth was so dry, short answers were easier.

She focused on looking strong and not crying. She was determined to look Bobby Joe Long in the eye when she answered, but she had to stretch her head far to the left to see around the judge's bench. She was asked to identify Long and pointed to the man she hated. Before she could even feel settled, she was excused.

Once back in the hall, she walked to a window and stood there to hide her tears. When she felt under control, she sat down to wait for the detective who would take her back to the motel. She was stoic, but trembling. She detested herself for being so weak. Suddenly the bailiff stood next to her. She hadn't seen him coming out of the courtroom. "Sorry Miss, but you have to go back in," he said.

Her mind was reliving her trauma. Like a zombie she followed him back into the courtroom not knowing what to expect. Mr. Van Allen was holding up a bag. He withdrew a pair of dirty, white pants, a black sweater and socks, no sneakers. For a moment, she just stared at the clothes. Then with a start she recognized them. They were hers, the clothes she wore the night she was kidnapped. They belonged to that child. That frightened child she was five years ago. It seemed like two lifetimes ago. She wasn't and would never be that tortured young girl again, but she cried for her. The bailiff led her from the courtroom sobbing. "I'll wait for my ride outside," she told him brokenly.

Bright sunshine greeted Lisa when she ran from the cold, unfeeling court building. She sat on a wrought iron bench outside and breathed deeply. The November wind rushed through the tall palm trees. The warm breeze dried her tears. All she wanted to do was return to Tampa and forget the terrible experience. She tried to keep from closing her eyes, so she wouldn't see the image of the white slacks and black

sweater. She could feel the blindfold and smell the after-shave he'd worn. The horror replayed in her brain. She swallowed hard trying not to throw up.

Lisa returned from Fort Myers looking forward to being held in Jimmy's arms. She felt the need she had for her grandmother, when she crawled up those rickety steps the night after the rape. Her experience in court, it was almost like being raped again. She wasn't prepared for the angry voice of the Public Defender. He sounded accusing, like she did something wrong.

Lisa ran into the house. She was so happy to be home. Jimmy stood in the living room holding the baby.

"It's about time. I missed another day of work." Jimmy said, passing the child to her mother.

"What happened to I love you, I missed you? Not you lost another day of work...I wasn't on vacation."

"You're too wrapped up in that thing."

"Jimmy, I was subpoenaed. It's a legal document you can't ignore. It's something I had to do. I thought you understood."

"Three days is a long time."

"I didn't know it would be so long. The waiting was terrible."

"Well, it's over now. Let's forget the whole thing. I'm sorry if I seem angry. I can still get a couple of hours in today." He brushed her cheek with a kiss and headed out the door.

"Well, my sweet darling, Mommy did miss you." Lisa swung the baby around. Jennifer gurgled with delight.

During the next few years, despite a growing rift between herself and Jimmy, Lisa tried to put the nightmare of Bobby Joe Long and her childhood to rest. She did not forget, nor did she want to. But she wanted very much to live a normal life.

Chapter 20

Speaking Out

By 1991 more women were beginning to report rapes, and a few talked about their rapes on radio and television. But their numbers were small. Most hid their rapes, or if they didn't, kept their identities hidden. The courts determined a point system to define the degree of rape. Counselors created a profile of the character traits of rapists and a prescribed way of treating rape victims. The Shield Law was instituted to protect rape victims from having previous sexual experience brought into court to undermine the victim's testimony.

I strongly felt that most of the public needed to be educated so no one could use rape as intimidation against victims. I believed the change had to begin with those who had experienced the stigma. The only way for that to happen was for rape victims to speak out against their rapists. So, three years after my rape, I volunteered as a rape counselor. I vowed, in addition, to work to help other people who were trying to change a system that blamed the victims.

To accomplish this, I went on a local television program about women going public with their rape experiences. When the program was over, I received a phone call from Tom O'Brien, a business acquaintance, who commended me for my bravery. He went on to tell me that he had been engaged to a girl who suffered a rape. His family constantly brought it up to him to convince him that in some way she was inferior. He said, "Your story made me realize that I shouldn't have been effected by their negative thoughts of my fiancée. I'm ashamed that I let their attitudes influence me."

Although I was grateful for his vindication of my position, the call reaffirmed to me the necessity of women who are rape victims to come forward with their stories. And I began to think of additional ways to use my own experience to benefit other victims of rape.

Having had such negative counseling sessions myself, I felt that was another area of need. I wanted to bring more openness and restore pride to those who'd been raped, and teach them the philosophy of being strong survivors, not weak victims.

Interviewed at a rape counseling center, my training began as twenty-eight of us volunteers watched an enactment of a rape. The film depicted a young woman whose car had stalled forcing her to hitchhike to work. We were warned it simulated a brutal attack. Afterwards, we were asked to express our deepest feelings. Of all the people who were to become counselors, only a few didn't blame the victim. Some comments were: "She shouldn't have hitchhiked," "She should have jumped out of the car when he told her he had been in prison," and "She should have bitten him on the penis."

To me, it was an example of the fact that even people who were concerned enough to want to help judged the victim. When I said I had been raped, I was told that if I were to counsel victims, I was never to mention my rape. If I couldn't do that, I wouldn't be allowed to participate.

Next the volunteers were placed in the same room with men who had been released from jail for crimes of incest, child molestation and rape. During the training session, the men preceded their comments with statements that acknowledged their guilt.

One man, who sexually molested his fourteen-year-old stepdaughter bragged about his recovery, but criticized his wife for still holding a grudge. He seemed to feel she was sick for not forgiving him.

One extremely good looking man stood up and announced he was the most dangerous man in the room. He claimed he raped girls and boys, as well as their mothers and fathers. He said he was a seducer, but had paid for his crimes by serving six years in a military prison.

Another rapist told us how he had been unable to cope with society. So he raped his mother! A few days later he broke into a house to steal and saw a couple sleeping. He got into their bed and performed oral sex on the woman. His wallet was found and so he went to jail, but his father still didn't think he was a rapist.

The only woman sex offender there claimed she performed oral sex on her infant, because her husband held a gun to her head. He also took a picture of her doing it. Years later, after she charged him with raping her daughter, he produced the picture of her and the infant in court. She went to jail.

In our classroom discussion, the other volunteers and I talked about that experience. I was the only one who felt the woman had been an abused wife. Most of the new counselors seemed to feel that males who committed these heinous crimes didn't really understand the terrible nature of their acts, but the mother was even more guilty. I was surprised they didn't have more sympathy for a woman who acted under duress with a gun pointed at her head. Many of the men who molested children had a wife or partner who refused to believe they could behave badly with other women or children.

After our training was completed, we were given our client list. Carol, the first client I met, was a victim of date rape. She was blond and beautiful, in her late twenties. She knew her assailant for only a month. The assault happened when she went to his home to have an intimate relationship. After the couple was in bed for about thirty minutes, five of his friends walked into the bedroom. He invited them to have sex with her. When she objected, he held his hand over her mouth and restrained her. They took turns as her partner cheered them on. She said one held back and offered to take her home after the ordeal.

Carol told her ex-husband about it when he brought their son back from visitation. He called the police. She claimed the police officer told her that if she pressed charges it would be the men's word against hers. She decided not to prosecute. Now her ex-husband believes she invited the rape. "I would like to take the rapists to court, even now," she said, "but I'm too fearful of the results. I could only face a court case if my husband threatened to get custody of my child."

About six months later, I went to a meeting at the

Victims and Speakers Group. Shea, a nurse, and the only woman I ever met with that name, sat with tears in her eyes as she explained the focus of the speakers program. "When women are taught to defend themselves, there will be no more rape!"

The naivete of her statement appalled me, and I suggested we should focus on counseling rapists as well as teaching women to fight back.

An attractive man announced that he was going to teach women how not to be raped. At first, I didn't recognize him as the pedophile, who had announced himself to be the most dangerous man in a room at my training session. Now he was concerned about women fighting back.

"Isn't that like sending a prostitute to teach nuns how to be chaste?" I later complained. "I believe if a pedophile is to be part of this group, he should be introduced as someone in therapy."

My statement started an argument. The consensus was that rapists knew how to find victims, so they were experts in informing women how to protect themselves. They couldn't understand my feeling that it was insulting to rape victims to put a rapist in such an elevated position.

I tried to show the counselors articles about groups like the one in New Port Richey, Florida, called EPAR (Enraged People Against Rape), or "rape" spelled backwards. The founder of EPAR said, "We are made up of men and women who have had it. We aren't going to take it anymore. We want the court system to be more responsive to victims. We formed after a group of young men entered the home of an elderly couple and gang raped the wife, while the husband was made to watch. Within days, two young children were

abducted from different homes in the middle of the night, raped, and left to wander the streets." The organizer claimed the group had three hundred members.

One member appeared on local television and described her rape. The night of the incident, she had heard a noise and went into her darkened living room to see what it was. She was attacked from behind. The rapist wrapped his belt around her throat and threw her to the floor. He tightened the belt until she was unable to scream and could barely breathe. Finally, she passed out. When she came to, her tongue was so swollen she couldn't swallow. The rapist had left when she was unconscious. She never saw his face, so she couldn't identify him.

Those were the kind of cases we were not to mention. My dissatisfaction with the Rape & Counseling Service at which I'd volunteered was growing. Then I received a certified letter from the director telling me that I wasn't sensitive to the counseling program, and they no longer wanted my services. Getting fired from a paying job is bad enough, but to get a registered letter, to be fired as a volunteer, made me angry as hell. Again, I called my friend, Ted Gordon, who was no longer on radio or television. This time it was to vent my frustration.

"The letter only proved to me that the professional counselors at our rape center didn't empathize with victims. They want simple answers and a paycheck!" I complained.

"That's what most people want. Lisa was critical of the counselors also. Now I understand why."

"I'd really like to talk to her. If I get furious, it must be worse for her."

"I've been meaning to contact her about you. I'll call her

today and ask her to contact you in the next few days," he said. "I think you both would be good for each other. In addition, Lisa needs a job badly. Maybe you could give her some helpful advice."

Chapter 21

Shared Feelings

I glanced around the lounge searching for Lisa Rhodes and Gayle de Pietro, a school counselor and friend, who Lisa had said in our phone call would be with her. I knew I would recognize Lisa because of the pictures which had been in the papers. Finally I spotted her at a table in the corner. "Hello, Lisa. And you must be Gayle," I said to the tall blond woman beside her. "Sorry I'm late. I had to park in the garage across the street."

Lisa smiled and said, "I've been looking forward to meeting you." She had a cheerful manner. When I'd spoken to her in October, she accepted that I didn't have a job for her with such grace that I'd been sending her leads ever since.

"I've brought you all the newspaper clippings from the murders and the trials," Gayle said, handing me a folder of papers. "They'll give you some history. I hope you don't mind my being here."

"Not in the least. Lisa said you'd been helping her put the past in place and get ready for Bobby Joe Long's new trial."

Gayle replied, "No one can understand the trauma better
than you."

I nodded. "Lisa, it seems like I already know you."

"And I you." The waitress stopped by and Lisa and
Gayle ordered tea. I ordered lemonade. "You must have so
many mixed feelings having to testify again."

"It is beginning to make me apprehensive." Lisa stroked
her chin. "I don't know how I'll feel seeing that man again."

I leaned forward. "How can I be of help?"

"Be my friend so we can share our feelings, the good and
bad. It's hard to do that with someone who hasn't been there."

"I'd like that too. If I had known you before, we
wouldn't have had so much in common. I had no idea how
our society views rape victims."

"I'd like to learn something about that," Gayle said, "but
please let's eat. I'm starving."

We were led to a table inside the small tastefully deco-
rated dining room. As soon as we ordered I began to air my
long repressed feelings about how rape victims are treated.

"Sympathy! If everyone didn't think you were forever
impaired, it might be more tolerable. Heaven forbid you ever
talk about it in polite society. In the Middle East and Africa,
they ostracize women who are raped. I don't think we are
very far removed, but we pretend to be more civilized and
compassionate." I couldn't tone down my anger.

"You're right, Joy. Inside I feel the same way about
other people's opinions, but I've never been able to express
it before." After we ordered lunch, Lisa said softly, "It never
occurred to me before I was raped that people had anything
but sympathy for rape victims."

I watched Lisa closely. She was not only pretty, but there

was a depth to her I was immediately impressed by. When I was raped, one thing which passed through my mind was...what it would be like for a young girl. Ten years before Lisa had only been seventeen. I understood what it was like to think that any moment you could be slaughtered. All I could think of was what the pain of a knife would feel like, and how horrible it would be for my family to see my bloody remains. "Lisa, you and I share what men in battle experience. We have both faced death. Our own," I managed to say, but my voice was choked by emotion.

"Why is that so hard for other people to understand?" Lisa said. She patted my hand.

"Unfortunately, we rape survivors are a small club. The members who didn't live can't tell what it's like. Outsiders often think those who didn't die had a romp in the hay or a shameful experience."

Gayle softened the moment. "You look younger than that statement. People Lisa's age don't know what a romp in the hay is. I do. I hope I never take rape casually. I suppose some people do."

I looked away from Lisa and focused on Gayle who was older than my first impression of her. She was an attractive woman with gray blond hair. She obviously was composed, but friendly. "I was married a long while and then I got divorced. Lisa mentioned you were too. I was married to a lawyer and have two children. I'll admit I try to understand people's lives through my experiences, but there are some commonalities in studies of previous victims. Lisa doesn't fit the mold. That's what makes her unique."

"I was married to an engineer and lived a protected life on two country acres only forty-five minutes from New York City, before my rebirth as a single woman. But Lisa's

experience is something I identify with because of my rape experience, though hers was more horrible. Nevertheless, how could I not have compassion for her. I feel her hurt."

"Yes, I can see why you do."

I gave a bitter laugh. "In fact, I reminded people at the rape support group so many times about not blaming victims that I was fired as a counselor."

"I thought you were in the advertising business."

"I am. I was fired as a volunteer. Their agenda was to teach women karate, etc., so they could fight back. They didn't want to know that sometimes you can't fight and survive."

Lisa broke in, "It made me miserable. I thought it was just my problem. Everyone kept telling me to get counseling, but I felt I was being criticized. I got enough of that at home."

"I'm surprised that a counselor wouldn't realize that," Gayle said.

"Do you understand why they do that?" Lisa leaned towards me.

"Unfortunately I do. I've spent a lot of time studying the problem after I'd become a counselor. I have come to think the ideas of volunteers and professionals are imprinted by the mores of our society, just as average people's beliefs are. They, like everyone else, are appalled by rape and fear it could happen to them. It's easier to think that fighting back will stop rape. When I was a young girl, the boys called me 'wild cat' because they couldn't intimidate me. They weren't rapists with brute strength holding guns or knives and ready to use them."

"So, you've found another way to fight back," Gayle said.

"We both have," I looked at Lisa, and her eyes met mine.

"Not hiding the truth."

Chapter 22

A Hero

During the next week or so, I went to the library and read old newsclips on Lisa and Bobby Joe Long's other victims. I also called Ted Gordon and asked to see him.

Ted's cluttered office reminded me of mine. There were stacks of books and papers everywhere. Video tapes and photo shots of his programs lined the walls. He put the pilot for his new show in the VCR so I could view it. Like many creative people, he was enthusiastic about his work. His interests and projects were many and varied. I couldn't help asking too many questions and, as ever, he was generous with his time. Finally, I got to the purpose of my visit.

"Ted, thanks so much for having Lisa get in touch with me. After meeting her, I was really impressed. She's terrific; levelheaded, cheerful, hardworking and more attractive than the pictures I'd seen in the newspapers."

"She's amazing isn't she?" Ted said.

"Despite all that's happened to her. Her voice always sounds happy and she laughs a lot. She's everything you said

she was. Definitely an optimist, who makes everyone around her view the glass as half full, not half empty."

"Of course," Ted mused "you met the new Lisa, not the timorous child she was nine years ago. She had a selfish grandmother whose terrible boyfriend pretended he was Lisa's father while he was sexually abusing her." He grimaced. "Polly Goethe was the first person to believe her and saved her from that existence, as well as putting the identity of Lisa's attacker and the serial murderer together."

"Polly's belief was undoubtedly a catalyst. I can imagine the determination it took to convince the male detectives that the rapist could be the murderer, but, in truth, Lisa was the hero. She kept her wits about her during the attack and was alert to every detail of her surroundings, as well as the physical appearance of her attacker. She refused to follow Bobby Joe's order and spoke the truth. Finally she led police to where he was located and described what he looked like so the police could find him and put him behind bars. Lisa was astute and brave from day one."

"Polly was pretty determined too. She had to get Lisa's confidence to encourage Lisa to tell the truth. At first, Lisa said he was black. She protected Bobby Joe," Ted opined.

"Never!" My voice was more forceful than I intended. "Lisa gave the police her assailant's description as a white man, six feet, 185-200 pounds, brown hair and a mustache, driving a maroon Magnum. It's in the old clippings dated the day she returned home."

"What about the abuse information."

"It took a few days for Polly to get Lisa to admit she was abused at home. She was afraid to tell that."

"A lot of newspapers implied there was a love relationship

between Bobby Joe and Lisa. Even I thought Bobby Joe
Long had affection for her. How else do you explain why he
let her go? Remember the stories about how he washed her
hair?"

"Strange love. The washing was for cleanliness and was
not a loving, caring gesture. And the rest of the time he was
threatening her with death. She did whatever he wanted so
he wouldn't kill her. And it worked—he let her go."

"I know. When Captain Gary Terry testified before
Congress about Lisa, he called it Bobby Joe Long's one act
of mercy. You can grant him that, can't you? After all he's
a human being with feelings."

I could feel my face reddening. "If that was true, he
wouldn't have savagely raped and then brutally murdered all
those women."

"No one can justify that, but if someone does something
positive it should be acknowledged."

"One good deed in the midst of a rampage of horror. It's
hard to give him credit for it. As for the newspapers thinking
Lisa had any feeling for Bobby Joe, that's a load of crap.
She, just as I, did anything she could to survive."

"Did you really say 'we have to stop meeting like this?'
You made that up," Ted said.

"Gospel, but it still amazes me that something could
strike me funny when I was about to have my throat cut."

"Did they ever catch that guy? You had so much information."

I shook my head and heard myself sigh heavily.

"It doesn't make me feel confident that the police try
their best. I want them to catch these rapists and then I'll feel
better. You were talking about how difficult it was for the

woman detective, Polly, to convince the male officers that Lisa's rapist was a murderer. 'Just a rapist', they said. Isn't that sad?"

"Lisa's upset about the romanticized version of her rape being publicized," Ted volunteered, changing the subject.

"You can paint the canoes any color you want to. There were three stories about the Long Island Lolita. You see why young girls are in trouble. In Nabokov's book, Lolita was thirteen. The newswriters did Joey Buttafucco a favor calling that girl The Long Island Lolita. I read that Buttafucco paid the light bill on the house of prostitution. It was too convenient that they had a video of her with another man. Lolita has come to mean seductress. I think it's the other way around."

"You have a one track mind."

"You don't?"

He grinned.

I thought about another problem. "What do you think about rape victims' identities being protected and their being encouraged not to speak out. I feel it increases the stigma of shame around rape."

"Neither of us could have imagined how much that exposure could have impacted your life. Do you regret finally speaking out?"

"No. Well, almost never." I added.

"I never thought of it as being anything but the women's experience, but it affects everyone who knows the victim," Ted observed.

I nodded. "I've never been comfortable with other people's reaction to my rape. In the beginning, I too wanted to hide and hated the attention. Then, when I was able to accept it

and needed to work through the experience, my friends and a lot of my family wanted me to forget it. I couldn't in my mind. I almost died. No one else but Lisa perceives being raped and attacked that way."

"I can understand why Lisa would."

"Lisa didn't know Long was a killer until later. No one knows about the man who raped me. My guilt over not wanting to report my rape in the beginning will always haunt me. I've contributed to that secretive attitude. But the thought that anyone could love her rapist makes me gag."

"I'm sorry, I didn't mean to sound as if I believe that. Even when I spoke of love between Lisa and the rapist, I didn't mean the type of love between a man and a woman. I meant a bizarre kind of love, as obsession perhaps, from the intimacy that happened. That's why Long meant to kill her, but couldn't. It's the reason he's in jail. Those twenty-six hours changed two peoples' lives."

"Psychologists call it the Stockholm Syndrome."

"Don't be upset by my reaction, Joy. It's great to be able to have a difference of opinion and still be friends."

Leaving Ted's office, I thought more about Lisa. Maybe I should tell the story of Bobby Joe Long's victims and especially Lisa. I fantasized that I would write about her strength and how she survives. I wanted to tell the world what a rape survivor was really like. I felt anger at the thought anyone would or could think of rape and love in the same context. Even the rapist. If it was only Ted Gordon, I could rationalize my anger at his opinion. But my own counselor echoed his sentiments. When she asked me if I loved the man who'd raped me, I had exploded. If she hadn't told me her own tragic story, I'd never have forgiven her.

As I got into my car, I remembered the detective who'd originally questioned me, when I reported my rape. He too had his own perceived agenda. Even my neighbor once asked me how many orgasms I had in four hours. I felt strongly that understanding how Lisa coped with all the bullshit might help others who'd experienced rape. Maybe even me.

During the next few weeks, Lisa and I spoke on the phone frequently and met just to talk on several occasions. Each time we spoke or were together we grew closer.

Chapter 23

Courthouse Blues

The Government Center Courthouse, circled by television news vans on Little Rock in New Port Richey, was easy to spot.

It was almost 9 o'clock, and I had to park my car in the far corner of the parking lot and walk around the building. As I passed one van, I asked the bearded guy rolling thick cable, "Do you know what number trial this is for Bobby Joe Long?"

He scratched his beard. "I know it's the third for his murder of Virginia Johnson." He shook his head as if to say, "Can you believe it?" I shook mine to concur.

I had to pass through a metal detector similar to one at an airport, and then rushed to Judge Wayne Cobb's Courtroom, Number One, expecting the room to be full of people and peeked in. I walked over to the bailiff. "What's going on? Where is everybody?"

"You can go in because they haven't started." He pointed to the door.

Judge Cobb sat at the head of a long table wearing a black robe. I found a seat at the foot. On my left was a television camera.

Only one camera was allowed at a time, and the stations shared the footage. I recognized the handsome, eloquent attorney on the judge's right as the Assistant State Attorney, Phillip Van Allen, because he had a cane next to him. He wore a gray suit that matched his slightly graying hair. His wavy hair was stylishly long, just below ear level. Next to him sat the conservatively dressed Assistant States Attorney, James Hellison, who would give the opening remarks for the prosecution.

I barely had time to look around when a door near the judge opened, and two sheriffs came in with Bobby Joe Long. A man walked up to the prisoner and stood talking. I assumed it was his Public Defender, sandy-haired, fiery and articulate, William Eble. He was a superior attorney, able to shift on the run and think on his feet. After a short conversation, Eble found a seat across from the State Attorney. Bobby Joe sat beside him. The bailiff whom I had talked to stood directly behind Long.

Eble addressed the judge. "My client doesn't want to sit in the courtroom. He wants to go back to jail. His mother didn't send him a new suit. He doesn't feel he is presentable in his blue one."

"It looks presentable to me."

"But he's wearing white socks."

I glanced over, camouflaging a smile. It is a trial about rape and death. I wasn't expecting such a trivial remark from an attorney, and from where I sat, I could see the bailiff's white socks. It amused me, but I didn't laugh. I turned my full attention to the man who had murdered so many women. He was only inches away. Bobby Joe Long looked better in the photographs taken nine years before. He had changed for

the worse. His nose dipped down and his rather pointed chin
swooped up. If he ever grew to be an old man, he'd have one
of those faces where the lips begin to recede. His best
attribute was his thick wavy hair, now slightly streaked with
gray. I looked closer at what he was wearing and shrugged.
The navy blue suit and light blue shirt were more than just
presentable. Poor Bobby Joe, his mommy didn't send him a
new suit.

Van Allen made it clear that if there was going to be a
trial, the prisoner had to attend. "If he doesn't want to sit in
the courtroom, he can sit in the holding cell."

Eble continued to argue for his client. He finally
exclaimed, "The holding cell isn't heated or cooled. In this
weather, he might be cold."

I felt myself stiffen. Long was cold. Who cared? If I
had remained outside, I wouldn't be privy to such ridiculous
information. Watching this trial wasn't going to be easy.
Now I knew why some people complained about coddling
prisoners.

Finally, they set about the serious business of picking a
jury to determine the guilt or innocence of Bobby Joe Long.
When they didn't finish by 5 p.m., the task was tabled for a
second day. It was difficult to find anyone who hadn't read
anything or watched the news. Meanwhile, the number of
spectators at the trial grew. The eleven potential jurors, who
survived the admonitions and questions about their knowledge of the history of the murder and rape cases were told to
go home and not watch television, read the papers or to talk
to anyone about the case.

Eble's questioning of prospective jurors was so intense it
sounded like the opening arguments in which he would be

making his case. At one point he said, "I'm not Perry Mason, and no one is going to rush through the double doors and confess." The whispers in the courtroom doubled in volume. In questioning a juror about an article in *The St. Petersburg Times,* Eble asked, "Did the headline use the word 'Serial,' but not 'Kellogg's'?" he cracked. The courtroom spectators broke into laughter.

Meanwhile, the judge tried to restore calm and seriousness. After having the State Supreme Court overturn the death sentence in the Johnson murder trials two times, Cobb seemed to take extra caution about the demeanor of the courtroom. He somberly explained the charges and the laws pertaining to first degree murder. Cobb told the potential jurors that to find someone guilty did not automatically carry a death sentence. There would be two parts to the trial: one to determine the defendant's guilt or innocence of the charges and one for sentencing. Each juror was asked if they had a strong feeling against the death penalty and, if they did, would it render them unable to come to a verdict. The last question the judge asked was, "Do you smoke?" The reason for that question was never explained. A short while later, I was taken by surprise when I was named in the trial. Eble asked if they had seen me talking to a CBS reporter at the pretrial hearing. All the potential jurors replied, "No."

In his questioning, State Attorney Phillip Van Allen focused on the jurors' ability to consider only the facts presented and not anything that was heard or read outside of the courtroom. He explained, "Aggravating circumstances must be proven beyond a reasonable doubt. Mitigating circumstances do not have to be beyond a reasonable doubt, and there is no limit to the number present." It was clear in his

forceful manner that he was going to leave no stone unturned in making this trial in the matter of Virginia Johnson the last.

I found the presumption of Long's innocence, after so many trials, difficult to take. Lisa's words to me as we'd gotten closer ran through my head. "I had looked forward to confronting the man who raped and terrified me for twenty-six hours, but my experience in testifying in Fort Myers left me feeling used. They asked me to identify my clothes. It brought my own horror back, and I cried on the stand. I had to wait outside the courtroom for three days, ten hours each time. I was only allowed yes or no answers. Did that man rape you? Yes. The dead women can't speak for themselves, and the living aren't allowed to talk. The courts are only concerned with the civil rights of criminals."

She had gone on to tell me that knowing she was going back to court prompted nightmares that she hadn't experienced since Long's trial in Fort Myers in 1988, and since she and Jimmy had separated, she had to deal with them on her own. In her dreams, she saw the bottom half of a naked woman and knew she was dead. She would wake up screaming, "Stop!" She confessed, "I truly believe part of me was killed when I was seventeen."

Lisa shared more of her haunted feelings with me each time we spoke or got together. "I'm angry at a system that terrifies me," she told me in an anguished voice. "Who knows when some jury will agree with the Supreme Court that overturned some of his convictions? I feel outraged that I'm expected to go to court, and I'm not offered help. I have to beg for assistance, and the criminal doesn't have to ask for transportation and a place to stay." My heart went out to her.

Another time she confided, "As a single mother, I barely

Susan Replogle knew Bobby Joe Long before he began his murderous rampage of rape and murder. When he raped and battered her, she told the police and he was prosecuted. She became the object of his rage.

Lisa McVey was on her way home from work on her bicycle when Bobby Joe Long kidnapped the seventeen year old girl. He subjected Lisa to twenty-seven hours of rape and torture. She is the only survivor able to connect 9 deaths.

Joy Wellman, host of a popular radio talk show in Tampa, Florida .

9 young women murdered by Bobby Joe Long

Ngeun Thi Long, 19, danced at the Sly Fox Lounge. She was found nude, bound and strangled on May 13 off of East Bay Road near Interstate 75.

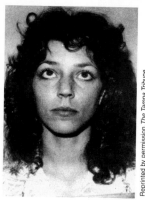

Michelle Denise Simms, 22, was found strangled and stabbed on May 27, north of Interstate 4 off of Park Road, within days of arriving in Tampa.

Elizabeth Loudenback, 22, was found strangled on June 24 off of Turkey Hill Road.

Chanel Devon Williams, 18, was found nude, dead of a gunshot wound on October 7 alongside Morris Bridge Road near the Hillsborough River State Park.

Karen Beth Dinsfriend, 28, was found partially clothed and bound, dead by asphyxiation on October 14 in an orange grove on the west side of Lake Thonotosassa.

Kimberly Kyle Hopps, 22, was found raped and strangled on October 31, 200 feet south of the Pasco County Line off of Route 301.

Virginia Lee Johnson, 18, was found bound and decomposed on November 6 off of Morris Bridge Road, two miles north of the Hillsborough Line in Pasco County.

Kim Marie Swann, 21, was found bound, naked and strangled on the north side of Orient Road overpass north of Adamo Drive on November 14, 1984. She had danced at the Sly Fox Lounge.

Vickie Marie Elliot, 21, was found with scissors she carried for protection on November 16, 1984 by police using Long's directions during his confession. Her body lay decomposing and undetected near the busy cross section of Fletcher Avenue and I-75, while her ticket to go home waited on her bed.

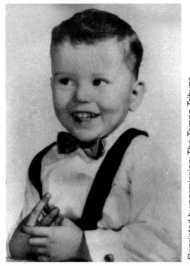

The youngsters at Beach Place weren't impressed with the news stories of the serial killer's difficult childhood – Bobby Joe is shown here as a child.

Bobby Joe Long's picture as a boy scout was printed by many newspapers and manipulated public sympathy in his favor.

The threatening letters Bobby Joe Long wrote while in jail.

Famed Miami Criminal Attorney Ellis Rubin, who volunteered his services, confers with his client, Bobby Joe Long, July 14, 1986 during the trial for the murder of Michelle Denise Simms.

July 19, 1986 Assistant State Attorney Michael L. Benito shows the jury the knife that slashed Michelle Denise Simms' throat before her naked body was dumped in a wooded area.

Sgt. Larry Pinkerton, who became Lisa's friend and 'substitute father' following her abduction has continued to support her through the years.

Lt. Gary Terry of the Sheriff's Department headed the task force that caught Long in 1984. When he testified before Congress in 1986 he said of Lisa, "Bobby Joe Long made two mistakes: first, he kidnapped Lisa, and second, he let her go."

Assistant State Attorney Phillip Van Allen spent 1,275 hours prosecuting Bobby Joe Long for the murder of Virginia Johnson.

Assistant Public Defender Laurie Chane looks pensively at the graying Bobby Joe Long during one of his quiet moments at his third trial for the murder of Virginia Johnson, Saturday, February 5, 1994.

Corp. Lee Baker's hair was only peppered white when he asked Susan why Bobby Joe Long hated her so after learning the contents of Long's letters written to the 'jail snitch.' "Pops" traveled 80 miles to witness Bobby Joe Long's fifth death sentence in 1994.

This map shows where four bodies of murdered women were found. Four other murdered women were added after red fibers connected their deaths to the same killer.

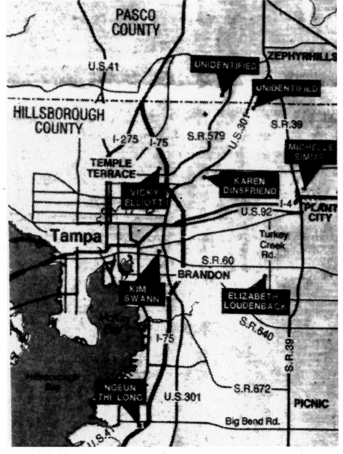

The Authors Today

Joy Wellman, a former talk show host, is now the head of an advertising agency in Florida.

Susan Replogle has become a successful interior designer and resides in Florida.

Lisa Mc Vey whose hometown treats her like a hero, has graduated from college and married.

make a living wage and am lucky to pay my rent. I haven't
been able to keep my telephone on at times. I feel isolated.
I'm scared, but I wouldn't want Bobby Joe Long to know.
That's what he wants. Then he would win."

"He won't win, Lisa. We won't let him," I said defiantly.

At the third trial for Virginia Johnson, Bobby Joe Long's
lawyers asked for a mistrial or a change of venue after a
week of interviewing one hundred twelve possible jurors.
Many young women interviewed said they could not consider
Bobby Joe Long innocent because of what they knew about
the case from all the flamboyant news coverage.

One balding man was so upset about Long being granted
another trial that the prospective juror loudly complained
about the waste of taxpayers' money. He was dismissed
immediately, and other prospective jurors were asked if they
had heard his remarks.

A plump woman with coiled gray hair was asked by
Bobby Joe Long's attorney if she knew the address on
Nebraska Avenue and did it mean prostitution to her? Eble
reminded Judge Wayne Cobb that Bobby Joe Long had a right
to a jury of fifty percent that had no previous information
about the case.

It turned out that over eighty percent of the possible
jurors had either read a newspaper account or seen one on
television. According to Long's attorney, the fifteen percent
who didn't read or watch television had to be illiterate.
"Bobby Joe Long deserves a jury of his peers." I wondered
how he could get them off death row. Long was granted a
change of venue.

Lisa called. "I need to talk. Could you come to my house?"

"I'll be there," I promised.

"Good, because I was so upset when Phillip Van Allen told me about the change of venue, I called Sgt. Pinkerton. We talked a lot about my feelings, and he said he understood. Anyway, afterwards I told him about you. He'd be happy to meet you. He said we should get together in some neutral place. Get this! My apartment!"

A few hours later, when I got to her house, she answered the door all smiles.

"I'm so happy to see you. Come in. We can talk a few minutes before Jennifer comes home from school."

I followed her into the neat, orderly apartment. A police officer was seated at the table. He was tall and trim with a straight chiseled nose, strong chin and much younger than I expected. He stood immediately and offered his hand.

"Joy, I wanted you to meet my friend, Larry Pinkerton. Excuse the mess. I just got home from my new job. Would you like some coffee?"

"Coffee, yes, but you lost your old job?" I was shocked.

"Yes, I had to stay home for days waiting to be contacted to go to court. It never happened, but I still had to be here, and the memories flooded back. You know I told you about the dreams. I was afraid to sleep. There was no way I could go to work." Lisa talked from the kitchen area as she fixed coffee.

"I'm so sorry. You told me how much that job meant to you."

"If only I got subpoenaed after my probation period was over. I was fired on the last day. I'm working at the super-market on the corner until I can get something better. Actually, it's more convenient. I can work the hours my daughter is in school or visiting her father."

I watched the young woman who was telling us the positive things about her new job and wondered how she had the strength to adapt to all the setbacks. Her sleek, wavy brown hair framed her pretty face and made her brown eyes look large and shining. Turning, I directed my attention to Sgt. Pinkerton, who was listening to Lisa also.

"I wanted to kill the bastard when he planned to escape. Everyone told me it was a stupid idea. Maybe it was, but it would have saved this girl a lot of pain. Ten years and it's not over."

I could hear the anger and frustration in the officer's voice. I said, "I wonder how she manages to bounce back and sound so cheerful."

"We all wonder! Lisa's told me you two have become friends. I've known her since she was seventeen. My daughter is two years younger, and I've always connected my feelings about Lisa to my love for my own child."

Looking admiringly at Lisa, Larry Pinkerton began to talk of his first impression of her. His voice was impassioned. "Policemen see so many people who use excuses to explain their bad behavior. Psychiatrists make a living doing it for criminals in our courts. It's enough to make you sick, but meeting one person like Lisa makes up for it. Over the years, I'm amazed at how she copes and goes on with her life."

I glanced at Lisa, who was smiling at him. Then I looked back at Pinkerton. "It's not only her bravery when Long attacked her, but when I think of what this girl endured with Marce I get angry all over again," he said forcefully. "Epileptic medication was another method Marce Rhodes used to control Lisa. She never had epilepsy. He convinced Lisa's grandmother that the girl was incompetent, bordering on mentally retarded. He used the idea that Lisa wasn't

mentally competent to speak to social welfare workers. When family members were present, his verbal abuse contained words like: worthless, imbecile, moron, retarded bitch. The more someone's mental capacity is diminished in other people's eyes, the less likely they will be believed. Can you imagine what torture that was for this beautiful, intelligent girl?"

I sighed. "I understand why you respect her so. I realize that your continued support is important to Lisa."

"I won't disappoint her like so many other adults did." He looked at Lisa and then at me appraisingly.

"Neither will I," I replied to his unasked question.

"You're both great," Lisa added.

Before leaving, he said, "I wish that Marce Rhodes could have spent his last days in jail. His disabilities should never have been an excuse to free him. He wasn't too disabled to commit his crimes. And as for Bobby Joe Long, the electric chair is too humane for him."

"I can't argue with that," Lisa said quietly.

"Agreed," I nodded.

Lisa walked Sgt. Pinkerton to the door. Watching them say goodbye, I realized that the police officer's life was forever touched by Lisa. I knew that Lisa felt he was the father she never had.

Before we could say anymore, Lisa's daughter, Jennifer, bounced in from school and sat at the table. Lisa poured her a glass of milk and put down a plate of cookies.

"Jennifer, this is my friend Joy."

The child was as gregarious as her mother. She smiled warmly at me. "I'm pleased to meet you. Now I'll know what you look like when I talk to you on the phone."

Mother and daughter gave their attention to the papers Jennifer brought home from school. It was obvious that anymore conversation about Lisa's ordeal at the hands of Bobby Joe Long wouldn't be appropriate and, when I finished my coffee, Jennifer and Lisa walked me to the door.

After seeing her as a mother, my admiration of Lisa grew. She put all her anxieties aside to create a happy home for her child. She didn't let the trials or her divorce interfere with the stability and warmth of her loving relationship with her child. She was an inspiration to me. She didn't just appear strong, her whole being radiated strength. Lisa's daughter reflected her mother's care and attention. For a little girl, she had a superior vocabulary and wonderful diction. She was also polite and well-mannered, just like Lisa. She adjusted amazingly well to her parents' separation and divorce. Like her mother, she too had strength.

Lisa didn't just put on a happy face to the world. Somehow she had managed to put her terrible experiences aside. Or, they were like the fire which filled a kiln, transforming clay into beautiful porcelain.

Chapter 24

Words of Truth, Words of Falsehood

Lisa received another subpoena to testify at Bobby Joe Long's trial for the murder of Virginia Johnson. The trial had been relocated to Ocala, eighty miles north of Tampa. Mr. Yearby, a detective, drove Lisa to Ocala, where she registered in a hotel. There she began her ordeal of waiting alone to confront the man who captured, raped and released her almost ten years ago. Although she was on edge, she finally managed to get some sleep.

This was the third time Bobby Joe Long was being tried for Johnson's strangulation death, and the second time Lisa was to be the only victim/survivor to identify him from the witness stand.

The next morning, Lisa went to the Marion County Judicial Center. There were guards at each door. Trembling, she entered one behind the witness stand and stoically walked towards it. She knew everyone was depending on her.

The law enforcement officers on the case, the woman

who discovered Johnson's decaying body, and the man at whose house Johnson had stayed had all preceded Lisa as witnesses. Now the jury of six men and six women sat watching Lisa being sworn in. She took her seat in front of the jury. Her long, wavy brown hair flowed down onto her white blouse. Sitting straight and tall, her large brown eyes glanced around. Catching sight of me, she gave me a quick smile.

From where Lisa was sitting between the jury and Judge Charles W. Cope, she could not see the graying Bobby Joe Long rocking back and forth in his chair. But I could, and I had watched him, laid back and detached, fall asleep several times during jury selection. A few minutes after Lisa took the stand, I saw him flash a furious scowl look at a good looking brunette woman, who sat down in one of the front rows.   Phillip Van Allen, the State Attorney, began questioning Lisa, bringing her back to the time she'd been kidnapped by Long. His voice was gentle.

Lisa calmly answered. The testimony covered her route on her bicycle.

"Did you cross Sligh Avenue?"

"Yes, there was a church parking lot. After I passed a white van, I was grabbed from behind and pulled off my bicycle and thrown to the ground. I screamed, and the man said, 'Stop screaming or I'll kill you.' He dragged me to the car holding a revolver to my head." Lisa's main job was to point out Long, which she did in a clear, unwavering voice.

When it was time for cross examination, William Eble, the Public Defender, was more stern. "How did he get you in the car?" His voice sounded angry.

Lisa replied, "He opened the driver's side and shoved me into the passenger side."

"Were there any obstructions?"

"I had to climb over the shift."

Eble began to spit his next questions out in quick succession, hardly giving Lisa a chance to answer. "Did you have your clothes on? Did you have your clothes off? What type of transmission?"

Lisa managed to reply, but grew visibly rattled. When she said, "Noisy," her voice cracked.

"What kind of locks?"

"No locks." Tears started to wet her cheeks. Bobby Joe Long watched her intently.

"Describe for the record what he was wearing."

Unable to repress her feelings, Lisa began to cry. Bobby Joe, holding his chin, whispered to the female Assistant Public Defender, Laura Chane, sitting next to him. She bent her head close to hear him, and he repeated his words to Eble when he walked by her.

Eble asked to approach the bench. The attorneys began to discuss some issues not privy to the jury. The argument before the bench gave Lisa time to get her emotions under control.

Judge Cope reminded the jury that Bobby Joe Long was not in court for the crime against Lisa. Then he sent the jury out of the room.

Eble faced Lisa and shouted angrily, "Did you lie in that deposition? How can you identify him? You never saw the man's face. You didn't pick him out of the pictures."

The questions cut through Lisa like a knife, her memory fading back in time. Lisa responded without hesitation. "I

picked the man with the thin eyebrows. I felt Bobby Joe Long's face, his thin eyebrows, his cheekbones."

Eble began to shoot more questions at her like darts.

"Did you see his eyebrows? His cheekbone? You didn't identify him at his last trial."

His face drawn like a mask, the blood vessels in his temples bulging, Eble kept hammering questions at Lisa. Finally, he turned to the subject of Polly Goethe.

As Lisa left the stand, Eble's voice struck out, asking the Judge for a ruling.

"Approach the bench."

After a brief discussion, they all agreed that Eble could write out five questions and present them to the Judge.

"I will direct the witness not to mention anything that happened in the car or apartment. Details of what Long did to Miss McVey are inadmissible. There will be no testimony about sexual battery."

Eble sat down next to Bobby Joe Long and his assistant. His face now looked relaxed, and he smiled.

After a short recess, the questioning of Lisa resumed with the jury present.

Eble narrowed his eyes, firing questions about the identification of Bobby Joe Long. He went over the time Lisa was with Long before the blindfold was put on.

"On page thirty-six in your 1985 deposition, you did not identify Bobby Joe Long's picture. Who showed you the pictures?"

"Polly brought them."

He went on with a few more questions.

"Remove the witness," Eble demanded irately, and Lisa was escorted off the stand once again.

A heated discussion ensued about Lisa's testimony on the stand. Attorney Eble objected to having the jury exposed to an emotional display from Lisa McVey. "We had twenty-three minutes of testimony and nineteen minutes of tearful emotion. I tried to depose that witness, but was blocked by the State."

Van Allen reminded him. "You had the opportunity to depose the witness if you informed the State of your line of questioning, as is required by the law. You made no attempt to do that."

The judge allowed Eble's request.

After Eble got permission to put Polly Goethe on the stand, he wavered, saying he didn't want to "open a can of worms" by his line of questioning. "I don't want any preju-dicial evidence of Mr. Long's other murders brought out in court." He made another attempt to get a mistrial and was denied. His motion for a recess was granted.

During it, Polly Goethe Horn (her married name) took the stand without the jury present. After briefly questioning her, Eble returned to the subject of Lisa.

The judge peered over his glasses and then looked down at the papers before him. "Do you have any more questions of this witness?"

"I want details of Lisa McVey, to see if her description is different from the written deposition."

"Her testimony is privileged to her," the Judge admonished.

"No further questions. If I lose, I don't want to be dis-qualified as inefficient," the defense attorney said irritably and returned to his seat.

The jury was brought back in and seated.

Sgt. Carsen Helms, one of the policemen who first sighted Bobby Joe Long on the north end of Nebraska Avenue on November 15, 1984, was called to take the witness stand after Polly. He testified in answer to Van Allen's questions that he'd stopped a white male in his late thirties with short brown hair driving a maroon Dodge Magnum.

Detective C.D. Wall asked to see the driver's license. It belonged to Robert Joe Long, 1584 Fowler Avenue.

On cross examination, Eble asked, "Did you identify him from a photograph?"

"No, a description."

"Point out the man you stopped."

"Right there," the officer pointed. "Bobby Joe Long."

"You took his picture. Did you have camera equipment in the police car?"

"No, we had to call for it."

"How long did you detain this man?" Eble asked and then, seeing a puzzled look on the officer's face, changed the question. "Keep him waiting?"

"Twenty minutes."

"Did you also photograph his car?"

"Yes."

The next witness, Harold Windseph, described himself as a corporal in the Hillsborough Sheriff's Office. "I am one of the officers who arrested Bobby Joe Long." After pointing out the defendant, he told how he and fellow officers brought Long to the Sheriff's Office in Ybor City.

At the end of Windseph's questioning by Van Allen, Eble and Long conferred quietly. "No questions." The witness was excused.

A published statement of one of the arresting officers not

present, was then read into the records. Van Allen was building his case block by block.

"Call Thomas J. Muck to the stand." In answer to the District Attorney's questions, Muck informed the court he had spent sixteen years in law enforcement and was a photographer. He was with Central Booking of the Hillsborough Sheriff's Office. "I took a series of photographs of the maroon Dodge Magnum."

Eble jumped up shouting, "Did you have a warrant?"

Muck's cheeks colored. "I don't know if we had a warrant or not."

The weary jury was excused after the lawyers rushed to the bench for a belabored conference before the bench. Eble then renewed all his objections and talked about bringing Lisa McVey back on the stand. "Did Bobby Joe Long admit to raping Lisa McVey?"

"The confession is valid without an admission of rape," the prosecutor interjected.

"We note the confession made in relation to Lisa McVey." The Judge looked at Eble and waited.

Eble's eyes glared.

"The prosecutor says he will go over all the gory details if I recall her."

"Testimony concerning the McVey details are excluded."

"I withdraw my request."

It was after 1 o'clock.

The Judge announced, "We'll recess for lunch."

"The Court will rise," the bailiff said.

In the hall, I stood with a group of press people viewing the trial. A cub reporter said, "I saw you taking notes. Are you writing a book about Long?"

"I'd be more interested in writing about Long's victims.

Lisa McVey managed to survive even after he started his killing spree. As a rape survivor myself, I empathize."

"Oh, I'm sorry," he murmured and walked away. Looking around as I walked down the corridor, I saw the luxury courthouse building flaunted lots of glass and chrome and soft gray carpet. I stepped into the shining black and chrome elevator and pushed the button marked "G."

William Eble, Bobby Joe Long's attorney, hesitated before stepping in besides me. "If you don't mind," he gave me a quizzical look. I assured him it was fine.

"You'll have the opportunity to tell me how Bobby Joe Long could be innocent," I said, fully aware of my sarcasm. Then I caught myself, "Seriously, is this trial going to last through the weekend?" The elevator stopped at the ground floor and the doors slowly opened.

"If I have my way it will," the young attorney said as he stiffly marched off to have a cigarette in front of the courthouse.

Now that I had the opportunity to talk to him, I followed. The noon sunshine was beginning to warm the winter day. "Tell me one positive thing about bringing Bobby Joe Long back to court over and over. If anyone can explain this treatment of mass murderers, you should be able to. My personal feelings are that, in Florida, death by electric chair comes a heck of a lot swifter to those who kill a store clerk, or a black man who kills a white person. Ted Bundy went to court so many times he became a celebrity."

"Bobby Joe Long hasn't had a fair trial, and he isn't getting one this time either," Eble protested. "The State's case is solely Long's confession. They shouldn't use it in this trial, but I've not been able to stop them. I'm just a public defender." He looked away and then irately snuffed out his cigarette after taking a last drag.

"Well, Ellis Rubin told the press that Bobby Joe Long had a fair trial."

"I've never seen that in print but," he shrugged, "Ellis Rubin is the only private attorney Long has had."

"Do you try as hard to represent someone charged with a minor crime?"

"Of course I do," he said stuffily.

"Well good. I think some innocent people need good attorneys, too." I had to walk away.

I strode over to the food stand on the corner where hot dogs were sold and bought one for my lunch. To me, a hot dog in the open air just smells better. I ate it slathered with mustard, onions and relish. It was so good that it took my thoughts off the trial for at least a few minutes. Then the court scenes rushed back. It was mind-blowing that so many people were employed to protect the murderer, and there was no one there to protect the reputations of the women he had killed. Even if they all had been prostitutes, though some clearly were not, they were lumped together and referred to by that demeaning term. And just the way the word "prostitute" was said was damning, as though it made such women fair game for murder. The whole thing made me furious. I regretted not mentioning it to Long's attorney. Oh well, he would only have spouted some ridiculous justification.

When I went back to the courthouse, Lisa was standing outside with Phillip Van Allen and the arresting officers. Walking up to me she confided how upset she was. "His attorney wouldn't let me say what I wanted, only what he wanted."

I squeezed her hand. "We'll have our time," I promised.

"I'm still waiting," Lisa said wearily. Then, as if giving

herself an inner pep talk, she added, "And I'm going to continue to wait until we do!"

The next person to take the stand and be sworn in was Lt. Randy Latimer. "I've been with the Sheriff's Department twenty-two years," he said firmly.

Van Allen was gracious, but grave. "Do you remember 16T984?"

The officer answered in kind, looking straight at the prisoner. "The license plates of Bobby Joe Long."

"Before Mr. Long's statement, was he advised of his constitutional rights?"

"Yes." He was a sharp officer I thought, wise to the ways of lawyers.

"Did he understand his rights?"

"Yes."

"Did he indicate he might need an attorney?"

"No."

Van Allen deliberately detailed and covered every aspect of the arrest of Long, rejecting any implications that Bobby Joe Long's testimony might have been obtained illegally.

Later, Detective Kenneth Hager described the site where Virginia Johnson's body was found. Eble cross-examined him at length, putting emphasis on the short distance Cromwell Road was from the Pasco County line. I wondered if he was inferring that Pasco didn't have jurisdiction over the death site. If that was the attorney's intent, nothing developed.

As the litany of witnesses fleshed out Van Allen's case that Bobby Joe Long had committed cold blooded murder, I grew tired and looked at my watch. The day was ending when Michael T. Malone, who described himself to Phillip

Van Allen as Supervisor and Special Agent to the F.B.I., testified. Assigned to laboratory investigation with intensive training in fiber and hair analysis, he qualified himself as an expert witness in forty-five states as well as the District of Columbia. Displaying large diagrams of human hair, he explained how the magnification could determine its individuality. Somehow I felt strangely affected when two hairs from Virginia Johnson's head were introduced as State's Exhibit B.

For what seem like an eternity after Van Allen had finished his questioning, Eble challenged the State's expert witness. He made him go over and over the hair and fibers, and the amount of fibers it took to determine a dye lot. How many miles of carpeting in one dye lot? And when he finally got down to splitting the fibers, I thought it apropos. How many angels could dance on the head of a fiber, I wondered. Of one red fiber alleged to be from Bobby Joe Long's car, Eble asked, "How much of the fiber does it take to test versus how much was left?"

At one point, Malone said, "This is not a fingerprint but it's very identifiable."

The next person brought to the witness chair, Sgt. Steve Moore, testified he had been with the Sheriff's Department for sixteen or seventeen years. "I vacuumed Long's car and put the contents in five plastic envelopes for evidence."

When Van Allen turned Moore over to Eble for cross examination, Eble examined the envelopes. He then asked the Judge for a copy of Long's confession.

"That will be two bucks," the Judge quipped.

Later, Corporal Lee Baker was asked by Van Allen if he had come into contact with Bobby Joe Long on November

16, 1984. The detective described taking hair samples from Bobby Joe Long and putting them in envelopes.

"Were they sealed?"

"Yes."

Another possible objection done away with. Van Allen was going to see to it that there were no mistakes. Long wasn't going to have appeal grounds this time if he could help it.

Steve Crib testified he was a detective for the Sheriff's Office and witnessed the carpet samples being stored. They were accepted as State's Exhibit U. He was the last witness for the day.

Court was to resume on Friday morning at 9:00 a.m. As I walked out of the courthouse, the sky was darkening. I could hardly wait for the next afternoon when Bobby Joe Long's confession on the CBS tape would be run for the jury. I couldn't imagine that reading it would have the same impact as hearing his voice and seeing his body language.

When court reconvened at 9 o'clock the next morning, Dr. Joan Wood was called to the stand. Her red jacket stood out in sharp contrast to the polished wood of the courtroom and more somber colors. Her dark hair was attractive, streaked with gray. In response to the questioning of Van Allen, Dr. Wood, adjusting her glasses, said she had been the Chief Medical Examiner since January 8, 1985. She was on the Board of Pathology and had performed 5,000 autopsies.

"Describe the scene you examined on November 6, 1984, please."

"I arrived at Cromwell Road at about 2:14 p.m. There was a large blackened area around the body caused by the decomposing of the body and bloody fluids that leaked out and stained the grass. The head and neck and upper torso

were twenty-four feet from the area. I had everything
flagged that didn't belong in the field."

"For what purpose?"

"To find all the human bones, clothing and everything
attached to the corpse."

A chill shot through me. How horrid such revelations
would be for Lisa. I was glad she wasn't there.

"Did you estimate how long the body was there?"

"From the decomposition, about ten to fifteen days.
Animals moved the bones. In spite of that, the upper part had
a necklace and earring on the right ear."

"Label that State's Exhibit item I."

The plastic bag with large red labels was shown to the jury.

"The forensic dentist removed tissue from the exposed
lips," Dr. Wood continued.

"Label that State's Exhibit I."

"There was cloth around the neck that was a white or
beige ribbed tank top. It had aqua horizontal stripes. There
was also a shoelace with a small loop in it."

"Like a leash?" Van Allen interjected. A gasp went up
from the spectators who anticipated what was coming next.

"Objection!" Eble cut in, his voice like a knife.

The witness continued, her voice flat. "I removed the
metal chain. I carefully cut the shoelace off and saved the
knot. It was looped twice around the neck. The internal
diameter was nine inches."

"State's Exhibit J."

While the plastic bag containing the items was introduced into evidence, Dr. Wood continued her testimony.
"The bikini underpants were not on the body. We know that
because they were not discolored with blood and body fluids
like the top. They contained no pieces of skin or pubic hair."

"State's Exhibit M," Van Allen said passing the plastic bag. People viewing the spectacle turned away.

"The semi-nude, decomposing body also had shoelaces around the wrists. The way the laces on the neck were placed the woman had been garroted. People think when that is done, death occurs from the lack of air. It happens from the drainage of blood out of the head. It takes two to three minutes of continuous pressure. If the blood flows both ways, it takes longer. The victim only becomes unconscious when the draining fluids are blocked." As Dr. Wood described the way the woman died, she spoke directly to the jury. Her concentration on them never wavered.

One motherly looking woman left the room clutching her stomach. As Wood continued to describe the victim's wounds, I thought of joining the spectator who left.

The shoelaces used to bind the victim's hands were labeled State's Exhibit N.

Eble started his cross examination by going over Wood's testimony about the darkened area. He asked about a struggle and whether the body could have been killed elsewhere and dumped in the field. Dr. Wood, holding her ground, answered his questions by repeating the testimony she'd already given.

Thank God, I thought, she couldn't be shaken.

"You cannot say the shoelaces that were around the wrists were probable homicide. Isn't it true that some people tie their hands for autoerotic sex?" Wood's retort was muffled by the spectators' audible giggles.

The next questions were fired in Eble's staccato form. Wood answered in the same manner, tit for tat.

"It is said that lack of oxygen in blood heightens orgasms."

"In saying probable garrotement, there was no evidence of stabbing? Gunshot?"

"There were no bones splintered."

"Did you test for drugs? Could you rule out a drug overdose for heroine or cocaine?"

"With her hands tied, yes."

"The woman was a prostitute," Eble stated, watching the jury. "Did she have any sexually transmitted diseases?"

"She had gonorrhea at least four times prior to her death."

Why the hell was that important? Did it make her less a victim? For a moment, I hated Eble for his insinuations.

"You didn't find any red fibers, did you?"

"No. Not in the field examination." She paused and Eble could not hide his slight smile.

Then the witness went on in the same tongue-in-cheek tone as Eble. "They were found later in her hair."

Hurray for Wood. I wanted to cheer.

"I have no further use of this witness."

"I'll bet you don't," I murmured half under my breath.

By 11 a.m. the courtroom felt warm and humid. When I walked outside during the recess, the heaviness of the air was palpable. Dr. Wood was talking amiably to some detective from the Sheriff's Department. The sparring of the courtroom vanished for awhile. Eble walked up to her and chatted about the humid weather. The shaded brown panther on his tie perfectly complemented his tan suit.

Dr. Wood challenged him jokingly. "I didn't know you were concerned about endangered species."

Eble looked down, his face serious. "It's nice isn't it. My daughter gave it to me." I wondered if Dr. Wood was

implying Eble's tie should have a woman on it. If she was, Eble didn't get it.

During the recess, a television set had been moved into the courtroom facing the jury box. The atmosphere and movie film quality of the trial increased! I positioned myself on the left side of the room so I could see both the screen and the defendant. Bobby Joe Long took his seat next to the young woman who assisted the public defender. Eble, small and athletic looking, paced back and forth not unlike a panther.

The jury was already seated. The Judge entered, and we all stood to the sound of the bailiff's command, "All rise, Judge Charles W. Cope."

Then came the part of the trial that the jury and spectators who hadn't seen the original broadcast were anxious to see, the accused murderer's television interview.

Van Allen requested permission to bring CBS camera operator Ronnie James to the stand and explain to the jury the interview they were about to see. Ronnie James testified that Bobby Joe Long was not promised anything or forced to give the interview to CBS News.

Just as the tape began to roll, Bobby Joe Long shouted into the quiet of the courtroom, causing shocked exclamations. "I'm just a stupid man, but I don't know how you can bring my confession into the courtroom when it includes other crimes." I stared at him closely. He looked bloated and haggard compared to the fit, happy looking twentyish man pictured on the television.

His protestations were juxtaposed to the mellow voice of Bobby Joe Long, talking on the tape about how he would become agitated periodically. "For periods of about a week, I feel I'm going faster. I sleep four-five hours a night."

A low pitched female voice asked, "Does it make you hate?"

Bobby's face had on its little bad boy expression. "I'd get in fights. You know, about the girl I let go, Lisa McVey. She didn't escape, I let her go! I used to stand in front of a mirror and see if I looked different. I thought everyone could see the difference when they looked at me. When the McVey girl happened, I began to think I was out of control. This was a girl on a bicycle. Did I drive away? No, I was so mad there was no thought, just anger. I don't know if you know how I got busted. The cops said they were looking for some hit and run. I knew they weren't taking pictures for some hit and run bullshit."

The voice of the young Bobby Joe Long on camera was pleasant, composed and calm. His face was animated as if he enjoyed telling his story.

I turned around to see the effect of the panorama of the tv screen on the spectators. Every eye was riveted on it. Except Bobby Joe Long's. He was intently watching the jurors.

His rambling voice went on, "I knew I was attracting attention. I was afraid. The task force. I could have moved to Lakeland or Mexico. I had twelve hundred dollars in the bank. I didn't want to stay in jail. When I let the McVey girl go, it was obvious that something was wrong with me. Someone will fix me. No one gives a damn. The cops know I want help."

The interviewer calmly asked, "Did you think of the victims?"

Without emotion, Bobby Joe answered, "No, I killed them....A, B, C, D. I'd stop....pull over....and kill." The gasps of the spectators in the courtroom were audible. "They were all the same. Streetwalkers. This was a working girl on a bicycle. I was wondering when it was going to stop. I was

losing control. A little girl on a bicycle. Then it dawned on me that things were really getting bad."

"Are you saying you wanted to get caught?"

"I never thought of getting a death sentence."

I stared at the man on the screen. My blood chilled. Into my mind came an even more frightening thought. Bobby Joe Long knew Lisa's name. He knew approximately where she lived. She was the one who identified him, and he knew it. The day after he let her go, the papers described and named him. At the time he was probably stalking Lisa and instead had killed the ninth woman only days later. Was it out of fury at Lisa? Most likely. Now he wanted his letting Lisa go be seen as an act of kindness. He wanted to use it to save himself. What if Lisa hadn't given the police a description of what he looked like and pinpointed his location? What if the police hadn't been combing the area looking for him? What if Polly Goethe hadn't made the connection between Lisa's rape and the murderer? Even in the few intervening days, he might have kidnapped Lisa again and finished the job. And how many others? To me, Bobby Joe Long hadn't protested too much about having his television appearance shown for a very calculating reason. He was using it to show remorse. Not a stupid or crazy man at all.

Eble walked slowly, deliberately toward the jury, his face set in stubbornness. "Ladies and Gentlemen of the jury, evidence which has been admitted shall," he paused, the effect was pure melodrama, and then went on, "only be considered for identity."

Van Allen had already started to rise when the Judge commanded, "Approach the bench." Then he added, "The jury is excused for lunch."

After the jury left the room and newspeople hurried out to post their stories, the lawyers battled over the admissibility of the tape. Long's attorney insisted it didn't connect him to the murder of Virginia Johnson. The State argued that they made a circumstantial case for his connection to her through the fibers and Dr. Wood's testimony.

Suddenly, Eble brought up another point. He wanted to call another witness: Sharon Martinez.

I wondered who Sharon Martinez was. Obviously a witness whom Eble thought could alter Long's damning admission.

The Judge granted Eble's request.

After lunch, Martinez, a statuesque blond who wore her hair in a pony tail, was called. She was dressed chicly in black, but appeared to be ill at ease, as she looked from the jury to the accused.

Eble smiled as he started to question her. He thanked the young woman for returning, explaining that he'd let her go home Wednesday. "I talked to you awhile ago. You met Virginia Johnson in 1984. You considered her a friend. Did she use drugs and alcohol?"

Van Allen, exasperated, protested, "Objection, leading the witness."

Eble changed the question, but not the subject. "Did you have occasion to observe her alcohol habits? Did she drink to the point of passing out?"

"Hearsay," Van Allen interjected calmly.

Eble wasn't about to stop without finishing. "Drink to the point of urinating on herself?"

"Remove the jury," the Judge injected, clearly annoyed.

"I renew my motion to dismiss," Eble said as the jury was leaving.

"Can I ask a question?" Bobby Joe Long interjected. "The Florida Supreme Court ruled other murders can't be included. I don't understand how other murders cannot come in with the videotape."

"The interview is not excludable because of the inclusion of other murders. That testimony put those ladies in your car. It put Miss McVey in your car," Van Allen said.

"I may not be bright, but the law says other murders can't be brought into court," Bobby Joe Long repeated.

"Violent felony kidnapping. 'When I saw them walking down the street...I killed them A, B, C, D," Van Allen said, using his cane for emphasis.

"Judge Cobb found insufficient evidence," Eble argued.

"The evidence is she left Tampa...ended in Pasco and was killed in Pasco," Van Allen noted.

"I cut my own throat on circumstantial third degree murder," Eble admitted.

"Mr. Van Allen," Judge Cope said, his voice taking on an iron edge. "My," he drew out the word and glared at both the attorneys, "reply is there is sufficient evidence for felony murder. Sufficient to bring in the others, because of the testimony of Lisa McVey. The circumstantial evidence on Virginia Johnson—I haven't ruled on."

As Eble continued questioning Martinez, more arguments ensued and other information was batted back and forth in an intense sparring match. Old laws...fibers...hairs...fibers aren't fingerprints...the abduction of Lisa McVey. But the witness didn't cooperate.

"I don't remember," she said looking confused.

Eble kept swinging. "Do you remember being in the Country Inn in Tampa and meeting Virginia Johnson and having her ask to move back in with you? You told her no."

"Yes, er...No," Sharon Martinez answered uncertainly, turning her head toward the Judge.

Eble struck another blow at his own witness. "You wouldn't let her move back in because you knew she was a drug addict. Did speed balls."

Van Allen was livid. "Objection, hearsay! The victim's state of mind is not an issue."

Eble strode to the bench. Van Allen remained seated, but he looked furious.

"Objection, hearsay! Remove the witness. The object is to trash the victim." Once again, the Judge excused the jury.

Van Allen's assistant and Eble began verbal fisticuffs. Eble kept pounding on the idea that the victim's drug addiction was relevant because she could have died of substance abuse. He claimed he wanted to disqualify Dr. Wood's testimony because she made no toxicology report and called Virginia Johnson a healthy female.

Van Allen struck back. "Sharon Martinez called the police when she saw that Long was arrested. She went looking for her (Virginia Johnson)."

"Her alcohol and drug addiction is not relevant," countered the State's Attorney.

"I don't want that testimony presented to the jury. I know why she called the police. I don't want to open the door to discussion about all the other bodies," Eble pleaded. "Her drug abuse is relevant. It shows the medical examiner wasn't thorough." He stared at the Judge, entreating, "A man's life is at stake."

"It could still be hearsay. Do you know that Miss Martinez had personal knowledge of Virginia Johnson's use of cocaine and heroine? Miss Herman, the nurse, also testified that there were zero medications and zero drugs and

no track marks." The Judge, studying the documents before him added, "I'll allow it under 8042C."

The jury was again seated, and Sharon Martinez was brought back to the stand.

Over and over Eble covered the same ground, using variations to question Martinez about meeting Virginia Johnson in a restaurant, and refusing to let Virginia move back in with her because she believed that Johnson was using drugs. But Martinez still hesitated. Then Eble asked Martinez about Johnson's working on Nebraska Avenue. Martinez responded that Virginia showed her money.

Once Martinez took the bait and the word money was spoken, Eble started asking her about the men Virginia knew, hammering on Hank Rojeges, a television repairman who lived near the area where Virginia's body was found.

Eble asked question after question about Rojeges' use of alcohol and his personality when drinking. "Did he drink a lot? Was he a nasty drunk?"

"Objection as to relevance."

"Overruled."

Eble fixed his gaze on Martinez's face. "Did Rojeges have a lot of prostitutes visit, and were they involved in unusual sexual activity?"

I was getting disgusted with Eble. It was obvious to me that even the most minor player's reputation would be sacrificed, not to mention the use of unproven accusations concerning the victim's drug and alcohol habits to prove her murderer's innocence. As was pointed out, she had been killed by a garrote around her neck with her hands bound, however, she obviously was on trial too.

"Irrelevant!" the State's Attorney protested.

The witness was excused and Dr. Wood was recalled.

"Do I understand that up to five minutes ago you knew nothing about drugs and alcohol?"

"Mr. Hagen told me last night that drugs and alcohol were an issue," she answered.

"So, she could have died of a heart attack. You can't rule out drug overdose," Eble responded.

With a heavy dose of irony in his voice and exasperation plainly written on his face, Van Allen pointed out, "There's a minute possibility the sun won't come out tomorrow, but the possibility of her dying from drug abuse is even less."

"Your opinion was based on a healthy person," Eble continued undaunted.

Finally, the Judge had enough. He told both attorneys to prepare their instructions for the jury.

"Without the videotape, the State has no case," Eble shouted.

Ignoring Eble's remark, the Judge said, "Advise the court if your client wants to take the stand."

"Can the court consider Mr. Long waiving being present during the closing arguments?" Eble asked.

Van Allen was plainly annoyed and used his cane for emphasis again. "We oppose having Mr. Long leave. He can't just come and go as he wants."

"I won't have Mr. Van Allen pointing his cane at Mr. Long. I know that Mr. Long and Mr. Van Allen can come to loud arguments."

"I'll go to the far end of the jury," Van Allen said quietly, but forcefully.

The time was 4:30 p.m. The spectators in the courtroom were restless. The arguments seemed to be winding down when court was adjourned for the day.

The next morning, the lawyers began their final statements.

Van Allen ended with a telling comment about Robert Joe Long. "If he didn't intend to kill, all he had to do was let her go."

Long continued his antics from the holding cell.

Standing alone on the side of the courtroom, I was so immersed in my own thoughts that I didn't see anyone walking up to me. I was startled when I felt a tap on my arm. I turned to see a pretty woman with a model-like figure, delicate features and long hair much like Lisa's. She asked, hesitantly, "Are you a reporter?"

I shook myself awake. She looked strangely familiar.

"No, a fellow victim."

The woman leaned towards me, seemingly wanting to talk. "Did you see how mad he was when he saw me sit down?"

I nodded. That was why she looked familiar. I remembered Bobby Joe's angry look when he'd seen her take a seat in the courtroom. "He seemed to really hate you. Did you know him before?"

"I once thought he was a friend. I trusted him. Then he raped and battered me."

"Do you want to go somewhere so we can talk?" I asked. She nodded. We walked awhile, introducing ourselves by name, and sat on a bench outside the chapel, near the security check. Susan began to tell me of how she'd met Bobby Joe Long through her boyfriend.

"At first, he seemed handsome, shy and polite. I'd seen him looking at me. I knew he found me attractive, but I was in love. Then my boyfriend and I broke up. I was alone, miserable and having more trouble than I could handle, so I called Bobby." Her words rushed out like she'd had them pent-up for a long time. "That was the worst decision I ever made."

"Is that when he raped you?"

"Yes, he forced himself on me. The more I protested, the more force he used. I told Dan, my boyfriend, but he didn't believe me. Later Bobby lived in his house." She gave me a deep searching look. "Why are you here?"

"A few years ago, I was raped and swore to help other survivors. I've become friends with Lisa McVey—one of Long's few survivors."

Susan grimaced, "I guess that's what you'd call me too. Despite what all these smart-assed attorneys are trying to imply, I know why he let McVey go." She stopped, looked into my eyes and seeing sympathy there, went on. "She must have been submissive. He couldn't stand criticism or being rebuffed, that's why he hates me."

"Go on, Susan." I reached out and patted her hand.

"After I recovered from the rape, I wanted to explain to my boyfriend, Dan, what happened. I didn't want him to think it was my fault. I called him and asked to come over. Dan wasn't there, but Bobby Joe was. He punched me and threw me on the lawn. Afterwards, friends who witnessed the attack took me to the hospital emergency room. It's all documented. This was before he went to California. When he got back, he found out there was a warrant out for his arrest for assault and battery. He called me on the telephone and threatened me. At the trial, his lawyer claimed it was my fault." She bit her lip, "It wasn't, I swear."

In the trial, he bragged in front of the Judge that he raped me. When the Judge asked him if he was admitting rape, he laughed and said no. The jury found he was within his rights to beat me because I was in my fiancé's apartment, and he lived there too."

"Susan, the papers described you as his roommate? Were you?"

"Before he lived with my fiancé, I let him stay with me when his children visited. He thought if we lived together it meant he could sleep in my bed when the kids were gone. I wasn't interested in him that way, and he left angry as hell."

I pressed charges when he beat me up. I didn't though after he'd raped me. He called the rape a sexual encounter. I came today hoping to hear the jury send him to the chair. He's an animal, but the courts treat him like some kind of god."

"I agree. He's a piece of work!"

"When he got caught, a detective came to see me and asked why Bobby Joe hated me so much. He said Long wrote a threatening letter to me from jail which they confiscated, so I never received it."

I stared at her more closely. "Many of the girls he raped and killed looked very much like you," I said shocked.

"I know." Anguish was in her eyes.

"Some girls he raped were only twelve or thirteen," I said disgusted.

"His favorite saying was if she's old enough to play, she's old enough to pay. Now that takes on more meaning. It didn't then. My ex-boyfriend even thought it was funny. Just one of the good ole boys. He refused to believe that Bobby Joe was the serial murderer until after the first trial. Now Dan doesn't want anyone to know he even knew Bobby."

"Did you dance on Nebraska Avenue?"

"At the Library and some other places. Believe me, all the women who dance aren't prostitutes. Nor were many of

the women he raped and killed. In fact, many of the women he raped were homemakers. And the dead girl found with the scissors in her vagina worked as a waitress in the hotel at the corner of Nebraska and Sligh Avenues. She was a decent person. I heard she carried the scissors for protection."

Her words touched a nerve.

"It disgusts me to hear the women he killed labeled that way, especially as it infers some justification for murder. People would be enraged if anyone talked that way about a dead animal. The ASPCA would picket."

"I thought I was the only person who felt that way." She squeezed my hand. "Bobby didn't like women. He used the word 'mother' like a curse."

"Did you meet his mother?"

"No. She owned some kind of clothing store and sent him clothes all the time. He never said much about himself or his family."

"Do you think he has brain damage, Susan? That's his attorney's latest ploy."

"Never! He got good jobs, but screwed them up. He wanted his own way all the time."

"Lisa gets terrified when the Supreme Court overturns the other trials. It upsets her so much."

She nodded. "I feel the same way. Especially since I found out about the hate letter from jail. I immediately bought a gun, I was so frightened. Two weeks after the detective told me about the letters, a man wearing a wig cut my window screen and raped me. I think he was a friend of Bobby Joe's. The worse part was I couldn't get to my gun." She sighed heavily.

"You couldn't get to your gun? So many people suggested

I get one after I was raped, but I felt even if I had one, I wouldn't have been able to get it or use it. Where did you keep yours?"

Susan shook her head. "Under my mattress. It gave me a sense of security, but when I needed a weapon to fight back, I couldn't reach it. It's difficult to explain even to the police."

I nodded, unable to speak. Silent tears filled my eyes. "Maybe people want to think victims do something to make themselves vulnerable. Wear short skirts or too much make-up or work at the wrong jobs for their own victimization. They try to forget they too could be attacked."

Her voice was soft, "I still feel vulnerable, but I never talk about it. My family wishes I could forget the whole experience."

"I don't think that's ever possible."

"I don't either, but maybe I could get on with my life if Bobby Joe didn't get tried over and over for the same horrific murders. It's as if time went on he could erase what he's done and go free." She stopped, took a deep breath and went on. "That's what I'm really afraid of."

"Lets hope it never happens."

As we walked back into the courtroom, Susan and I made plans to meet again. And I said, "You really need to meet Lisa."

She nodded. "I've always wanted to. I've read so much about her heroism."

"I'll arrange for us to get together."

Chapter 25

Three Victims Meet

Susan arrived at my office for the Sunday outing at the beach I'd suggested. Her smile disappeared when she saw I was alone. "Isn't Lisa coming? It's taken me hours to get here."

"She's usually on time, but she's late today. Would you like a soda?" I took a cold can out of the cooler I'd prepared for the beach.

Susan settled on the couch after she put her towel and traveling bag down. "I've wanted to meet Lisa for so long. Ever since I read about her. I know we'll get along if I have a chance to talk to her. Did she agree to come because you pressured her?"

"That wouldn't work with Lisa. Even though she's vulnerable, she has a strong will. Maybe it's curiosity or the lure of the beach. She loves it just as I do."

More than a half hour passed.

"She's not coming. I just feel it." Susan threw her head back and clenched her fists.

I felt frustrated. Watching Susan, I realized that her reasons for wanting to meet Lisa were greater than mine. I wanted to cement a relationship between the three of us for the purpose of unity. Susan's motivation was emotional. I was beginning to think that Susan was right, until I saw Lisa through the glass door. She pushed the door open with her usual gusto. I felt relieved.

Lisa carried into the room a paper cup from McDonald's. "Hi Joy," she said. She wasn't even looking in my direction. She stood over Susan inspecting her. "Is this Susan?"

This meeting wasn't getting off to the best start. I stepped forward and put my arms around Lisa like she usually did to me. "Lisa, I'm so glad you could come. Let's not talk now. I've got some sodas and fried chicken for the beach. It will be so much nicer in the sun." I handed Lisa three sand chairs. She didn't protest.

Susan jumped up, grabbed her things and followed us outside in silence. Competing with the sound of the rushing cars was impossible. I juggled the cooler and picnic basket uncomfortably, waiting for an opportunity to cross.

The beach, warm and inviting, set the stage. Settling our lunch on the blanket and removing our coverups involved comments about the task at hand. If only we could ease into conversation. "Let's start over. This is Susan, Lisa."

Whether it was from habit, conditioning, or her natural good humor, Lisa smiled. She didn't offer her hand, but things were improving. My belief that large bodies of water have a calming effect just might be true. My spirits lifted.

Susan's figure in a bathing suit was supple and trim. So was Lisa's. I could see why Susan believed Lisa looked like her. They both had broad shoulders, lovely cleavage, slim

hips and long legs. Their hair color would have been the same except Susan highlighted hers. I watched them taking each other's measure. Lisa put the beach chairs down between them. Susan settled in one.

"Lisa," Susan said seriously, "I've always wanted to talk to you. I've suffered so much because I knew that man. I thought we'd have that in common." Nervously she fumbled in her bag and put on her sunglasses. "It's been much worse for me."

"You don't have to lose jobs going to court. It's my testimony they want. I can't say no, because no one else positively identified him to the police," Lisa said. I'd never seen her so abrupt.

"I did for battery," Susan's soft voice raised. "Did you read his letters?" Susan added. "One implies ten women died because I rebuffed and sued him."

Lisa leaned her face close to Susan's, and I could see her expression softening. "Joy suggested I read them. I can't. It makes me sick to know what that monster had in his mind."

"I know just how you feel, but then you don't know that he wanted me murdered even if it took years. He is relentless. I want to let other people know what he's really like so he will never get out," Susan said.

"Don't even think he could be released. And don't say it," Lisa interrupted. "I've been assured he'll never get out. Phillip Van Allen told me that."

"I'll never feel free until he gets the chair. At the last trial I watched him crow he'd be out on appeal. It's like a nightmare that murderers are being freed on technicalities," Susan replied.

"I told a news reporter that I wanted him to get the chair

three years ago. But I want to concentrate on positive things so I can survive. I have to stay centered, to be there for my daughter," Lisa stated.

"Well, letting people knowing what a serial killer is really like gives me hope. To me, it's the most positive thing that I can think of." Susan's voice strengthened.

"I think so too. I care, you care, Joy cares. Other people are just beginning to realize that victims suffer. I know I have to speak out for those poor women who met their deaths every time I hear a lawyer trash them in court," Lisa said with determination. "But it's tough."

I looked at Susan. Her passion surprised me. She had that Southern, ladylike, quiet manner every other time I'd talked to her. Then I looked at Lisa—she was the spirited one. Since I'd come up the ranks of talk radio, I was used to being considered aggressive. I continued my thoughts out loud. "What is it they say? Men are determined, women aggressive, and media women impossible. I think you're both terrific."

Lisa lay back against the beach chair. "I'm also very scared at times." She blinked back tears.

"Lisa, I can understand." Susan stroked Lisa's hand like a mother speaking to a child. "I thought I was alone too until I read about you. At first, all I could think of was getting even with Bobby for what he did to my life. I'm not ashamed of those personal feelings of retaliation, but what we need to do is greater than that."

"I know what you mean. But spending our time and energy telling the world what happened to us because of a serial killer sometimes feels useless, especially when all the newspapers I see talk about his needs. What about my needs? Don't victims have rights? I wait days to spend two

hours in court. He gets days, weeks, years with public defenders and armies of doctors. We're left to try to piece together our lives. We're used for his purpose and not the other way around," Lisa retorted. "And it's frustrating."

"I know. Still it's time for victims to speak out. To show what the court system does to victims. We're not alone anymore. We have each other and Joy. And if we don't speak out, Bobby Joe wins!" Susan added.

I watched Lisa and Susan sharing their feelings. Their ability to voice inner emotions they'd always restrained , I hoped would be a catharsis.

"We're in this together for a greater purpose than our own feelings. Call it whatever you want: an accident, a tragedy or fate. We have to give the dead our voices." I paused to look at Susan and Lisa. They were staring at me with moist eyes.

Chapter 26

The Television Scene and The Real Scene

The romantic view I once had of American courtrooms I'd learned from television. It didn't prepare me for the circus-like atmosphere of Bobby Joe Long's trial for the murder of Virginia Johnson, where he was able to shout, clown around or say anything at anytime. "You bring me down here just to pull my chain," Bobby Joe Long now yelled from his hide-away.

It was March 11, 1994, and we were back in the same courtroom for the sentencing hearing. Mrs. Long, Bobby Joe's mother, sat in the witness chair. Her short brown hair with gray streaks was almost the same shade as his. Thin, tired, and frail she looked more abused than abusive.

Amazingly, when Eble questioned Long's mother, his face didn't take on a purple hue with bulging blood vessels, but looked kind. He didn't sneer or speak in an irate voice. I wondered if it helped lawyers if they were schizoid. If Eble lived his life as the type "A" personality he appeared to be in the courtroom, he'd never live as long as his client. Most of

the time, he looked like a heart attack waiting to happen. Now that angry self vanished. He was almost gentle as he asked the witness to describe Bobby Joe Long's childhood.

Mrs. Long spoke sadly of living in a series of people's homes where she and her young son shared one room. Her explanation sounded more reasonable than the sensational news stories about a boy having to sleep with his mother unless a lover took his place. Eble began to ask about a motorcycle accident Bobby Joe had at nineteen. The accident was pivotal in the attorney's case to show brain damage; so he covered the same territory over and over in different ways.

I wondered if Eble would bring up the enlarged breasts Bobby Joe had operated on when he was thirteen? His mother had testified about the operation in a previous trial. What had been Bobby's and his friends' reaction? What was Bobby Joe Long's image of himself as a man? How many young boys have to have breasts removed? It had to have a serious impact on his developing self-image as a man. What about his hormone development? Was his father there, and what had happened to him? Bobby's ex-wife and mother were here in the courtroom. I looked over at his loyal ex-wife. Petite and neatly dressed, she had a mild mannered and unassuming demeanor. What thoughts about her ex-husband coursed through her mind? What would she tell her two children about him? No one asked about or spoke about his father. Hours and hours worth of words and so few questions were answered before the day was over.

The next morning, as soon as I entered the courtroom, I knew immediately what would be the event of the day. On a low wooden wall that separated the spectators from the attorneys, sat a plastic brain. I felt like I'd entered the twilight zone.

Dr. Frank Wood took the stand. Eble began to bring out his credentials by questioning the doctor. His litany droned for twenty minutes non-stop. Neuropsychology...I heard Duke. Teacher of Human Behavioral Studies, North Carolina...Brain and Language...Metabolic imaging...

"Move this along. No objection to witness," Van Allen finally said.

If Van Allen thought he could end it that easily, he soon knew differently.

Eble continued to rattle off Wood's schools and articles. "Development Disorders, Archives of Neurology, Journal of the A.M.A... Lecture Neuro Imaging... National Institute of Health... Brain Language... University of Toronto... Harvard... University of California... Oxford... Johns Hopkins... First Award Mention... twenty times testifies head injury, dysfunction, competency... Bowman and Gay Code of Ethics." Eble paced as he read another twenty minutes from a long list to put the credentials in the record.

Judge Cope read through the papers. "He needs more references in imaging, M.R.I.'s."

Dr. Frank Wood responded, "National Institute of Health Grant, Committee of Peers. Everything is carefully diagnosed. We don't have strong norms yet."

That statement started thirty minutes of debate about what constitutes normal P.E.T. scans...normal M.R.I.'s. Then Van Allen got into the discussion asking, "How much formal medical training..." On and on the list wound. After hours of questioning, Woods was finally accepted and began to speak on Eble's premise that Bobby Joe Long's brain was dysfunctional.

He turned on the projector and showed, by overlapping his

fingers, the different slices of the brain. "You can look at an image and see misalignment." He pointed to what looked to be the right side. "Head well-sized in thirty-one slices. The reason we start at the top of the head is to get to the bottom and the different paths through the brain to crystals. Overlapping slices three millimeters."

Almost as if he was speaking of a thing, not a man, Dr. Wood outlined his perception of the abnormal brain of Bobby Joe Long. Afterwards, the lawyers got in their perspectives, philosophical and otherwise.

"What is abnormal?" Eble asked. He stood up as if he were going into battle in a Socratic forum.

"Twenty-four. Greatest abnormal. Two scans. Defect in the absorption in the temporal lobe. Lower glucose consumption." Dr. Wood pointed to a picture, not a well-visualized color scan. He then pointed to the right hand side of the M.R.I., which was in shades of gray. "This should be closed like a donut." Dr. Wood reacted to the Assistant Public Defender.

The Judge's law professor reaction came next. "What's normal? What's not?" Judge Cope asked, staring at the images reflected from the slide projector.

"Show the Judge on the brain model." Eble left his place at the table, gingerly picked up the plastic brain sitting on the wooden partition and handed it to Dr. Frank Wood.

"Levels inside the gap between twenty percent to thirty percent areas are not even in brain temporal 1 lobe. Inside abnormal lobe. Taking the temporal lobe apart," Dr. Wood said, struggling to take the plastic model apart.

"Part of his brain is actively missing?" The Judge half stood and peered down from the bench at the smooth unrecognizable pieces of the plastic brain.

I could imagine the Judge would think that. The rest of

the scene was just as unreal. Dr. Wood responded unshaken.

"Not at all—less metabolism. The ganglia nuclei bundle. This brain, any brain. Number of slides show damaged nebula. Normal emotions." Dr. Wood set the plastic pieces aside and went back to his computer-generated images.

"What do you base the information on?" Van Allen rocked back and forth in his seat, pensively holding his large book of brain pictures.

"How would that effect the human brain?" Eble coaxed from his seat at the defense table.

"Objection as to brain function." Van Allen said again.

"What effect on human behavior?" Eble urged his witness leaving his chair again.

"Object." Van Allen pointed his cane at Eble.

"Research shows going to behavior conclusion!" Eble shouted in response to the State's Attorney's objection. His face flushed.

"That belongs in behavioral science," Judge Cope admonished.

"Research on observation and behavior," Eble responded still standing near the defense table. His partner, Laura Chane, was left standing at the podium. She remained silent.

"Bottom line physical organ of dysfunction. What he found, I have not heard qualifications to allow him to do so." The Judge's voice rose for the first time that day.

Laura Chane interjected, "I don't know if I was aware it was not given."

"Monkeys show gross change emotions—passive—hypertensive," the doctor said, looking from one attorney to another.

The monkey/human analogy continued with further

descriptions of monkeys with an injury to what the doctor called the amygdala. "They put inappropriate things in their mouth." He went back to explaining his slides. "See in six B, slice twenty-four and six C, slice twenty-five."

"Is there something that tells us that is Mr. Long's brain?" The Judge finally asked. "The pictures are all Mr. Long?"

"P.O. 1384 I replaced with Mr. Long."

"Pictures are all Mr. Long?" The Judge tried again.

"Yes."

The exchange continued, back and forth like a monkey swinging from branch to branch. Back to P.E.T. scans, M.R.I.'s and repeated discussion about what was normal. Again the same material about nineteen people who used cocaine versus fifty-four who were normal. My mind floated away. I had to keep reminding myself that this examination of the prisoner's brain was the reason he was supposed to remain alive, but the value escaped me. I tried to refocus on Dr. Wood, who was in the middle of commenting.

"...meeting of the Public Defenders," Dr. Wood answered.

His words got my attention. It shocked me to hear that expert witnesses presented themselves to attorneys in such blatant ways; it was unreal. But that some sold themselves to attorneys on both sides was even more objectionable.

"You were asked by the attorney to come to the Public Defenders meeting to show P.E.T. scans?" Van Allen continued.

"No, Hal Smith. Dr. Dunn's report made note of problems within normal left brain area," the doctor answered, referring to doctors who examined Long during the trials.

"Biological in nature or result of injury?" Van Allen asked.

"Motorcycle accident, left side of helmet dented. Mr. Long was unconscious for six hours. Mother and wife noticed increased sensitivity," Dr. Wood replied.

After a barrage of questions from Van Allen, the doctor talked about his opinions of what was normal.

Judge Cope observed. "Fifty-nine is a small number. Do you feel that's enough to establish norms?"

"Sixty-five," Dr. Wood contradicted. "Yes."

Eble jumped up and started his litany of studies. "Rappaport. The University of Pennsylvania results...The research was funded by the National Institute of Health. Half of the sample was part of the review to get funding."

I tried to adjust my attitude to listen objectively. After all, the reason for examining Bobby Joe Long's brain according to Eble was that such an examination would give society clues to understanding the reason for serial killers. I couldn't accept it. Not only was the court system rife with absurdities, but this charade was based on a government grant. If only such funds were put to a better use than saving the Bobby Joe Longs of this world, I thought, as I pushed open the double doors eager to leave the morning behind me. It was like a reprieve that the court had adjourned for lunch.

Later that afternoon, after we'd returned to the court-room for more testimony from the good doctor, the bailiff entered with a note from Bobby Joe Long. "You just got a message," the bailiff stated as he delivered the note to Eble.

Eble said, "No, not now!" He read the note and put it on the desk.

The tempo picked up with arguments between the

experts, the attorneys and their assistants while the Judge
tried to umpire.

"Objection," Van Allen said perfunctorily.

"Overruled," the Judge said.

"Yes sir." Eble continued to go over Dr. Wood's testimony
frame by frame...Symmetry versus asymmetry...He asked the
doctor to define what asymmetry meant. "You agree it means
there is a difference."

After many questions, Eble finally hit one which got a
response that was different from previous testimony. To
Eble's question about how the doctor would determine the
metabolic values in P.E.T., the doctor answered, "In the
spinal fluid." Traditional medical procedures didn't impress
the attorney. Eble hammered on Dr. Wood's morning testimony. Finally, he changed that attack by reintroducing the
studies of his prospective witnesses Rueben and Rachel Gerr.

"Are we going to talk a little about Mr. Long?" Judge
Cope inquired. His voice sounded frustrated and weary.

"If Van Allen hadn't said P.E.T. scans," Eble justified.

"We are here to discuss the use of P.E.T. and Mr. Long."
Judge Cope may have wanted to get more specific, but the
questions and answers continued to be shuffled. More objections, overrulings and more testimony were recycled until the
witness was excused.

"Call Dr. Daniel Sprehe."

"Strike Daniel J. Sprehe," Eble yelled instantly. "I registered objection October 14, 1993. Dr. Merin is different. I
did authorize him."

Eble pointed to Dr. Sprehe, and addressed the Judge.
"Opinion on confession illegally obtained."

"I hear objection. He was appointed by the court," the
Judge explained.

"That was in Tampa. I object to use by Pasco."

"It's been argued before," Van Allen said, matter-of-factly.

"When have I heard this last?" the Judge added shaking his head, and then looked directly at the defense attorney.

"Case law," Eble said vehemently, his face taking on a scarlet color.

"Ad nauseam. Moreover, the State didn't put rebuttal. It became a mite rule and additional review became moot." The Judge continued this explanation as to how the defense attorney's performance could have avoided it.

"Ad nauseam," Van Allen observed almost like an echo.

As if he hadn't heard, Eble continued his argument. "Ellis Rubin should not have allowed it in the Tampa case. Never requested a motion of insanity in Pasco..."

Eble's arguments turned to the previous cases in Hillsborough, Pinellas and Pasco counties. He went over them one by one. No wonder the State's Attorney echoed ad nauseam. Hearing the same horrific details all day created a gnawing in the pit of my stomach.

Suddenly, the Judge interrupted, "Mr. Long wants to clarify his position." The Judge indicated to Long in the holding room and halted the arguments.

Eble walked to the holding cell door in front of the defense table. Bobby Joe Long stood as the sheriff removed the handcuffs. He was dressed in his prison-red jumpsuit over a gray sweatshirt.

"My rights have been violated by the Florida Supreme Court by letting this individual participate." Bobby Joe Long pointed his accusing finger at Dr. Sprehe.

"We have an agreement," Judge Cope responded in a quiet voice.

"McVey was allowed to testify. I waived my rights to..."

The name "McVey" got my attention. He began to talk of Lisa's kidnapping.

"You studied that case," the Judge interrupted.

"Justification was used as a means of identity."

"They were mistaken," Bobby Joe Long said emphatically.

"I'm glad you're here." The Judge guardedly smiled at the irate defendant. "Evidently, Dan Sprehe was not on the list of witnesses."

"He violates plea agreement! He lied as to my very case! I deny him! He's usurped my rights! He lied!" Bobby Joe Long shouted.

Every time I looked at Bobby Joe Long, I felt uncomfortable. The knowledge of all the women he'd raped and murdered never left me for a moment. As his angry voice filled the courtroom, the terror of my own rape passed before my mind, my anguish, my fear. I tried not to think of it but to refocus on this monster. How terrible it must have been to be controlled by him. He used the word "lied" like it was worse than murder. Meanwhile, he obviously had wiped the slate of his conscience clean.

"McVey was not a Pinellas case. Tampa," Van Allen addressed the Judge.

"It still befuddles me that you allowed that case to come in on this case."

"Do you want to sit in on..?" the Judge questioned.

"My plea agreement has been violated!" Bobby's voice roared over the Judge's quiet one.

"When I asked Judge Cobb..." the Judge tried again to calmly respond to Bobby's accusations.

"Florida Supreme Court says they can't use other cases to make this one! I wish you'd stopped them! They violated it with McVey and CBS!" Bobby shouted, turned and opened the door to his private observation cell.

"You don't want to stay? Do you want to take the stand?" The Judge managed to ask.

Eble quickly stepped forward and held up his hand to his client. "Don't answer that question! I raised that point." Eble continued the argument in the angry tone of his client. "No provision to sit in court and listen to..." He began to shout precedent cases. "Fickle and Dickle. Supreme Court has this issue."

"Rules of Discovery apply," the Judge responded to the previous cases.

"Supreme Court ruled Dilbeck. Been up on review. Presently in Marion County," Eble said defiantly.

"What he can testify to in those two issues, I have not ruled on," the Judge answered in a conversational tone.

"Court ordered investigation of insanity at time of Simms' trial, not Virginia Johnson. Made to have an examination on a different case," Eble argued.

"When can the doctor be allowed to testify on competence to stand trial?" the Judge queried.

"Maybe I should have yesterday, but I didn't. If I do something like this relevant to Dr. Sprehe, then I've not represented Mr. Long," Eble responded sheepishly.

"Assume for the purpose of competence. It's an issue," the Judge explained.

"Are you going to hear under Judge Cobb?" Van Allen said relying on the previous ruling.

"Not all those when we argue this case. They try to protect

this witness," Eble's angry voice railed at the prosecuting attorney.

"Already ruled under Judge Cobb," Van Allen tried again.

"Parker and Lovett, Magen and Grant," Eble spat back.

"You said that wasn't available to you," Judge Cope reminded Eble, in response to the case Eble referred to.

"Lovett published January 1994," Eble continued to argue against the doctor's testimony.

The passion of his argument caused him to pace up and down repeating some of his earlier statements about previous cases. It was clear he wanted to avoid the psychiatrist. He went to great lengths to tell the Judge how careful he had been not to open the door to mental competence and Long's other offenses.

"Until I put an expert on, he can't testify," Eble stated confidently like he had won his point.

"According to Long, he killed victims to eliminate witnesses." Van Allen quoted Dr. Sprehe from previous testimony used to show that Long was sane. There was no response from Eble or the bench.

The Judge explained, "In the penalty phase, I can introduce a psychiatrist. Since you've agreed to Dr. Merin."

"I object to Dr. Merin," Eble said ignoring his previous statement.

"Overruled!" the Judge responded emphatically.

"Motion for a new trial!" Eble yelled back.

Judge Cope had just about enough. He rose to his feet, an angry expression on his face.

"Meet me in chambers."

When he and the lawyers returned, the mood had quieted.

The doctor who inspired the impassioned pleas walked slowly to the witness stand and took his time finding a comfortable place to settle his stuffed briefcase. Under the bright ceiling lights, his white hair was even brighter than Eble's blond. His glasses made his blue eyes even bigger and brighter. "I'm Dr. Daniel Sprehe, physician specializing in Psychiatry.

"In how many cases have you been called to testify?"

"Three thousand five hundred murders and fifty serial murders."

Nothing prepared me for those numbers. They blew me away. I wondered why Eble hadn't mentioned that in his lengthy arguments. If Dr. Sprehe got $3,700, the Chicago psychiatrist that the newspapers claim was paid and didn't show up, had to be a wealthy woman. My calculator responded with $13,135,000. I wondered if the pay was less for a common murderer, say $3,500!

"Have you examined documents?" Van Allen asked.

"Objection! He gave up the rights to use those."

"Prison records? A letter Mr. Long wrote?" Dr. Sprehe asked.

Eble responded accusing the doctor. "Illegally obtained communication. You're really not going to use that letter. Letters of crime admissibility shouldn't have been used under Judge Wayne Cobb. His opinion is tainted."

"Sustained. I don't know anything about letters. Open your question on what information the doctor relied on," the Judge deemed.

"Letters obtained by the 'Jail Snitch'—relied on illegally! Obtained illegally!" Eble shouted, staring at the State Attorney, Phillip Van Allen.

"Judge Cobb based on so-called 'Jail Snitch.' The law of the court can be relied on," Van Allen returned.

The Judge enunciated each word clearly, "It's not going to happen under Judge Cope. Motion to review."

The letters of the 'Jail Snitch.' Suddenly, I bolted upright. They had to be talking among other things about the letter Susan had mentioned. The one in which Bobby Joe Long had stated his murderous plans for her. I strained to hear every word.

"Prison records...This letter the defendant wrote—if you're not sure the letters are so critical as evidence, leave them out. Have you relied on the document?" the Judge admonished the doctor.

"Why are you bringing the letter in?" the doctor asked the defense attorney.

"Dr. Merin approved by Judge Cobb with no provision in the law! CBS tape overruled Dr. Merin!" Eble shouted.

I watched the Judge and Van Allen to see if they understood Eble's reasoning. I just hoped that the prosecution would be able to include the information in the letters. Eble began ranting about the illegally obtained confession for what seemed the hundredth time. He quoted dates in 1984 and October 28, 1985, and complained that it was the report of experts that put Long in jail, not the crimes.

The doctor on the stand kept looking from one man to another and back to Judge Cope. Every time he opened his mouth to answer, Eble objected.

"Give your opinion not relying on the letter," The Judge directed again.

"You can base on other experts?" the doctor asked sounding puzzled.

"Opinion of rumors is not a mental health issue. Not relevant. Don't need to open." Eble took up his familiar pace as he argued. His face contorted as words shot from his mouth.

"I have an opinion," the doctor said.

"Are you saying you can set it out of your mind, and render a brand new one?" Eble spun on his heel and faced the doctor.

"No," Dr. Sprehe responded quickly.

"In that interview you talked about nine homicides." Van Allen attempted again to let his witness testify as the Judge reviewed the transcripts.

To add to the confusion, Bobby Joe Long began to shout from his hideaway. His attorneys ran to see what all the screaming was about.

"Get one of those attorneys back here right now!" a grim-faced Judge Cope commanded.

Was he concerned about the safety of the attorneys, or that there could be a mistrial if one of Long's attorneys wasn't present?

"Can I explain the problem of talking to a serial murderer?" the doctor asked, addressing Judge Cope.

"Virginia Johnson only. Disregard the nine other homicides."

Eble inquired, "Can I go back for a minute and see Long?"

More yelling from the holding cell overpowered the courtroom. For the first time in a long time, Judge Cope smiled a wry smile. "Eble is communicating with him."

Laura Chane looked anxiously toward the cell door. "I request that Mr. Eble be observed." I realized I wasn't the only person who felt uneasy.

"Get Mr. Eble back in," the Judge demanded. "How long are we going to be with this witness?"

"At this rate, one minute," Van Allen responded. "I've spent 1,276 long hours of penalty on this aggravating case!"

At that moment, Van Allen was unaware his words were a double entendre. I muffled a giggle. The Judge, suppressing his own smile, let Van Allen's words pass without comment.

"Aggravating circumstances, murders in Hillsborough cannot be admitted. Rebuttal mitigating circumstances," Cope ruled.

"You can't use Hillsborough for mitigating!" Eble shouted as he ran back from visiting his client. "No way. Dr. Sprehe cannot remove from his memory, can't set aside his mind information from the police report."

"Don't," the Judge's voice boomed, "go over the death reports of nine women. Can he set aside everything he has said about Bobby Joe Long? I heard him say he couldn't." Cope paused and the corners of his mouth twitched. "Maybe I was mistaken," the Judge added.

"Are you asking for an opinion based upon Hillsborough County Plea Agreement? The agreements included facts. A five-hour interview," Dr. Sprehe asked.

Judge Cope had enough. "Can you render an opinion based on the facts in the Virginia Lee Johnson case?" Judge Cope demanded. "Based on other than hearsay of confession, other than murders of nine women in Tampa."

"I don't know. If you talk about a giraffe, I think about a giraffe."

The Judge couldn't stifle a half cough, half laugh. "Can you be uninfluenced?" Judge Cope inquired.

"Witness is not able to extract opinion," Eble added quickly.

Van Allen tried again to enable his witness to testify. "Can you tell the Judge what you said about the murder of Virginia

Johnson? The kidnapping, rape and murder examination performed under the court order?"

"Rape was never proven!" Eble shouted almost in the doctor's face. Sprehe drew back and waited.

"Objection! What did he say?" Van Allen used his cane to stand up, and he hit the side of his head in disbelief.

"Overruled," the Judge said quickly.

"He went into details about Virginia Johnson. That information was influenced by letters and jail documents," Eble argued.

In a calm voice, the Judge asked again, "Can you render an opinion uninfluenced by documents?"

"Can I explain the problem of talking to a serial murderer?" Dr. Sprehe asked again, sounding distressed.

"Sentence is not to be taken into account of serial murders. Disregard all the activity in total, only Virginia Johnson."

"No. Notes and a little bit about Virginia Johnson." Dr. Sprehe looked from the Judge to Van Allen.

Bobby Joe Long's shouting changed to screaming.

"Can I go back there a minute and see Long?"

Cope shook his head vehemently and motioned to Chane, who ran over to Long, placating him. Meanwhile, the Judge ruled that the doctor's testimony was adverse to the interests of Long because of the plea agreement Bobby Joe Long made for eight Hillsborough murders he admitted to. After hearing another barrage of arguments from both attorneys, the Judge excused the exhausted witness. Cope looked as if he wished he could follow him out.

My opportunity to hear about the letters to Susan was lost, and it was getting later. The dinner hour passed, and I expected the Judge to call a recess; instead he asked for the

next witness. The testimony went on. It was now 8:00 p.m.

Still another psychiatrist was called. Dr. Sydney J. Merin told the court he had been in practice in the Tampa area for thirty-six years and an expert witness three thousand times.

This time the large number didn't give me a jolt. At least he didn't say three thousand murders.

"You had occasion to examine Mr. Long?" the Judge inquired.

"October 25, 1988." Dr. Merin smiled as he settled back to testify.

"Are you able to..." The Judge's voice was lost to the louder one coming from the holding cell.

"Ah, ah, ah," Long called out, as if he was being stabbed.

This was becoming the theater of the absurd.

"...not influenced by eight bodies." The Judge tried to continue the examination in spite of the clamor.

"Yes." The doctor added his voice to the cacophony. Bobby Joe was screaming again.

Cope was through being conciliatory. "Interrupt the summary counsel. Mr. Long cannot control himself particularly well with these two doctors, as well as a few others. The court awaits Bobby Joe Long's counsel to return." And then Judge Cope added, "...both counsels."

I struggled to keep from laughing out loud. The Judge had gotten his sense of humor back and was making a joke of the situation. If I heard even a titter now, I wouldn't be able to restrain myself. Bobby Joe Long was like the troll under the fairy tale bridge who shouted every time someone crossed it. He was controlling the courtroom.

Eble was determined to go on.

"Your assistant did some psychological testing?" the Judge asked.

"Nine tests." Dr. Merin looked directly at the Judge either so he wouldn't miss a word, or so he wouldn't respond to the scene going on about him.

"He didn't talk to Mr. Long about any other cases and, under a court order approved by Judge Cobb, you rendered an opinion?" the Judge asked after reviewing the paper in front of him.

"Yes," Dr. Merin answered quietly.

"Judge, this doctor has testified and can't render an opinion," Eble objected.

"On the tests he was given." Judge Cope sounded firm, but looked toward the holding cell. "Mr. Long wants to come into the courtroom."

"I can," the doctor answered Eble.

All eyes and focus were on Bobby Joe Long as he sauntered into the courtroom in his prison red and faced Judge Cope. "I want to say how this man got involved in this case. I had an agreement with this man. I want to tell you it happened on this one issue. I had a lawyer with me when it happened."

"This is important to you, Mr. Long." The Judge's voice was compassionate.

Old arguments railed once more, with the attorneys, the doctor, and Bobby Joe Long joined in the long fiery sideshow.

Almost simultaneously, the doctor wanted to refer to his notes. Eble claimed they were from Dr. Sprehe, whose opinion was tainted by the letters, and he argued patient confidentiality. The State Attorney claimed court-ordered doctors were to report their findings to the court. The

Judge read the transcripts. Eble maintained he hadn't opened the door to the doctor's testimony.

"I don't want to look at that pig!" Long screamed out.

A frustrated Van Allen wiped his brow. "Can Dr. Merin be excused?" he asked wearily.

Bobby Joe Long had won his battle with the State's psychiatrists.

His bravado performance merited no extended applause. Within three hours, the jury, chiefly on the strength of the testimony of the State's experts about hair and fiber, Lisa's testimony and Long's video confession, rendered their verdict. They found Robert Joe Long guilty of murder in the first degree on February 6, 1994. For the next few days, they heard of Long's other crimes while Long cursed Van Allen for presenting them. On Thursday, February 10th, after voting on the issue, the jury recommended Long to be put to death in the electric chair.

Chapter 27

The Center Ring

It was the day of sentencing, March 18, 1994. Lisa had to be at her new job. So since we'd all agreed that at least one of us would always be present, Susan and I went to see the final act. The somber octagonal room, polished wood reflecting the stately display of grandeur, was intimidating to the general public. But for insiders, the scene was still a circus-like spectacle. The bailiff, court stenographer, sheriffs, and Phillip Van Allen's faces were tense, but they cracked a few jokes, warming up the crowd for the main event as they waited for Judge Cope and the defense attorneys.

Looking toward the room where Bobby Joe Long was held, an atmosphere of tension prevailed. One of the deputies commented, "You can bet he'll be putting on a show. It's his last performance for a while."

Bobby Joe Long responded from the waiting cell. "What the hell is holding things up?"

"We're scared of him now. He says we're late." The

deputy leaned his face close to the news reporter's camera and then stepped forward.

"Who gave him a watch?" Van Allen enjoined.

"His brain ticks," a reporter quipped.

"He's complaining he'll be late going back to jail," the joking deputy interpreted the shouts of Bobby Joe Long.

"The Judge will be ready to roll in five," the bailiff announced holding up his five spread fingers.

The deputy grimaced into the television camera. "I can't see you, but you can see me. How long does it take to say "May God have mercy on your soul?"

William Eble entered, striding quickly past a white-haired man, and he addressed Van Allen. "You've got Pops here? We'll be out of here in thirty minutes."

"You mean thirty minutes dragged into two hours," Van Allen sounded resigned.

Eble ignored the remark and joined his client in the holding cell.

Meanwhile, the court reporter moved the three brown boxes marked "Appeals" from the camera's view.

"It probably doesn't make any difference now, but the appearance of these on camera once almost got a mistrial."

"I have seven," the white-haired man responded.

I thought he looked too young to be called Pops. He was trim, and his face was boyish with almost no lines.

Susan and I sat together. She glanced over at Pops and whispered to me, "That's the detective who came to see me and asked me why Bobby Joe Long hated me so. His hair was pepper and salt then."

"Look what this case did to him," I joked. Susan smiled, but her eyes were weary and serious.

Eble strode out of the holding cell followed by Chane. He addressed Pops, who was sitting closest to the defense table. He grimaced. "They gave him a cheeseburger." Van Allen rolled his eyes, and Susan shook her head.

"All rise. The Honorable Judge Charles Cope presiding."

The Judge entered the now quiet courtroom. The jokes and comments ended abruptly. The official nature of the proceedings invaded the carnival atmosphere. Judge Cope sat down and rifled the papers in front of him.

Two deputies brought Bobby Joe Long into the room. He was dressed in jeans and a bright yellow sweatshirt. His eyes darted to Susan, and he gave her a glaring look.

The Judge looked up and said formally, "Good morning."

"Nothing good about it," Long shot back.

The Judge's eyes narrowed. "Counsel, any legal reason Long shouldn't be sentenced?" he asked soberly.

"Not that we haven't argued," Eble responded.

Judge Cope sat back thoughtfully and then began to speak. He enunciated each word.

"I have carefully weighed aggravating and mitigating circumstances and found Robert J. Long guilty on all counts. He will be delivered to the State of Florida for execution. Governor Lawton Chiles will name the time and place of execution."

"I'm Bobby Joe Long, not Robert J. Long," the defendant called out as he was escorted to the holding cell. He looked over at Susan again. His eyes and lips narrowed.

Susan watched him close the door. She shivered.

"If he ever gets out, he'll kill me," she said softly.

"We have to make sure he never has the chance."

She clasped my hand. "For Lisa's sake too."

I nodded.

"I probably shouldn't have come."

I shrugged. I was aware of how much Susan wanted him to know she was a witness to his death sentence. "I can understand. Lisa really wanted to be here too, but she couldn't afford to lose her new job."

Our attention changed to the holding room where Long was creating the usual clamor.

"Does my appeal go to the Sixth Circuit? I'm under the impression that the court's responsible. Do I send it to you if it goes back to Marion County?"

"I'm appointed by the Supreme Court. If it helps the public defenders. You can send it to Ft. Myers and the 2nd District for CBS."

The business of nailing down where to send copies of the sentence took a few minutes. Everyone on the prosecution team sat quietly, waiting for the legal formalities to end. Susan had become silent. I knew what she was thinking.

"Mr. Long wants to challenge the constitutionality and the legality of the death sentence in the Florida Supreme Court, and he wants his sentence reduced. We acknowledge the one hundred page limit on briefs." Eble paced back and forth as he objected to the death penalty for his client and noted where to send his seventeen-page brief. "I'll file this," he said, waving the papers in the air. "He wants it filed and will let the appellate lawyers do as they see fit. I'll file in Pasco."

The Judge calmly accepted the new brief. A long discussion ensued about oral and written arguments and court procedures. During the interchange between Eble and the Judge, Bobby Joe Long reappeared, grinning broadly like a victor. Susan winced. "He's managed to win appeals on the other two convictions. Look at him smirking."

His attitude conveyed his belief that it wasn't over yet, not by a long shot.

The Judge read from the briefs in front of him and repeated some of the wording. "I represent to the court a ten-day wave of oral argument." He looked down from the bench into the prisoner's eyes. His own clear voice unyielding. "Present in the Court of Florida...death penalty unconstitutional. Legality subject to Appellate Jurisdiction...Memorandum of law...is that correct, Mr. Long?"

"Yea."

"Thank you, Mr. Long."

"I'm not accepting this motion at all. Subsection three not timely. Motion one. Not timely. Memorandum of sentence!" Van Allen objected, as if he'd just realized that the defense attorney had made a new plea.

"My client wants to fail relying on merits. Benefit of memorandum. Van Allen, can we do that?"

"April 1st," Van Allen replied. As the negotiations were already concluded, Corp. Baker began to walk out of the courtroom.

"I want to see Bobby and for him to see me," Susan whispered and stood up. First I looked at Long, and then I looked back at Van Allen. He was getting up wearily and leaning heavily on his cane. His handsome young face looked tired. It struck me that he and Bobby Joe Long were growing old together. It was over. I walked outside.

Susan walked outside and was talking to Lee Baker. As she spoke, she tossed her head and her long, burnished brown hair flashed in the sunlight. She reminded me of Scarlet O'Hara in her white cotton dress covered with delicate pink roses. The short sleeves and low-cut neckline revealed

smooth alabaster skin. Susan lowered her dark lashes and talked expansively. A paper in her hands fluttered about as she explained something. "Joy," she motioned me over, then resumed talking.

"Yes, this was the drawing of the man who ripped open my screen, came in my house and raped me two weeks after you came to ask me why Bobby Joe Long hated me."

"I wasn't aware of that," Baker answered, wrinkling his brows.

"I bought a gun after our conversation, but it was kept under my mattress. Here is the report. The guy had dyed hair under a baseball cap. He had blond pubic hair."

"That was so long ago. It doesn't ring a bell."

"To you it's ten years; to me it's yesterday!" Susan was turning pale, obviously upset. She looked at me beseechingly.

Wanting to back her up, I said, "Prisoners get in touch with people on the outside who will hurt their former victims. Women are especially afraid of that."

"Long was kept pretty isolated. I don't think he could have been involved. You were his girlfriend weren't you?"

Susan, who had calmed down, said emphatically, "No, we were friends. I let him stay in my apartment for a few weeks when he had his children visit. I hate it that people, especially those in the media, call me his girlfriend. I never was."

"But he started his killing right after a public defender overturned your assault and battery charges against him, at the beginning of February, 1984. The first body was found in May."

Susan looked at him, horrified. "My God, do you really think that his retrial for assault and battery against me started his killing? What would have happened if he had lost the

case? He didn't even get prison for pulling a gun on a woman in her car. He just got probation. Now we know he had a record going back to his days in Miami."

"Not many people knew. In fact, his wife was one of his big supporters until we showed her some pictures he kept of his own children naked. His friends were fooled too."

Susan flinched.

I turned to Baker and said, "I heard you say you have nine boxes of information on this case. Could you find the letters you told Susan about...the ones written to the 'Jail Snitch?' Lisa's asked about them too. I'd like to read them. Knowing the contents of the prison information has become an obsession ever since I heard Bobby Joe Long screaming not to have the contents revealed in court. And Susan told me many of them held threats about her."

"Here's my card. You have to clear it with Legal first. If it's all right, I'll be glad to get you copies."

Baker wrote the number for the Legal Department on the back of his card. I turned it over when he handed it to me. He was with the Hillsborough Sheriff's Office, Homicide Special Investigations Division.

Susan and I watched the detective leaving. "I need to talk more to you," she said. It was lunch time. We walked over to O'Callahan's just across the parking lot from the Ocala Court building. There was a dining area outside in the warm sunshine. Since it was the day after St. Patrick's Day, I thought they would have corned beef and cabbage. They didn't. I settled for a corned beef on rye. Susan had a Reuben. We enjoyed well-frosted glasses of iced tea while waiting for lunch to arrive.

"I came today hoping it would be Bobby Joe's last hurrah, but I fear it isn't. I can tell he doesn't think so either."

"How long can the charade go on?"

"What an evil man Long is. It's hard to believe that at one time my friends and I accepted him as just another guy. Dan thought Bobby Joe was just a good old boy when he'd repeat, 'If she's old enough to play, she's old enough to pay.' He said it so often, we didn't listen to the words or think about what lay behind them. Now it makes me sick."

"Pedophiles are good at convincing adults they are trustworthy," I said soberly.

She bit her lip. "I did think he would show some remorse today."

"Hardly. In fact, he was angry he had to give up his comfortable jail cell to hear the Judge's sentence."

She sighed. "The tortured deaths of those unfortunate young women have become just an inconvenience to him."

I looked at her for a moment and then asked, "What was it like to dance on Nebraska Avenue?"

Susan pondered a moment before responding. The question seemed to surprise her. "When I started at Diamond Lil's, I was terrified. I needed money to pay my daughter's and my bills. I had a lot of lessons, loved to dance, and had no real training for any profession. For me it was just the way to get enough to support my child. And a lot of the others had similar reasons, though some of the girls had illusions of getting on the stage."

I shielded my eyes from the sun and looked intently at her. "I wanted to go to the Sly Fox Lounge where two of his victims danced, so I could see it. The placed was closed."

Her eyes widened. "I danced at the Sly Fox. Actually it was one of the better places to dance. It had an elevated stage. There were two girls dancing at all times. The customers couldn't get to you."

The waitress brought our sandwiches. The corned beef was piled so high it took concentration to eat without spilling any. Susan seemed to handle her Reuben better.

"All the news articles about Long's victims make them seem like party girls or addicts or prostitutes. In court, it's even worse. How does it feel to hear attorneys talk so disparagingly about dancers?" I leaned toward Susan.

"Terrible. You'd think, by the way they talk and the way the media reacts, I'd have track marks up my arms." Susan held out her arms as she spoke. "It effects the way I even think about dancing. I never thought dancers would be labeled prostitutes just because they were dancers. The girls who did that usually had a drug habit or were supporting some tattooed bum who had one. Drugs were easy to get in clubs. Some men would even put cocaine in your hands. I don't even smoke! I played naive so I wouldn't have to deal with the drug scene. I have a guardian angel on my shoulder and my daughter to think about." She paused and then in a bitter voice said, "No one says anything about the men who go to the clubs. I've always had a problem with that. A lot of them were used car salesmen who worked on Nebraska Avenue, but they came from all walks of life."

"Remember," I said grimacing, "when that television reporter got nailed for being with an underage prostitute on Dale Mabry? The first time he was arrested all the viewers jumped to his defense and he kept on reporting the news. Then he repeated his offense less than a year later on the same street and they finally got the message. He's not the only jerk. One radio show host runs nude clubs in other areas of Tampa. No one calls him a pimp. Men get away with a lot and aren't blamed by the public."

"You're darn right," Susan said, her annoyance showing. "One club used to have a sign saying, 'We're proud of our Bush Gardens.' Everyone knew about the nude dancing there. One night I went there with a friend of mine. The girls danced nude in a kind of playpen surrounded by men. They offered to let us see a better show in the back room, but that wasn't for me. That owner wins all his court cases against naked dancing. I never danced nude or even topless, but I got nailed anyway. One night, I turned my back to the audience, flipped my sheer skirt and got a citation from the police for dancing nude. The liquor authority has some rule that, if even part of the buttocks is revealed, a girl can be arrested, but girls can be totally nude if the customers don't drink liquor. So at nudie clubs the customers drink orange juice."

"Well, it is Florida. I guess orange juice is sacred."

Susan laughed. "My family tried to warn me about dancing in the clubs. I thought my mother and brother were alarmists. I loved dancing and getting paid to do it. It meant my daughter and I could live more comfortably. I'd close my eyes, forget where I was, and become the dance. The applause was my reward."

"We do teach little girls to want that attention, don't we?"

"Yes, we also teach them that they're nothing without a man. When I danced on Nebraska Avenue, I'd just broken up with Dan and was carrying a big torch for him. I dated Bobby Joe out of loneliness and frustration. It's true, I called him. But that's no excuse for what Bobby Joe Long did to me or the others."

"One poor girl got blamed for her own murder." Susan closed her eyes for a moment as if visualizing the scene. "In court, Bobby Joe Long's attorney wanted everyone to think

that girl killed herself with her hands tied behind her. I guess she drove herself to the murder spot, too. Eble's argument was plain ridiculous."

"If I wasn't sitting there, I wouldn't believe it either. You'd think he'd be ashamed. The court reporter told me he's a wonderful family man and a great father. However, it's not just men who think women ask for it. Laura Chane was just as vindictive about Virginia Johnson."

"Long's attorneys didn't seem to care about what they said to slander the victims in order to serve their murderous client. I would like to be a voice to remind such people that the victims were living and breathing human beings. Not that it would help. Nevertheless, I don't think I can stand the negative image they created so vividly of those murdered women and, by implication, of those like me who survived. My family didn't want me to even go to the trial. They wanted to protect me from all those hurtful slurs and graphic bloody details."

"Families want to help. They don't realize that not facing reality usually adds to your burdens. Still it's tough. Because of my own rape, hearing about the victims upset me, and I don't have as much reason as you and Lisa do."

"The people who love me have no idea how angry I am about the unfair way Lisa, I, and all the victims of Bobby Joe Long were treated by the media and courts. Even Baker asked if I was Bobby Joe's girlfriend, and the newspapers tried to imply Lisa and he had a love affair." She shuddered, "*Love*. Bobby Joe Long doesn't even know what the word means. *Terror* was the operative emotion."

"I'd bet my life on it," I replied.

Chapter 28

Hate Letters

The activity of uniformed officers and people passing through the four groups of double entrance doors at the red brick Tampa Sheriff's Operations Office in the old Spanish section called Ybor City set it apart from the sleepy atmosphere of the nineteenth century cigar factories, antique shops and quaint restaurants. I looked around the halls to find the cashier so I could pick up the letters written to the "Jail Snitch." My eyes were drawn to the Memorial Wall opposite the entrance. The pictures of officers who died serving the community were a grim reminder that victims of crime weren't all civilians.

Once I got the envelope, I rushed home to read the mysterious letters. I felt they would give me insight into Bobby Joe Long's psyche. My curiosity was heightened by my knowledge that Bobby Joe Long didn't want the contents revealed in court even ten years after he wrote them. I settled myself in a comfortable reading spot on the end of the couch and put a cold Diet Pepsi on the table nearby.

Opening the manila envelope, I shuffled through the letters until I found one signed by Bobby Joe. It was addressed to Detective Price Latimer.

Do you remember me?

Yeah, I'm sure you do!

Well I have a favor to ask you guys, and I hope you don't let me down. I need something to wear in court, etc. In my clothes you confiscated (I swear none of my clothes or shoes is either HOT or even warm) there are a couple of things I could really use.

The things I'm asking for have never been involved in any crimes, and I'd appreciate it very much if you could arrange for it to be in my property here so I have something to wear to court.

Check them out with Microscopes if you want. I'm telling the truth.

I'll make a list on the back of this, and even tell you where they were bought. (If I can remember.)

What I've said is true and I would appreciate a little help on your part very much!

Bob Long

1. Dark blue - 3 piece suit (pants vest coat) - bought at J. Byrons in Miami years ago, Cindy was there when I bought it.

2. White long sleeve "Calvin Klein" dress shirt. I'm not sure, but I think it got it at J.C. Penneys.

3. Black - Soft leather lace up - "Porto Fino" brand dress shoes. Bought them at Knapps in Westland Mall in Hialeah!

4. One pair of black socks.

5. Light to medium blue, solid colored tie!

Come on guys, cut me some slack! I don't like looking like shit when I go to court.

Bobby Long.

Long's preoccupation with his clothes and image fit the character sketch I was beginning to fill in. I picked up another one.

Hi

I just wanted to thank you guys for bringing me my stuff. Too bad we didn't get a chance to talk!

Maybe some other time.

Bob Long.

I placed the letter under the pile, remembering his pretrial hearing in November of 1993 and his attorney's pleas that he didn't want to appear in court wearing white socks. I scanned several more letters looking for his thoughts about Susan and possibly Lisa. With the next one I hit pay dirt.

Do me a favor man —

Call me Bob —

Only the fuckin hillbillies up in W. VA. call me Bobby Joe.

There's one cunt in Tampa I'd give my balls to do. Her time's gonna come, someday, some how. It's Susan Replogle. She has a kid about ten or eleven, and if I know her a guy's living there. Details? SLOW - PAINFUL, and I want her to know who initiated it!

This bitch fucked me over royal, and she was on my list. Hey, a year, two years, five years, she was on my list for sure. Your people do her and I'll know this is for real. She's about five feet, seven inches tall and 129 - 130 lbs. Black hair, brown eyes. Has American

Indian blood in her. She's my best buddy's sister-in-
law, and he warned me about her, but I didn't listen.
Remember that cunt's name - Susan Replogle. It
would make my day! I'll be checking the obituary
and I just want her dead and to know I'm involved
"before" she dies. Fuck her for a week, first tear her
ass up; I don't care as long as she dies! SLOW.

This bitch has fucked me over every possible
way, cost me a lot of money, a lot of aggravation and
headaches. Even tried to set me up for rape, one I
didn't do...and about the third day I was in here I got
served papers for a civil suit by her for an undis-
closed amount, but over five grand. I've been thru
two trials for battery, not guilty both times, though I
did knock the fuck out of her throwing her out of my
house, and she did everything she could to get them
on the rape, but luckily other people were there and
saw what really happened...If these guys do her ass
"Great!" If I get out of here one day, I Will!

Nobody's ever fucked me around like this bitch. I
almost killed a guy because of her, and she pulls all this.

Reading the cunt's obituary, man I'd be high
for a month.

Bob

So Susan had been right. His rage at her not only had
exploded into violence with others, but he wanted to kill her
even now. No wonder Susan was panicked at the thought
Long might escape. She knew that if he did, his number one
target would be her.

There was a postscript to the letter and it was just as chilling.

Jay Buddy, you know and I know I'll "definitely"

get the chair, you have a good shot at it yourself.
They're going to fry Billy Boy eventually, it's just
gone fuckin crazy.   OK I never claimed to be
insane...But the State wants blood.   They'll get it
too...You can fool yourself if you want to, but in your
own mind you know I'm right. Unfortunately. You
know that's why I'm gonna go the escape route.

Listen, I don't know much about your charges
or what you've done. I know when I look in your eyes
I can see a killer. Yeah, it's crazy, but for a long time
now I've felt people could see that in my eyes. I've
done some cold blooded shit both known and
unknown. It doesn't bother me a bit to kill someone.
If the boys from Columbia can get me out of this I'll
owe em, and I pay my debts.

Columbia, Peru, both sound great.   Fucking
Peru has some of the most beautiful pussy in the
world! I'm serious.

I'd work for these boys, do ANYTHING they wanted!

I know some guys in Miami from Columbia
(should say I "knew") they're some bad cocksuckers!
Cocaine Cowboys. We're talking Ingram submachine
guns, execution style killings. Bad boys. That was a
while back. Too fuckin hairy back then. Trying to
establish territories and shit.

That's what I meant about some of the boys I
grew up with being dead, or just vanishing from the
face of the earth. Some shit that used to go down
would make your show Miami Vice look like Mother
Goose! Believe me!

Corporal Baker had told Susan that Long hated her.

Nevertheless, Long's vicious letter shocked me. To me, the letter held a greater meaning. The furor inside him sounded like a revelation of his motivation, not only for getting Susan but for killing ten other women. I believe he concealed his desire for Susan's death in a multitude of victims. He said his plan to finally kill her might take two years, five years. How many deaths would have happened before he felt safe enough to kill Susan?

My eyes were drawn to a star in a circle on the left margin and the words, *THE RAPE,* were underlined twice. Bobby Joe Long's handwriting slanted to the right, which in the parlance of graphology, indicates openness. He used slash marks over his 'i's and longer slashes cross his 't's and 'A' was often represented with '&.' He used underlining and exclamation points for emphasis. I pulled another letter from the pile. This one gave insight into Long's need for notoriety and power through rape.

O R, you wanted a story of one of my victims, this was one of the top 10 for sure. It's all true, it's one of the charges in Orange County.

You wanted a novel, I'll give you a chapter, one of many.

I'll tell you about the last rape that didn't end up with someone dead. She was 13 (there were two younger - 12 in L.A.) and one lived in Fla. (sic)

How it worked was the standard process I used in about 30-40 of these things in 3 states. It was really fool-proof & if I'd just stuck with it & not gone the cunt's way - killing people, I'd still be out there. It was like a hunt.

Really! I would pick certain ads in the local

paper of wherever I'd driven. I never worked in the county I lived in, and go to the classified ads and look under furniture household items. Pick the ones with beds for sale or bedroom furniture for sale because in order to see the bed or the furniture, you would get a good chance to check the place out & make sure it was just her, or her and very small kids and babies. This all started back in 75-76 and I'm telling you it was perfect. Never even came close to getting caught. For years I was referred to in the Miami Herald as the "Classified ad rapist", but I worked Dade, Broward, Palm Beach too, then moved up here and hit Manatee, Pinellas and Orange Counties. Its worked in W. Va., California and Kentucky. It was so good I never should have switched!

Anyway it got to the point when I could scan the ads, and just by the way it was worded, know the approx. age, naturally I wanted young ones, but sometimes the older ones would be good enough and they usually had nicer jewelry and more expensive shit. Mostly I did it for the "thrill" the "high". I don't have to tell you anymore about that feeling, I'm sure. So, I'd go wherever I targeted, get a local paper, scan the ads, write down 10 - 15 numbers, go to a pay phone, and start calling. If they sounded real old, 50 or more, I'd just hang up. If they were older but sounded good, (you can tell a whole lot the way a woman laughs or doesn't laugh for that manner (sic), and if they were "worth while" I'd get the address and make sure "they" were gonna be there. I'd always hit early in the morning 9:30 -10:00, husbands

& kids gonna be gone for hours, and eventually I worked up a routine where I'd even know when the hubby was coming home, by saying "We really need this stuff fast "yuk" Lets say I like it and it's what we're looking for, how soon would someone help me load it up!

By their answer (either my husband gets home around 6, or well Ill (sic) Ill (sic) be here all day) I knew pretty much what I was dealing with. So out of 10 or 15 numbers I'd have it narrowed down to 3 or 4, usually "one" I'd put a star by, for the first & best sounding one. It was usually right on the money. This was one of 3 ways I used that were perfect. I'll tell you about the other ones some other time. For now I want to tell you about *****, the 13 year old.

I was checking out the Orlando paper and found this ad Canopy bed for sale. A bell went off as soon as I read it. It was summer & school was out, I usually worked these during the school so the women would be home alone, but I was getting the "urge" and when I read this ad, I knew there was a young girl there, who else sleeps in (sic) Canopy beds, so it was just a matter of getting her on the phone she answered and I asked for her Mom. She her Mom was at work and I said well when will she be home? She said 5 or 6, it was like 8:45 or 9:00 in the morning. So I said well I'm calling about your ad in the paper, is there anyone around older I could talk to? She said she was 13 & she could tell whatever I wanted to know because it was her bed. To put it in your terms - "Bingo" she was mine! She had a real sweet teeny

bopper voice and we bullshit around on the phone a bit, yeah I can lay a line when I need to, and she gave me very precise and accurate directions, I said in (sic) be there in about 30 minutes or I may wait till later and bring my wife to see if she likes it too for my daughter. Anytime I could mention a wife and kids, it made them feel more comfortable & safe thinking I'm settled down married with a daughter. She said her Mom usually came home for lunch at 12, if I wanted to wait and talk to her, I said no I really just want to see the bed, I'm in the area and work weird hours so I'll come over now, while I have the time. She said, okay! So I took off, figuring I'd get there by 10 or so and would have at least an hour to do what I was gonna do to her. From there it was just a question of what she looked like, and I was pretty sure by her voice & the way she, spoke, she wouldn't be too bad.

I got there, went up (always wore a sports jacket, women trust you much more) knocked on the door, nice house in a nice suburb, no cars in the driveway, no people-neighbors-out doing yard work or any-thing. It looked good.

She opened the door, I was knocked out.

This 13 yr. old had a body like - well any women would be proud to be built like her about 5'5", 110 lbs., long reddish brown hair, pretty face, not beauti-ful, but pretty, the real clincher was she had on a blue bikini top, nice tits, and a pair of shorts. Just a very tasty little morsel all around. She just opened the door, I said hi I called about the bed she ran back to the phone telling me to come in, she would be right

back. She got off the phone, while I was waiting, I was taking it all in. There was nobody else home. She was a sweet thing! Perfect!

She came over said something about her girl-friend on the phone and started down the hall to the bedrooms. The whole end of the house was bedrooms (3) and the other end was a garage, no concern there! I checked the rooms as we passed em, and she was chit chatting some shit about the bed, me following her. I had fold out buck knife, just for effect, I'd never hurt this kid, or any of the others. The worst I ever did to any of them was one punch to a couple who'd fight at first, after one punch, they were resolved to it, and accepted it, and knew I was for real & would hurt them. Give a bitch a choice between getting dicked or getting hurt, you know what she's gonna pick.

She never even saw the knife, I just pushed her right onto the bed, face down as soon as we got near the bed. She didn't resist, at all, I told don't worry, I'm not gonna hurt you. Then I showed her the knife and said, unless you make me hurt you! Same line I've used basically in all of em. I had her put her arms behind her, and untied her bikini top, she was going oh God oh God. I said, "Baby, don't be scared, I promise you I'm not gonna hurt you! It was true, it calmed her down.

I got her top off, she was like on her knees with her waist up on the bed, face down. She smelled good! She felt great! Theres (sic) nothing like a girl who just turned woman-firm, right, sweet, I know of what I speak!

I used her bikini to tie her hands, not behind her but so they would be at her sides, no further, It was something I learned from experience.

It made them feel controlled, but I never tied them real tight, and I never tied their hands behind them. They got in the way if I did, and besides this way they could use one hand in the front of them on me or on them. while the other hand was pulled behind them. Can you picture it? Then I picked her up and put her on her back, up on the bed, and started on her shorts. Most woman I'd cut all their clothes off! It was a turn on to me, and several times to them. Plus the intimidation factor of me using a very sharp, nasty looking blade. You could shave with any of my blades. Psychology - and it worked, none of them ever tried anything after the thing was started. They believed I would use the knife! I don't think I ever would have, plus I carried a gun in the back of my pants, under my sports jacket. In case a hubby or boy friend or whatever showed up. It never happened. This method was fool proof, If I ever get out of her, I'll go back to it. It's too good to pass up.

Anyway as I'm taking off her shorts, she says "Your not here for my bed, are you!"

I said "no, what do you think I'm here for?" She said "Me!" I said, "That's right!" and then I saw the pussy and it was a little girl pussy it had a lot of hair light brownish colored, but very hairy. She was firm with very muscular legs, but it was all firm, the tits were not huge but I'm tellin you no woman would be ashamed of them firm, beautiful, big brown nipples. I

mean the brown covered the whole end of the tit, and the nipples were hard!

She knew what was coming!

I kissed her mouth, like I know she's never been kissed before-deep-hard, then I told her to kiss me, she didn't know what I meant at first as a lot of them didn't, but a lot of them did too! I told her again - stronger - KISS ME! YOU KISS ME! She got it then and gave me her tongue. I know she'd never been kissed like this, most women I have known and dated were amazed at what I'd do to their tongues, no shit. I've been told more than once that it was the first time they'd been kissed like that, she's gonna be real disappointed in the way her little school boy friends kiss her for a longtime.

She was getting into it!

Then I moved down to her tits, I told her they were beautiful, she thanked me, blew my mind. I told her to tell me all the things she was gonna do for me. I did this to all of them, some of them would start the penis and vagina shit,***** did, I said NO, not that, tell me like you'd tell one of your girl friends, I don't want to hear penis, vagina, or intercourse. I want to hear cunt, pussy, cock, prick, suck, fuck, screw, ball everything you can think of and don't stop telling me till I say so!

Man I've seen married women have a much harder time than this 13 yr. old. She cut loose with some really good stuff. She watched me and her tits.

She liked it, she'd lift up the one closest to my mouth by raising her shoulder, so I could get at it better.

She was really into it now. Her story was gettin real dirty, then when she started to slow down, I told her I was going to wait for her Mom to come home from work, and I was gonna do her while her Mom watched. I told her I was gonna make them do things to each other, but for her to tell me what! She did and she had a little problem at first, then I started licking her belly, it was tight and nice, then I started licking her thighs, first from one knee, all the way up, just passing over her cunt, breathing on it, and down the other thigh to its knee - then back, the other way. When I got right up to her pussy with my tongue, I'd just rub thru her hair, wouldn't touch her cunt, just breathe on it. Her breathing was changed, when I got by where she thought my tongue was gonna hit her pussy, shed (sic) tense, expecting it. This was standard, did it to all of them, they were never dry by this time, they were ready, ***** was ready, she was telling me she would eat her mothers (sic) pussy and her mother would eat hers, I asked if she knew what 69 was she said yes, I told her I was gonna put her & her mother in 69 and (with her on top) fuck her just above the mothers face, so Mom could see my cock going in and out of her pussy, so Mom would see her baby wet and lubricating my cock as I put it in and out of her real slow! Then I asked her what else I could do to her in that position? She said "Butt fuck me."

I said tell me about it, then I went to work on her pussy with my tongue. She was soaked, her clit was like a little rock, I was running my tongue up the

and they're fucking him, not him fucking them. Just a little personal preference. I liked it like that.

The young ones like *******would always say "But I don't know how! I'd (sic) "guide" them how, tell em faster or slower, no matter what position - This wasn't my favorite position!

It was sweet and this was when I'd get their ass. I'd spit on it, right on the asshole, then while I fucked em in the cunt, my finger would go in the ass, usually thumb if its doggie style like ******. Something else I learned from all these girls, The young ones like ****** had no trouble when I'd start on their ass - a couple of times their pussy would be tighter than their ass anyway - but I like butt fuckin these bitches. Even if it's just for a few minutes. A lot of the older (30-35) yr. old housewives had never had it up the ass. The way I did it they liked it. Not at first, but after a minute of so when the sphincter muscle of the ass loosened up, they'd always like it. The young ones always took it much better, never questioned it, I think they "expected" it. I still can't figure the "older ones" would be so surprised at it sometimes. The young ones - never! And it never hurt them even at first! Very strange, I'd have thought it the other way around!

After a few minutes of this, I was ready to blast off. This girl was sweet meat, and was into it real good! I had her start telling me about what her and her girl friends said about fucking. She did! Then I asked her how often she played with herself, and what she thought of to make her cum.

At first she said she never did that. I slapped her hard on the ass and told her not to lie to me again! A lot of them said that, than after one slap, they'd tell me! Man these girls think of some weird shit, and once they'd let it go. Brothers, fathers, niggers, getting raped, getting gang banged, fucken (sic) a dog. I heard it all! ****** said she thought about a girlfriend licking her all over. No wonder she had such an easy time telling me about her & Mom. I found out Mom was 33, built real nice, big tits, Blondish (sic) colored hair, black pussy hair. A little better than average looking, according to******.

I was still considering if I should wait for her and do this to both of them. I'll tell you now, I've had 3 chances this being one of them, and for one reason or another, I never got to do a Mother Daughter.

I would have even settled for a brother.

Just something real, make some sweety go down on her brother & him on her, then make em fuck! Never got that either.

But back to ******. I rolled her on her back and now she had no trouble I slid right in. Man I was hot and sweaty, her too, I took my shirt off, so I could feel her tits & sweat on me. I always did that too.

Then I had her kiss me, eyes open, looking into my eyes while I pumped her, about 4-5 minutes, bam, that was it.

I sat her up on the side of the bed, had her lick & suck my dick clean. Her blood and pussy juice & my cum. I had to physically move her head & just told her to suck, suck hard. She did, and I was up

again real fast. Most of the time once was it then grab a few things and split, real fast! These virgins, too good to pass up, had all 11 of them - twice.

Now I took her in Moms room, mom kept a little Ruger 22 by her bed. Ahh! paranoid of a stranger in the night!

Put ****** down on her knees, it was suckee time! Giving head was something practically all of them said they weren't too good at, or didn't know how, or even married bitches telling me they never did it.

****** learned real fast, her eyes on my dick going in and out and growing with every stroke. I had her do 10 real slow from tip to base strokes, then 10 as fast as she could tip to base, and just keep on like that. I liked that. I've had head like that driving down the road for an hour or more, because just when I'd get ready to cum, they would go over the real and mean real slow. It would lie down a bit, then fast, ready to blast then slow. After a few minutes of this, (she had a great set of lips on her, natural made for fuckin) I told..."

Nothing I read in his earlier letters prepared me for the jolt I felt reading about his rape of a thirteen-year old girl. No wonder Corporal Baker had made a special trip to Ocala to see the death sentence being pronounced. After Long was caught, police found items taken from the home of the thirteen-year old rape victim in Long's apartment.

The man who wrote such a detailed description of how to rape women for fun and profit was now sitting on death row for murdering ten women. Even though he had been caught

and sentenced, the horror he had perpetrated could never be erased. These letters were an incisive look into his twisted mind. Pictures of the bloated, burly man screaming to have his way in court had been another.

Why had he written these commentaries when he must have known that they were incriminating and referred to murders? He had written them before he learned about appeals and before he discovered his power in the courtroom. But even then the need for his power to be affirmed was there. The thirty-one year old murderer, who had described in these letters written in 1984 his heinous crimes with obvious relish and enjoyment, shouted and screamed to keep the judge from learning their contents ten years later. William Eble, Bobby Joe Long's attorney, had referred to the man who turned the letters over to the police as the "Jail Snitch." I wondered reading them now whether that prisoner hadn't provided more insights into the mind of this "Serial Killer" than all the expert witnesses and psychiatrists our court system could provide.

I went over the key points: Long blamed a woman for his murders. "The cunt's way - killing people." He started raping in '75-'76... "never even came close to getting caught. For years I was referred to as the Classified Rapist."

He had started raping when he was twenty-two. That meant Long's siege had lasted nine years. I had read the comments of his companions in California. He bragged to them about tying up young girls. No one seemed to care enough to tell the police. Susan said he bragged in front of the judge at his first trial for assaulting her, that he raped her, and recanted. Yet I too had been secretive when raped. How could I feel the other victims should speak when I was so reluctant to tell about my own rapist? I was as guilty as anyone.

Then another emotion flooded my senses — anger at this grotesque man, who imagined his young victims enjoyed being tortured and raped and intimidated. Anger — for everything in our society that led this demented person to that conclusion. Rage — for the hours hundreds of people spent studying him. For what? Would it protect the next child from being raped by another Bobby Joe Long? I doubted it.

Thoughts of the suffering Susan and Lisa had endured accosted me. No one had cared when Long battered Susan. They'd criticized her for prosecuting him. Did anyone in the court care what Lisa had to go through every time she had to testify? She had spent twenty-six hours of torture with the monster.

If these documents in my hands were read in a courtroom, some smart-ass attorney would probably claim it was just Long's imagination. That rationalization was untrue. It was Long's warped mind that blamed a woman for the murders he'd committed. As for the rapes, Long seemed to think rape was masculine and wanted to share his conquests with other buddies.

There were so many evil elements to Bobby Joe Long, and they were all equally unbelievable.

The only laughable parts of Long's letter came when he asserted his citizen rights to privacy in his jail cell. He bragged about his protests against a midnight guard's opera music, but lamented that he was a lone complainer and pleaded that other prisoners back him up. "Please speak up when the noise is too loud. I hate to be singled out like that!" Many notes referred to drugs in trade for Marlboro cigarettes. In my haste, looking for more letters about Susan

and Lisa, I almost skipped some about his elaborate escape plan. Part of his words hadn't survived the copy machine, so I had to guess at the few sentences missing.

Hey,

Today after I read the paper & sent it back to you, your buddy a tough white guy-short loud saw me put it up on your vent.

I tried to call you to let you know it was there, but before I could this guy came and picked it up and starting reading. Since he had found a note yesterday I heard he was O.K. I signaled him I had a note in there for you and he motioned like "Don't worry about it!" But man, what if someone else - the wrong someone had done that!

I guess we'll just have to make sure from here on that when something with a message is being passed we're both at our slots -ready!

Just read your note. I know who they are too......the visiting room today and then got worried.

It's getting to the point where I'm afraid I'm going do something I shouldn't...It wouldn't be the first time. I owe you for the pills. Two tabs & the 150 mg of the other shit sounds good, but exactly is it?

No I don't want to go for anything else (downers etc.) not now anyway! They put me back on med. I think my lawyer worked it out.

Hew what I was talking about body hunting it was gonna be me with 2 detectives for a walk I going to tell a detective I've got a body hidden in the back. I pretend like I'm looking for something, and have a gun planted.

But the more I think about it, may not be such a bad way to go.

They wouldn't know what hit em.

I have it all planned out, and I think it would work.

I sent the two guys a letter yesterday and will be talking to them soon. I'm sure.

They're like buzzards, when I start talking, the drool! And eat it all up.

What would it take to get a gun planted $$$$ wise? Are we talkin quality or Saturday night specials. I'd have to have a cannon, that's why I specify large caliber and revolver - 41, 44, 45 nothing smaller! Try and find out about the wire between the two buildings.

No chance for a hack saw blade?

I've looked at the way there wooden frames are put together, I think by cutting 8 Rivets on this one the whole thing would come apart. It wouldn't hurt to try you know! Thanks again for the pills yesterday. About the wire, if you can see it - wave.

Maybe you could sort of make a diagram of what you see outside your window? Mostly what I want to know is - is this building and the smaller one story building outside my window rolled over with wire or does it have a fence and wire there.

I looked at the diagram at the bottom of the page. He'd drawn a sidewalk on the north. A cell marked "me" was close to the corner of the tallest building, and there was an extra cell between another cell marked "you". The words "open yard" were written between the two buildings.

I wondered why he was trying to map the buildings if he

was planning to get out with the ruse of another dead body. It
had to be his backup plan. I read his words... "They're like
buzzards, when I start talking, they drool and eat it all up!"
Could they be the two he referred to in the visiting room that
was in the portion of the letters I couldn't read? Was one of
them Susan's rapist? I felt frustrated but continued.

**I did try to "feel out" the two detectives I told
you about for the hunt. I wrote them a note asking
them to bring me my 3 piece suits, shirts, tie, shoes,
etc.... for court. Two days later here they both were,
with my shit....drooling!**

**They all think I killed some cunt in some bar
across from bush gardens, and they're (sic) pretty
sure about one in Orlando. Man all I have to do is get
word to those two drooling fuckers, they'd (sic) be
here I an hour ready to go! Dripping & Drooling! I
think the 'HUNT' is the only real chance...I know if I
can think of the right place, the 'HUNT' would work.**

Escape. The very thought was horrifying. And as for his
intimidating threats, they were even more so. I shuffled
through note after note about the 'HUNT,' read Long's plans
for getting Latimer, Baker, and Price, and felt my hands shaking. When I finished with everything Long had written, I
began to read the notes in a second handwriting. It had to be
from the "Jail Snitch," the other prisoner who Long had been
passing messages to. The prisoner had passed the notes on to
the police. The prisoner's comments about Long added
more to the picture of him emerging from not only his cor-
respondence but that of a man in jail with him.

Hey Chief
Here is a little commentary on the notes I've

received from "Mad Dog" Long since we met on Thursday January 10th.

Date Received

Thurs. 1/10/85 1. Speaking of Sgt. Price, I had written back to him in response to his remark in an earlier letter that he could give me information to use to take another certain Sgt. on a "hunt" like he was planning. I said I'd be interested in hearing what he had to say, especially if it involved Price. The boats - I had asked him if this creek or whatever was big enough for a boat to make a waterway escape. Last paragraph, back side of page 1 is in reference to Susan Replogle (or whatever her name is).

Thurs. 1/10/85 2. He's worried about them moving me out of here - I am too. Don't let it happen- not at this stage of the game! Something interesting in this letter-referred to one of his "Drooling" buddies as his "Biker Buddy". First time he's ever mentioned that. With reference to Susan Replogle's brother-in-law as his best buddy, that's 2 clues to the possible eighteenth of the 1 or 2 people-he's protecting from involvement at all costs. He communicates with certain people thru a P.O. Box that his P.I. checks occasionally for him and then delivers to him personally. His ex-wife is also a mystery he's protecting her too for reasons unknown.

Fri. 1/11/85 3. He's chompin at the bit...I wrote back some B.S. to calm him down and told him I was mailing the map out tonight. I also told him that "before this month turned February, you'll read "Miss Cunt's (Susan Replogle's) obituary in the

paper and we'll have a date set up for the safari." Also fished for the information he has for me to "blast myself a Sgt." and tried to find out if his vulture buddies were involved in any of the murders he's charged with. Waiting right now to get my note to him. In his last letter last night, he said he wasn't writing any more until something happened, so I never wrote back. Sure enough, tonight he's breathing down my neck. Hope to find out some important things tonight.

Sat. 1/12/85 3:30 A.M. 4. Cindy & Holly - Cindy is his wife the other (Holly is an Italian girl in Ft. Lauderdale who works for the Florida State Bar Association). They both know a lot of shit but they would never talk. I talked to him for the last 4 hours. Right now, I don't even want to turn any of this over to the police. I'd rather just keep anything from happening and do whatever time I have to do rather than play Judas for 30 days of gain time or some petty shit. He's got enough problems the way it is.

Monday AM 1/14 I wrote back told him "my people" Viscoe among others. Also that my "investigator" knows people who know my people, etc. and to lay out the line to use on Baker. Also probed about Holly and Cindy.

5. Monday 1/14/85 6 P.M. Didn't respond to my "feelers" but in case I haven't learned more by the "the letter" from "my friends" at the end of the week ought to do it. I've got another letter written to him now ready to deliver and will hold off to see if I get an answer tonight.

6. Mon. 1/14/85 8:45-Midnight Damn-got

(another) and forgot to even sent the letter I'd written
him. He's got it now so I'll get an answer tomorrow.
Gonna close this up and get it in the mail.

Suddenly I understood. Susan's obituary? No wonder
Corporal Baker hadn't shown her the letter. Long not only
wanted his friends to rape her, he was still actively trying to
get her killed even from jail. Of course, he hadn't killed her
when he was on the loose murdering women. Her death would
have pointed straight to him, and he knew it. In jail, he'd be
safe from implication. I thought back. The guy who'd come
through Susan's window must have been one of Long's biker
buddies. He'd followed Long's instructions to get Susan and
sworn he'd return. Another irony, Susan had been raped less
than two weeks after Corporal Baker asked her why Bobby Joe
Long hated her so much. And she hadn't even had a chance to
use the new gun she'd bought for protection. It's no wonder
women who are raped are terrified; they could be menaced
even from death row!

How many more lies, I wondered, had Bobby Joe Long
told his prison confidant? Was it possible that Long believed
his own nonsense about a woman making him murder?

Monday 1/21/85 3 p.m.-Got this letter-not much.

Nothing new on the kinky female killer except
she went "back" to California.

5 PM -Just talked to him for a few minutes - he
said a guy named Mike in Clearwater is who he is
trying to get hold of. From the things he said at vari-
ous times in the last few weeks, I wonder if "Buddy &
his brothers are just "crazy" friends - seems like Mike
is (one of 2) that "helped" him on 2 of the murders. He
just wrote an extremely long letter to Cindy (ex-wife)

and Holly (ex-wife's roommate & friend of his) and is "wrote out" for now. Probably tomorrow - maybe late night - before I hear from him. (I enclose newspaper clipping about the 200 rapes he spoke of).

2. Monday 1/21/85 6 PM

He's chompin at the bit for a "letter" from my "cocaine cowboys". Might be a good thing if he got busted with the pills and they stopped his medicine - he's so nervous he'll spill his guts to get 'accepted.'

3. Mon. 1/21/85 10 PM

I had written, probing for the unknown accomplice with a story about a possible back-up plan which involved a robbery to get $$$. Definitely know the female that killed the first girl and started his string of murders - "Lisa". So she was here in April, May, or whenever the first girl got killed, but has since went "back to California," presumably L.A. I can't question him anymore about her right now or I'll scare him off.

4. Tues. 1/11/85 4:30 A.M. I had written last night to calm his ass down and reassure him that my "C.C's" would come thru I just like to have an ace in the hole (back up plans). I didn't get to give it to him until I served breakfast at 4:00 this morning and wrote right back. The "Tony" he speaks of is his "P.I." After reading this one, it left the impression "Mike from Clearwater or Buddy" was never involved in any murders with him. I'm sure though - both from the previous letter and from talking to him verbally - "Lisa" killed (or helped killed) his "first" Hills Co. victim. The "letter I'm writing on should hopefully clear the subject up. He's real edgy.

Stunned, I rose from reading the letters. They left nothing to the imagination as to the diabolic cunning of Bobby Joe Long. The letters bound his crimes together. They clinched his intention to find a way to permanently silence Susan and his plans to get her killed. They showed the rationale behind his brutal treatment of Lisa. They tied in his rapes and his hatred of women. They gave insights into his depraved mind better than all the brain examinations during the trial. Reading his words illustrated how Long reacted to men in authority as well as how he depended on outward appearances.

His cowardly fear of being alone was apparent in his complaint about the opera music he heard in jail. His ability to control himself was detailed in the notes about Baker, Price and Lattimer. His plans to kill police officers foretold what he was capable of with a big enough gun.

His own words, more than all the experts during the past thirteen years debating his sanity, proved what Dr. Sprehe said on the witness stand. Bobby Joe Long didn't have brain damage. In my opinion, he was also just a completely evil monster.

Long's words and thoughts made me wonder how law abiding people could ever be fully protected from killers, whether in jail or out.

I could understand now why Corporal Baker had been anxious to come to Long's sentencing hoping to see him get the chair. He and the other detectives who worked so hard on the Long case must be as frustrated with the appeals as the surviving victims and their families. They knew the Bobby Joe Long locked in prison didn't have any redeeming qualities.

I got up and walked over to the phone. Lisa and Susan would be waiting to hear about the contents of the letters. I

winced thinking of what I'd read and now had to tell them. Some of the revelations would make them even more frightened than before. Still I couldn't, wouldn't hide the truth. However, thinking more about it, I didn't want to discuss Long's letters with them over the telephone. I asked Lisa and Susan to meet me for dinner.

Chapter 29

Government And Madmen

During the 1994 election for the governor of Florida, the issue of convicted killers on death row played a pivotal role. The primary reason was a television commercial for candidate Jeb Bush that focused on a mother who complained about the killer of her child being on death row for fourteen years. Wendy Nelson made an impassioned plea saying that her family had been repeatedly victimized by a system out of control. Her daughter's killer had two trials and was sentenced to death three times. She observed, "We become victims all over again as our sense of loss and trauma become invalidated by a system that was supposed to protect us."

Her message was lost in the political competition which erupted between Jeb Bush and Lawton Chiles, who was running for re-election. Chiles called the advertisement "reprehensible," and a group of lawyers defended the Governor by saying he had "done more to streamline death row appeals than any governor since the death penalty's reinstatement in 1979."

Additionally, Chiles' media group created more advertisements defending the Governor saying he had signed as many death sentences as other governors, and the laws were responsible for the appeals system. Chiles castigated Jeb Bush for daring to bring up the case during an election campaign.

I was shocked at the fervor of his objections. If an election wasn't the place to create change in a democratic society, when was it proper? Moreover, I admired Mrs. Nelson's ability to bring attention to her tragedy through the political process. But eventually her appeal had few, if any, long-term effects.

Governor Chiles was re-elected, and Bobby Joe Long was placed in the Governor's custody on March 18, 1994.

William Eble, Bobby Joe Long's Public Defender, filed papers for Long's appeal against his death sentence for the murder of Virginia Johnson that same day.

Chapter 30

Chance After Chance

Susan, Lisa and I wanted to see for ourselves the documents which were used to set aside so many verdicts against Bobby Joe Long. More telling than the trials themselves, the subversion of the appeals process in the case of Bobby Joe Long had gone on and on. The first appeal, No. 67,103, was dated November 12, 1987 and received on November 16th.

For reasons expressed below, we find we are mandated by the United States Supreme Court decisions in Miranda v. Arizona, 384 U.S. 436 (1966), and Edwards v. Arizona, 451 U.S. 477 (1981), to vacate appellant's conviction and sentence and remand for a new trial.

After a perfunctory description of the charges against Bobby Joe Long in the murder case of Virginia Johnson, which included the information that Virginia was a prostitute, the document summarized the task force capture of Long owing to information supplied by Lisa McVey. The cursory information on Lisa as a victim included an inaccuracy – that she was abducted from her apartment, not her bicycle. The

appeal focused on what happened to Bobby Joe Long after he
was arrested:

*Long was arrested on November 16, 1984 pur-
suant to a warrant on the abduction, kidnapping and
involuntary sexual battery of Lisa McVey. After his
arrest, Long was transported to the Hillsborough
County Sheriff's Office for questioning. Initially,
detectives read Bobby Joe Long a form Miranda waiver.
Long reviewed the waiver and signed it. According to
detectives, Long spoke freely for approximately the
next hour and one-half, answering questions and
cooperating with the police, who eventually obtained a
full confession in the McVey case. At this point in the
interrogation, one of the detectives left the room to
retrieve snapshot photographs of recent murder victims.
After his return, the detective asked Long if he had ever
picked up prostitutes in the area. Long responded, "I
would prefer not to answer that." The detectives
immediately began to show Long the murder victim's
photographs. Long's attitude changed at this point
and he remarked to the detective, "The complexion of
things have sure changed since you came back into the
room. I think I might need an attorney." The record
is clear that the officers continued the interrogation. A
portion of the suppression hearing testimony of one of
the investigating officers reflects the following:*

*Q. Okay. After Mr. Long said he'd rather not
answer the question about Tampa prostitutes, after you
showed him the pictures of some prostitutes in Tampa,
do you recall at that point Mr. Long saying, "I think I
might need an attorney?"*

A. Yes sir.

Q.   Were those his exact words the best you recall?

A.   No, they weren't his exact words—he looked at myself, made the statement, "The complexion of things sure have changed since you came back into the room."

Q. And?

A. And he continued by saying, "I think I might need an attorney."

Q.   Complexion of things had changed, hadn't they?

A. Yes sir.

Q. You told him they hadn't

A. I said, "Nothing has changed. I'm still being honest with you."

Q. Were you — were you being honest with him in fact?

A. Nothing had changed for me. I was pursuing the interrogation.

Q. You told him nothing had changed. After he said, "I think I might need an attorney."

A. That's true.

Q. Did you attempt to clarify that?

A. Yes sir. I told Mr. Long not to try to fool himself or me, that the interview being conducted in regards to Lisa McVey would eventually turn into the investigation of homicide of the nine women.

Subsequent to this exchange, Long made a full, explanatory confession of Virginia Johnson's murder.

The precedent determining decisions were listed and defined. Miranda v. Arizona 1966 indicated that, in any

manner and at any stage of the process the accused wished to consult with an attorney, there could be no further questioning. It is affirmed in Edwards v. Arizona. In People v. Plyler the law requires the immediate cessation of police interrogation. The cases of many states gave way to listing all the equivocal cases including Singleton v. State, 344 So. 2nd 911, 912 Fla. 3d DCA 1977. Long had said, "Maybe I better ask my mother if I should get an attorney." There was no question the first trial on appeal related to the detectives not supplying an attorney in a timely fashion.

The document relating to the Pasco County Circuit Court should have been self-explanatory, but wasn't.

An appeal from the Circuit Court in and for Pasco County, Ray E. Elmer Jr., Judge - Case No. 8402275. James Marion Moorman, Public Defender, Tenth Judicial Circuit, and W. C. McLain, Assistant Public Defender, Chief, Capital Appeals, Bartow, Florida for Appellant. Robert A. Butterworth, Attorney General, and James A. Young, Assistant Attorney General, Tampa, Florida for Appellee.

"Why were the appeals only on the Pasco trial of Virginia Johnson?" Lisa asked. "Didn't the same breech of Miranda effect all the Hillsborough cases? Was my testimony the only one unaffected by the Miranda decisions because Bobby Joe Long agreed to answer questions about me? Why was I never called to testify in the Simms trial?"

I had no answer.

The next appeal Bobby Joe won was No. 69,259, dated June 30, 1988, seven months later. The appeal from the Hillsborough County Circuit Court Judge John P. Griffin, Case No. 84-13346-B, was prepared for the Appellant, Bobby Joe Long, by Ellis Rubin and David M. Rapport of the

Ellis Rubin Law Offices. Robert A. Butterworth, Attorney
General and James A. Young, Assistant Attorney General,
Tampa Florida for Appellee.

*We recently reversed appellant's first degree
murder conviction and death penalty for a similar
offense in Pasco County. Long v. State, 517 So. 2d
664 (Fla. 1987). Evidence in both cases arose in part
from the same confession given to law enforcement
officials by the appellant. We find the guilty pleas
valid and affirm the multiple life sentences, as well as
the sentence for the probation violation imposed as
part of the agreement. However, we find it was error
to use the prior Pasco County conviction as an aggravating circumstance in the penalty phase proceeding in
view of our subsequent reversal of the Pasco County
conviction. Consequently, we remand only for a new
death sentencing proceeding.*

"This is shocking. I can hardly believe it," I said to both
women.

"Look," said Susan, "his death sentence for Simms' murder
was overturned in Hillsborough, but they found his guilty plea
valid." There were even more pages in the Hillsborough appeal
– repetitious description of Long's crimes against Lisa and his
interrogation in Hillsborough. The appeal read:

1. Miranda v. Arizona, 384 U.S. 436 (1966).

2. The plea agreement reads, in pertinent part:

*The State and Defense do hereby stipulate to the
following plea negotiations in the above-styled cases
subject to the Court's approval.*

*In exchange for the Defendant's pleas of guilty
to the following case numbers the State would recom-
mend to this Court the following plea negotiations:*

Paragraphs 1 through 9 of the plea agreement set forth the sentences agreed to for nine separate incidents that include seven murders, eight sexual batteries, eight kidnappings, and one probation violation. The agreement provides that two life sentences in the first incident would be concurrent with each other but would be consecutive to one life sentence without the possibility of parole for twenty-five years, each of these sentences arising out of the first incident. All the remaining sentences were concurrent with this sentence.

3.   Case Number 84-13346B (victim Michelle Denise Simms) Defendant will plead guilty to all three counts of said indictment. The court will withhold imposition of sentence on all three counts until the completion of a second phase proceeding before a jury impaneled for that specific purpose. After an advisory sentence is recommended by the said jury, this Court will impose a sentence of death or life without the possibility of parole for twenty-five years as to count III of said Indictment 84-13346B.

The parties further agree as follows:

1.   Defendant waives his right to contest the admissibility of any statements he has given law enforcement and such statements are admissible at the sentencing hearing case Number 84-13346-B if otherwise relevant;

2.   Defendant waives the right to contest the admissibility of evidence seized from his car or at or near his apartment, and specifically waives his right to contest the admissibility of a knife found in a wooded area near his apartment in the sentencing hearing in case Number 84-13346B;

3. To the extent any sentence imposed as to any plea of guilty as to any count contained in this agreement, the parties recognize the negotiations may require sentences which depart from the guidelines and waive any issues caused by such departures;

4. The manner of voir dire of the sentencing is to be determined by the court;

5. The number of peremptory challenges is to be determined by the court;

6. The State of Florida shall not rely upon the pleas of guilty entered in any other case in the Thirteenth Judicial Circuit as aggravating circumstances in Case Number 84-13346B, but may introduce into evidence and rely upon any other conviction of the defendant previously obtained, including those in Pasco, Pinellas, and Orange Counties;

7. Upon acceptance of pleas of guilty to counts I and II of Case Number 84-13346B, the sentences imposed on the defendant as to those counts shall run concurrently to the sentence imposed on Count III of that indictment.

"Oh, my God...Lisa, you have every right to be afraid every time the monster goes to court and tries to gain his freedom. Where did all the newspaper writers get a figure of 623 years for his incarceration? Concurrent means simultaneous — parallel. Could he walk in twenty-five years? He's been in twelve years. The death sentence seems to mean nothing, and twenty-five years isn't a long time to be incarcerated for heinous crimes. His death sentence for Simms and Johnson were vacated! What effect did any of the juries have on the outcome?"

The vision of the death sentence given on March 18, 1994

and Assistant Public Defender William Eble preparing for a new plea against Florida's death penalty flashed across my mind. The three of us felt angry. We had to force ourselves to continue.

On December 11, 1985, Long moved to withdraw from the plea agreement based on the unavailability of a crucial defense witness and his earlier misunderstanding regarding his right to appeal the confession's admissibility. A hearing was held on the motion during which the appellant testified as follows:

> *Dr. Morrison was the key to this thing as far as I was concerned. She was the main ingredient to the defense when I pleaded, with this plea bargain that took place a month or so ago...*
>
> *My counsel advised me that she should be here. Went on what my counsel told me. They were mistaken. They were wrong. I don't know. But I know that they told me something that has not come about. I have no faith in anything in this now. I have no faith in my counsel. I have faith in the doctors. I don't know what to do.*
>
> *Before this thing I pleaded, I was under the impression that further appeals as to my confession would not be jeopardized, that I was giving up the right to appeal that suppression of the confession. I found out Monday, that indeed, I am giving up all appellate rights to challenge this confession. I wasn't aware of this.*

It should be noted that this proceeding took place while the judge was attempting to seat the Penalty Phase jury. The trial court, after the testimony on the plea, determined that

appellant should be allowed to withdraw his previously
entered guilty pleas. The trial judge stated:

> *But I believe that there is a mistake on his part of
> a misapprehension. It's uncontroverted he felt that Dr.
> Morrison was going to be here to speak on his behalf.*
>
> *That was one of the basis this Court finds for
> him entering into his plea agreement. That was a mis-
> apprehension on his part. No misapprehension at the
> time of entering the pleas, but was under the belief, it
> is this Court's finding, that she would be here or some-
> one of her stature.*
>
> *For reasons unconnected with the defendant and
> really with the Public Defendant's Office, that — it's
> on the record — has chosen not to be granting the
> motion which I am going to do.*
>
> *I am going to grant the defendant's motion to
> withdraw his previously entered pleas of guilty.*
>
> *I believe Mr. O'Connor made another telling
> point that I was also going to comment on, that he
> knows by withdrawing this and by my granting this
> motion, he is now laying himself open, unless future
> plea agreements are worked out, to potential eight
> death penalties. And I think that would be a strong
> factor to prohibit him from asking his attorney to file
> this motion for permission to withdraw the guilty
> pleas. It substantially even dangers (sic) his future
> life, and I believe it is another factor which indicates
> to me the truth of the matter that his entry into this
> plea agreement was based on, among other things, two
> factors: That he would have the right to appeal on the
> matter of the confession, and that he would have*

someone like Dr. Morrison here to speak on his behalf
at the penalty phase of the trial.

Therefore, the motion for permission to with-
draw previously entered pleas of guilty is granted.
With the granting of that motion, I believe that it ter-
minates further activity with this particular jury that
we have spent so much time trying to seat.

"Long got this appeal because Dr. Morrison didn't show
up in the penalty phase," I said. *The Tampa Tribune,* dated
Sunday, April 28, 1985, gave information about the doctor.
'A Chicago psychiatrist, Dr. L. Helen Morrison testified that
Long shared a bed with his mother for years as a child, but
remembered being kicked out of it whenever she brought
home a man.' The Metro section *of The Tampa Tribune,*
dated January 13, 1985, referred to the doctor's refusal to
return. *'Both O'Connor and Benito agreed in court that*
Morrison would be investigated for a possible grand-theft
charge. O'Connor estimated Morrison had been paid about
$3,900 in county money.' The same article contained infor-
mation that the doctor sent a letter claiming she wasn't paid.

"Whatever happened, the error cost the taxpayers a new
trial," Susan interjected.

"Long's attorney made a point of qualifying whether his
client could make the decision to set aside his plea bargain.
He was granted a forty-eight hour continuance so Bobby Joe
Long could think about retaining the plea already in place,"
I said.

"Look at this," Lisa pointed. "These are the notes taken
from the court transcript. Mr. Benito, the prosecutor, was
mislabeled." She laughed.

THE COURT: All right sir. Is it your intention
to now withdraw your guilty pleas and to reiterate the

plea agreement that was previously entered into and read into the court record by this Court at an earlier date.

THE DEFENDANT: Yes sir.

THE COURT: All right sir. Have you had time to seriously consider the consequences of that withdrawal of your motion to your previously entered plea of guilty? Have you thoroughly discussed it with your attorney?

THE DEFENDANT: Yes sir, that's all I thought about for the last forty-eight hours.

THE COURT: I can presume so. Do you feel that you have confidence in the advice that has been given to you by Mr. O'Connor or any of his associates from the Public Defender's Office?

THE DEFENDANT: Yes I do.

THE COURT: All right sir. Do you feel that it's in your personal best interest, after thinking about it over this period of time, to reiterate the plea agreement that was previously entered into?

THE DEFENDANT: Yes, I do.

THE COURT: All right sir. Another point at issue was that you were concerned about preservation of the right to appeal your confession.

THE DEFENDANT: Yes sir.

THE COURT: There was a great amount of discussion on that yesterday. Do you understand, sir, that if I allow this plea bargaining to go forward...that you are giving up your bargaining right of appeal on any issues in these matters? Do you understand that, sir?

THE DEFENDANT: On any issues?

THE COURT: On any issues, yes sir.

THE DEFENDANT: I wasn't aware of that.

MR. BENITO (DEFENSE ATTORNEY): On any issues as to...this particular plea agreement, if any appellate issues arise in the second phase you can appeal that.

THE DEFENDANT: Okay.

THE COURT: Obviously. Maybe I misworded it. Anything that is behind us.

THE DEFENDANT: Okay.

THE COURT: We are not talking about the punishment issue we are going to try this week.

THE DEFENDANT: Yes sir. I understand that.

THE COURT: Especially, the matter of the confession, that you are waiving your right to appeal. Do you understand sir?

THE DEFENDANT: Yes. Yes, I do.

THE COURT: All right sir. Also, one of the issues that you mentioned yesterday was that you felt that you based your agreement to the plea bargain on the fact that you would have a forensic psychologist, Doctor Helen Morrison, specially, in this case, here to testify as a keystone witness for you at this second phase of this case involving Michelle Simms, that this plea agreement is not based on a guarantee of a forensic psychologist being one of your expert witnesses at this penalty phase whenever it's heard.

Do you understand that?

THE DEFENDANT: Yes, I do.

THE COURT: All right sir. So that would not be an issue at any other time. Do you understand?

THE DEFENDANT: Yes.

"At the time of the plea, Long had already been tried and

sentenced to death for the Virginia Johnson murder," I said. "The new sentencing proceeding was set for July 9, 1986. Before those proceedings began, appellant's new counsel filed a motion to again set aside the plea agreement, directly affecting the appellant's right to a fair penalty phase proceeding, because the agreement expressly provided for the introduction into evidence of Long's confession. The trial court denied the motion to set aside plea agreement."

Lisa nodded and continued, as if she knew what I was thinking. "The penalty phase proceedings commenced July 10, 1986, and the State presented evidence of Long's confession with regard to the killing of Michelle Denise Simms and Virginia Johnson. The State also submitted a copy of the judgment entered in Pasco County for the Johnson murder. The State presented two expert witnesses, who concluded that Long, at the time of the Simms murder, was not under the influence of extreme mental or emotional disturbance, nor was his capacity to appreciate the criminality of his conduct or to conform his conduct to the requirements of law substantially impaired. *One of the State's experts did testify that, when the appellant killed his victim, he was also unconsciously killing his mother by extension.*"

Susan went on. "The appellant presented four expert witnesses who stated Long was under the influence of extreme mental and emotional disturbance at the time of the murders, and was unable to conform his conduct to the requirement of the law."

I shook my head. "Bobby Joe Long's mitigating circumstances, a troubled family life and the head injuries which led to brain damage and mental problems, were all alluded to. In spite of the fact Long had four experts to the State's two, the jury recommended the death penalty by a vote of eleven to

one. The Court, however, found the statutory aggravating circumstance. I think I'm going to gag. Wait until you see the end of this one."

"*—Far outweigh the two mitigating circum-stances determined by the court to have been fully established,*" it concluded.

"*Facts justifying the imposition of the death penalty are so clear and convincing that virtually no reasonable person could differ with this conclusion.*"

"Look at this," Susan broke in, pointing to the page.

"*Long's contention is that the trial court erred by: (1) denying any motion to vacate the plea agree-ment; (2) admitting the penalty phase proceedings, the confession, and knife found pursuant to the confes-sion; (3) denying his motion of continuance; and (4) imposing the death penalty.*

She went on, "*Because they reversed the death penalty for Virginia Johnson, they had to do the same for Long's penalty for killing Michelle Simms. The same Superior Court Judges had their names on both appeals.*"

McDonald, C.J., and Overton, Ehrlich, Shaw, Barkett, Grimes, and Kogan, J.J., concur.

"*Later, the same Judges' names appeared on the Hillsborough appeal,*" I said, "*Barkett, J. concurs in result only in the convictions, but concurs with the sentence.*"

"We need to read the appeals that initiated the recent series of trials for Pasco County. Hillsborough was covered under plea agreement." Lisa looked at me, and I met her eyes.

Both appeals arrived at the Department of Legal Affairs

on October 19, 1992. The first page read:

We reverse the conviction and sentence and remand for a new trial.

In the end, the Supreme Court Judges were in agreement, but Kogan qualified his agreement.

Barkett, Overton, McDonald, Shaw, Grimes, and Harding concur. Kogan concurs in result only as to conviction, and concurs as to sentence.

"The original opinion which entitled Long to a new trial was based on *Miranda v. Arizona* and *Edwards v. Arizona*. This appeal came from the trial in Fort Myers. That was the trial at which you became traumatized." I turned to Lisa.

"I remember some people found the medical examiner's words strange," Susan said, her eyes widening as she went on reading:

"Additionally, she could not tell whether the victim was conscious or unconscious at the time of death."

"Of course, to find that really ironic, a person would have to sit in a hot, humid courtroom many hours listening to the Chief Medical Examiner, Dr. Joan Wood, describe how unconsciousness doesn't occur by stopping air in the windpipe. It only occurs when the body's fluids cease flowing...up to three minutes. It is hard to imagine anyone being conscious and dead." I grimaced, shaking my head. "The mistakes are ludicrous."

"Look at what happened to me. I waited three days to testify," Lisa said. "See what they've written about me here."

After the victim's identity had been established, the State introduced testimony, over the defense counsel's objection, from Lisa McVey, a woman who had been raped by Long. In connection with that

rape, Long was convicted of kidnapping and sexual battery. The court instructed the jury that the evidence of these other crimes was to be considered only for the limited purpose of proving Long's motive, plan and identity.

McVey testified to the following. In November, 1984, she was working in a donut shop in Tampa. On November 3, she got off work around 2:30 a.m. and began to ride home on her bicycle. Before she got home, she was abducted at gun point and blindfolded. Her abductor dragged her into the passenger seat of his car, loosely tied her hands, and told her to strip. She did so because she was blindfolded, and never saw her abductor.

"Another meaningless phrase! Of course the gun and his size had no effect." Susan's jaw tightened. We read on:

However, from underneath the blindfold, she saw that she was in a maroon car with white interior that had the word "Magnum" on the dashboard. Judging from sounds, it appeared they were driving interstate.

They arrived at an apartment building. She had gotten dressed again and her abductor took her up a flight of stairs. Once inside, he raped her four or five times in rapid succession. She saw and felt a gun and believed he had a knife. Several hours before daybreak, the rapes stopped and her abductor slept most of the following day. He untied her hands and feet before daybreak. However, she did not try to get away because she felt if she cooperated he might not kill her.

Around three o'clock in the morning, her abductor awakened her, and told her it was time to go,

and asked where she lived. On the way, they stopped at an automatic bank teller machine. When they stopped, she could see a Howard Johnson's and a Quality Inn located nearby. Her abductor then dropped her off in a parking lot at the intersection of Hillsborough and Rome. He told her to describe him to the police as an "ugly man with a beard." However, as far as she could see or feel, he appeared to have a pockmarked face, a mustache, but no beard, small ears, and brown hair. After he left the area, she walked home and called police.

"The report on my testimony, called by everyone so important, was also so fouled up!"

"Nevertheless, the document was important for another reason; they didn't say it gave the monster another set of trials," I said, incredulous.

The investigating officer stated that the police located the only automatic teller machine in Tampa that was near both a Quality Inn and a Howard Johnson's. The bank recorded a transaction on its automatic teller machine at 3:49 a.m. on the day the victim was taken to the parking lot. Bank records revealed that the personal identification number used in the automatic teller machine transaction belonged to Long. The officer also testified that a motor vehicle records search indicated that Long owned a Dodge Magnum automobile. Further testimony reflected that two other detectives received information that a maroon Dodge Magnum automobile was possibly involved in another rape. On November 5, 1984, they saw such a vehicle and asked the driver for identification.

The driver produced a driver's license that identified him as Long. The officers then fabricated a story to see if they could get Long to consent to a search. He declined, but did allow them to photograph him and the car.

Susan said, "The police work involved reminded me of police drama shows on television and movies." The test followed the arrest and the F.B.I. fiber and hair analysis to the CBS news interview, introduced by the prosecution as Williams Rule evidence. The defense objected. Evidence was presented regarding each murder victim and information about the early murders.

One decomposed body had been found with a ligature around her neck and with her wrists bound behind her back. Testimony reflected that the cause of death was strangulation. The second victim was found, nearly nude, in a wooded area. Her hands had been tied behind her back with a bloody, green T-shirt. Articles of her clothing were lying in a limb of a tree. Her arms were tied together, her throat had been cut, and she suffered severe head injuries. Three photographs of the victim were presented to the jury. Testimony regarding the third murder reflected that the victim had been found semi-nude in an orange grove, and she was bound with cords and shoelaces. Two photographs of this body were presented to the jury. Finally, evidence of the fourth murder victim was presented. Testimony showed that the victim's nude body was found on the side of the road. There were no ligature or bindings found on the body or at the scene, but there were ligature marks on the neck and forearms.

*The medical examiner concluded that her death was
caused by strangulation. Next, the State presented hair,
fiber, and tire track evidence from each of the crimes.
Defense counsel objected to tire track evidence
because no such evidence had been present in the
instant case. Nevertheless, the trial judge allowed the
evidence. Additionally, the fiber analyst expert testified
that the fibers taken from each of the victims matched
the fiber found in the mass of blond hair found next to
the victim in this case. Evidence of other fibers, not
present in this case but present in the other cases, was
also introduced, and testimony connected these fibers
to Long. Similarly, hair sample evidence was presented
that connected the victims to Long.*

"*Evidence of other fibers, not present in this case, but
present in other cases, was also introduced and testimony
connected these fibers to Long.*" Accurate or confused mix-
ture? Perhaps in certain parts, both, I observed. The new
trial in Ocala spent hours on a red fiber found in Johnson's
hair. To me the trials appeared to mirror each other.

*Finally, the State introduced into evidence the
fact that Long had pleaded guilty in accordance with
the Hillsborough County plea agreement to each of the
Hillsborough County murders outlined above. The
State rested. Long's counsel moved for a mistrial
based on the State's use of Williams Rule evidence.
Counsel argued the murders were not similar enough
to the charged crimes to justify admission of evidence
regarding the murders. Additionally, counsel noted
that the court had heard nearly three days of testimony,
but that only four hours of that testimony actually*

related to the murder at issue. Counsel contended that the Hillsborough County murders, rather than the crime for which Long was charged, had become the central feature of the trial. The motion for a mistrial was denied. The jury returned a guilty verdict recommending the death penalty nine to three. The Judge sentenced Long to death and this appeal followed.

Long claims that the trial judge erred by allowing the State to introduce: (1) edited portions of the CBS videotaped interview of Long while denying Long access to the remaining portions of the videotape; (2) the televised portion of the CBS videotape because it referred to the criminal propensity and because it referred to the Hillsborough murders that Long claims were improperly introduced as Williams Rule evidence; (3) evidence of other crimes that became the overwhelming feature of the trial; (4) irrelevant and highly prejudicial Williams Rule evidence of a rape for which Long was convicted; and (5) evidence of four Hillsborough County murders to which he had previously confessed.

For reasons expressed below, we find that several of these claims have merit, and consequently, that Long is entitled to a new trial.

Accordingly, we reverse Long's conviction and sentence of death and remand for a new trial at which: (1) the CBS interview may be admitted into evidence provided the entire videotape is available for viewing for the Jury; (2) evidence of the murders to which Long entered guilty pleas in the Hillsborough County plea agreement may not be admitted under circumstances of this case; (3) testimony concerning the McVey incident

may be admitted to identify Long in this case so long as details of Long's treatment of McVey in his apartment and his subsequent plea of guilty in that case are excluded; and (4) evidence of the Hillsborough County pleas and convictions resulting from Long's plea agreement may not be admitted as aggravating factors given terms of the plea agreement.

I ran my hand across my forehead, which was perspiring. "William Eble's complaints about Lisa's emotional testimony were based on this Supreme Court ruling. The words are logical, but have other meanings! Over the years of game playing, the original reason for the game was lost as were the original rules. How long will the misplayed game go on? Who is it protecting: the defendant, the public, the police, the lawyers, the judges, the expert witnesses?"

Both women looked at me and shook their heads sadly. Lisa said, "No one knows."

"Here's another one: Supreme Court decision No. 74,512, Robert Joe Long, Appellant vs. State of Florida."

Appellee appeals his sentence of death imposed after a new penalty phase proceeding. We have jurisdiction. Art. V, S 3 (b) (1) Fla. Const. For the reasons expressed, we affirm his sentence of death imposed in accordance with the Jury's unanimous recommendation and reaffirm the validity of Long's guilty pleas...

"That appeal was prepared by the same Public Defenders, James Marion Moorman and A. Anne Owens, Assistant. All the Supreme Court Judges were the same and all concurred. Judge Lazzara was the only one dissenting. A unanimous jury for the death sentence must have had some impact on Hillsborough County's not reviewing the Simms' trial for a third time," I exclaimed.

At the outset, we note that the defense does not dispute that Long murdered the victim in this case, Michelle Denise Simms. The defense argued that Long is severely mentally ill and has been diagnosed as having bipolar brain disorder and temporal lobe epilepsy, which purportedly resulted from brain damage caused by a series of head injuries. According to the defense, these illnesses caused a condition described by one of Long's mental health experts as "sexual sadism." Because of Long's mental condition, the defense sought a life sentence in the penalty phase proceeding in this case. The jury was not persuaded and returned a unanimous verdict recommending the death sentence. The trial Judge agreed and sentenced Long to death for first degree murder.

Long now challenges his death sentence. To properly address the issues Long raises, it is necessary to set forth a chronology of events given the number of crimes and homicides for which he has been convicted. In addition to the murder in this case, Long confessed to seven other murders in Hillsborough County (See Long v. State, No. 74,017(Fla. Oct. 15,1992). He has also been convicted of sexual battery in several other cases in which the victims were not murdered.

"The events covered by the trials are repeated under *Evidence Presented in the Penalty Phase Proceeding.* Part of his confession is especially chilling."

Evidence of Long's November 16, 1984 confession, in which he gave the following account of Simms' murder, Long purchased some rope, cut it into sections, and put it in the glove compartment of his

car. He put a weapon in his car and drove along Kennedy Boulevard in Tampa looking for a prostitute. When he pulled up next to the victim, she asked if he wanted a date, and when he asked how much, she said, "Fifty dollars." He agreed, she entered the car, and they drove for a distance of half-mile to a mile. Long then pulled a knife, made the victim undress, reclined the passenger's seat into a prone position, and, at knife point, tied her up. Long further stated that he then drove fifteen to twenty miles to eastern Hillsborough County, where he raped the victim. Afterwards, he talked to her, intending to take her back to where he picked her up, and he told her he would do so. He stated that, instead, he drove her to the Plant City area and tried to strangle her. After the strangulation attempt failed to render the victim unconscious, he hit her on the head with a club and threw her out of the car. He then cut her throat and left her alongside the road. He stated that he also threw her clothes out of the car.

The State also presented, as aggravating factors, testimony regarding Long's convictions for two other crimes of violence in which victims survived. It is important to note that both of these convictions occurred before Long entered into his September 1985 plea agreement in the Hillsborough County murders. The dialogue of the plea agreement clearly established that any prior convictions not the result of the plea agreement would be admissible against Long on the penalty phase proceeding. The first crime of violence occurred in Pasco County on March 6, 1984, a little

more than two and one half months before the murder
in this case. The circumstances presented to the jury
reflected that Long saw a house with a "For Sale"
sign in front of it. Long was convicted of kidnapping,
robbery, and sexual battery for this crime on April 17,
1985.

The second conviction was also for kidnapping,
sexual battery, and robbery. This crime occurred on
May 29, 1984, approximately two and one-half days
after the murder at issue here. In this instance, the
victim stated that she received a telephone call con-
cerning a newspaper advertisement to sell furniture.
The man told her he was a salesman for IBM. Long
pleaded guilty to this offense on July 12, 1985. Two
months before his guilty plea in the Hillsborough
County murders...

"Wasn't holding a gun on a woman a serious crime?"
Lisa asked wearily. "It appears the State won't bring up
Susan's assault charge because Long's guilty charge had
been changed with an appeal through a Public Defender paid
for by the taxpayers."

"Look at all this testimony about Long's difficult childhood. The notations that he slept with his mother on and off
until he was twelve years old and disapproved of her occupation and dress. She was a waitress and barmaid and wore
hot pants, boots and sexy outfits. Is that a reason for murder?"
I asked frustratedly. We poured over the next few pages
together.

Two mental health professionals testified on
behalf of Long. The first was Dr. John Money, a pro-
fessor of medical psychology and pediatrics at Johns

Hopkins University School of Medicine. He testified that Long had the disease of "sexual sadism," a brain disorder that, according to Dr. Money, caused Long's criminal behavior. Dr. Money also diagnosed Long as having temporal lobe epilepsy. He indicated that this was a peculiar kind of epilepsy because it does not cause seizures; instead it causes one to enter an altered state of consciousness. Dr. Money stated that temporal lobe epilepsy often occurs with paraphilia of sexual sadism. He explained that an overlapping syndrome is a manic depressive disorder in which a person experiences alternating periods of extreme high or mania and melancholy or despair. It was his opinion that a head injury could be one hundred percent responsible for sexual sadism. Dr. Money also stated that the change in Long's sexual behavior from normal to hypersexual following his motorcycle accident and related head injuries were characteristic of sexual sadism and could result from damage to certain areas of the brain. He stated that Long's description of his feelings during the two rapes for which he had been convicted and during the murder at issue indicated that he was in an altered state of consciousness brought on by the temporal lobe epilepsy. Dr. Money explained that sexual sadists become sexually aroused by inflicting pain, but that such an individual is also capable of having sex in a normal fashion. Dr. Money expressed the view that, although Long knew what he was doing when he killed Simms, he had no control over his actions and that, in his opinion, Long lacked the capacity to appreciate the criminality of his conduct.

He also expressed the view that Long's ability to conform his conduct to the requirements of the law was substantially impaired when he killed Simms.

The second mental health expert who testified on Long's behalf was Dr. Robert Berland, a forensic psychologist. Dr. Berland interviewed Long on several occasions and subjected him to psychological testing. He determined that Long was above average in intelligence with an IQ of 118. He diagnosed Long as having four kinds of disorders, two of which were non-psychotic—paraphilia and antisocial personality disorder—and two of which were psychotic. The two psychotic disturbances consisted of an inherited bipolar or manic depressive psychosis and an organic personality syndrome caused by damage to brain tissue. He believed that the second psychosis may have been caused by Long's motorcycle accident or his chronic amphetamine abuse following the accident. He explained that, when brain damage is added to an inherited bipolar disorder, the psychosis is worsened. Dr. Berland, concluded that, in his opinion, the evidence suggested there was no substantial impairment of Long's ability to appreciate the criminality of his act in murdering the victim in this case, but he found that Long was substantially impaired in his ability to conform his behavior to the requirements of law because of his mental condition. In Dr. Berland's view, Long was under the influence of extreme mental or emotional disturbance when he killed the victim and Dr. Berland believed that Long killed her in a fit of rage.

The State, in rebuttal, presented the testimony of Dr. Daniel J. Sprehe. Dr. Sprehe had been appointed

*by the court to evaluate Long because his counsel filed
a notice of intent to rely on the insanity defense. Dr.
Sprehe was directed to determine Long's competency
to stand trial and competency at the time of the
offense. He based his conclusions on several face-to-
face interviews with Long in 1985, as well as a review
of relevant records, police reports, and Dr. Sprehe's
and Dr. Money's findings. Dr. Sprehe stated that Long
told him he had with him a rope, a piece of wood, and
a knife when he killed the victim, and that he would
not have killed her had a policeman been standing
there. He further stated that Long told him he killed
the victim to "eliminate a witness," and that Long was
not sure whether he hit her with a board to kill her or
so she would not suffer. Although Dr. Sprehe stated
that Long did suffer from a severe antisocial personality disorder, it was his opinion that Long did not suffer from a mental illness or disease. Additionally, Dr.
Sprehe believed that Long's capacity to appreciate the
criminality of his conduct or to conform his conduct to
the requirements of law was not substantially
impaired.*

"This appeal doesn't include the interview when Bobby
Joe Long told the reporter his first victim reminded him of
Susan. Eble and Long's frantic arguments in the courtroom
silenced the man, but I have the impression he based his
opinion on the jail letters," I said.

I read the next passage aloud. "Long claimed that the trial
court erred in: (1) denying Long's motion to withdraw guilty
pleas; (2) allowing the testimony of two detectives regarding
the details of two other rapes as crimes of violence in

aggravating; (3) allowing Dr. Sprehe's testimony during rebuttal because he was appointed to determine competence and sanity rather than determining aggravation and mitigation; (4) denying defense counsel's motion to exclude Dr. Sprehe's rebuttal testimony regarding Long's alleged statement that he killed the victim in this case to "eliminate a witness;" (5) permitting Dr. Sprehe to testify that Long knew right from wrong; (6) denying Long's motion to prohibit television cameras without an adequate hearing; (7) denying Long's motion to preclude mention during voir dire that the jury verdict was advisory, failing to give the jury instruction that the jury verdict is binding in some circumstances and denying Long's motion for a mistrial; (8) allowing the State to make closing arguments that were not based on the evidence in the case and by urging the jury to consider factors outside the scope of jury deliberations; (9) considering transcripts of expert witness testimony because the transcripts contained references to other murders committed by Long; (10) finding that the murder was committed in a cold, calculated, and premeditated manner without pretense of moral or legal justification; (11) failing to consider and find nonstatutory mitigating factors which were reasonably established and were not rebutted (sentencing Long to death because it is unconstitutional to execute the mentally ill); and (12) sentencing Long to death because the trial court found both mental mitigating factors and should have found nonstatutory mitigating factors, all of which outweigh the aggravating factors. We have examined each of these assertions and find that only four merit discussion."

"Long's claim that he was not told that his confession and pleas could be used against him in his Pasco County case as

Williams Rule evidence and as aggravation in the penalty phase if that case was retried was moot." I shook my head. "I'm frustrated beyond words."

"Ditto," Lisa said.

"Agreed, but to what avail?" Susan asked.

I began reading out loud. "In our decision in *Long v. State, No. 74,017 (Fla. Oct. 15, 1992), issued contemporaneously with this opinion, we reversed Long's Pasco County conviction, in part on the ground that his Hillsborough County pleas and confessions were improperly introduced into evidence in that case. Additionally, we held that, upon remand, Long's pleas and confessions could not be used against him in aggravation during a new penalty phase proceeding. We, therefore deny this claim."* My throat was dry.

I said hoarsely, "The rapes were admitted as evidence because they came before the plea agreement. Long's attorney stated the police reports were correct, and that the defendant was provided a fair opportunity to rebut any hearsay statements. Dr. Sprehe was first appointed to determine both Long's competency to stand trial under rule 3.2II and his sanity at the time of the offense. Dr. Sprehe's psychiatric examination of Long occurred only after Long had placed his sanity at issue and after his notice to counsel. Dr. Sprehe was to determine whether Long was sane at the time of the offense. He was allowed to testify in rebuttal to direct mental health testimony. Again, those precedent setting cases of a psychiatrist testifying about Long's sanity was at issue."

"The United States Supreme Court just ruled that if the request for an attorney isn't direct, there isn't any reason to stop questioning, but I'm sure there'll be a new ruling altogether in a few months from now," Susan said disgustedly.

"Remember how I was so angry watching Eble question Lisa and then complain about her emotionalism. I just learned he was trying to stick to the Supreme Court guidelines."

"Did you know, there are some errors in the Supreme Court appeals? One distorts Lisa's testimony," Susan said.

"Errors happen more often than they'd like to admit. Court reporters aren't perfect," I added.

"It says she testified that Bobby Joe Long had a pockmarked face. If he gets another appeal, could that statement be attributed to her?" Susan asked.

"Anything is possible unfortunately," I said frowning.

"I'm terrorized every time he gets an appeal. I'm afraid some jury will let him go. In Ocala, the jury voted seven to five for the death penalty. His odds are improving." Lisa took a deep quivering breath and let it out.

"Van Allen said, 'he won't get out!'" I tried to comfort her.

"Maybe not, but he's making one heck of an attempt, and I'm wondering if his opportunities will ever end. It may be a good system, but bad people are allowed to mess it up. Did he give the women he murdered even one chance to appeal their death sentences?"

"Not even one," I said looking from one of his victim/survivors to the other. "You two were just smart, lucky or a combination of both."

Chapter 31

A Calm Sea

Memorial Day weekend is the signal for all the Florida land-bound inhabitants to head for the beach. Since my office is on the beach, I headed in the other direction to stay with friends on the Gulf of Mexico. Returning home, I was surprised to hear Susan's voice on my answering machine. I called her. After we'd exchanged greetings, she said she had decided to pay me an impromptu visit along with Lisa.

"By the way Joy, did you know that Lisa has been dating a man, Zack, for quite a while now? I think it's pretty serious."

"She has mentioned him a few times, but I didn't know it was very serious."

"Well, I think it is. Anyway, we'll see you soon."

"I'm looking forward to seeing you both," I said and wondered if that was entirely true.

"We'll be there tomorrow."

They both arrived together. Lisa kissed me affectionately, the glow of love in her eyes.

Susan broke in, "My trip was a last minute decision. I'd

been thinking about you and Bobby Joe Long." She paused and laughed, "Well, not together."

"I'm glad," I replied.

"I keep thinking about how Long's lawyers are just now using the insanity plea so he can get away with murder," Lisa interjected.

"Imagine if all those expert witnesses who testified about his brain injury could realize the guy was so in control of his mind that he didn't try to kill you after he won the appeal? He would have been a suspect. He was too smart for that," I said.

"Ten years and he still scares me," Susan said shaking her head.

"How could experts read the 'Jail Snitch' letters and believe he was killing randomly? To me, the letters show he killed the others deliberately so he could do Susan in at some later time," I said.

"Zack and my family keep saying to forget I ever knew Long. But how can I forget he almost killed me?" Lisa asked.

Susan looked at her compassionately. "Why should you?"

"That's the conclusion I've come to also, especially when I think of the other victims who have no voices to speak."

"Bobby Joe Long told Corporal Baker that he killed Michelle Simms because she reminded him of Susan. He suspected that she had Indian blood."

"Because I have Indian blood he was figuratively killing me!" Susan paused and then said softly, "Lisa even looks like me."

I nodded slowly, concentrating on Lisa. "She does have long dark hair and brown eyes. I recognized the resemblance that day we went to the beach. His first victim had long dark hair also."

"To the bargain Bobby Joe Long used the courts to get even with me. I'm still angry about the way I was misunderstood by people I thought were friends."

"The media didn't help making out that all Long's victims

were dancers and tramps. I know why you were mortified." Lisa bit her lip pensively.

"Yes, for a while, like you I thought I should let it all fade away, and at least my daughter wouldn't hear what happened to me. But I am completely convinced that that won't happen."

"What changed your mind?" I asked.

"The letters and realizing that the appeals could go on and on. I thought I didn't want my daughter to hear about all this, but I've decided that more importantly, I don't want her to be afraid of speaking out if something horrible for which she is blameless happens in her future life. I want other people to know the truth, too. Not some imagined stuff. You know, like those poor women who were raped and killed? All those stories about prostitutes. Who knows what future jerk won't write that Long should get out since he only raped and killed prostitutes? I'd be furious. Not only for myself but for them. They were girls. They were women. Whatever their state in life, they were human beings."

She looked thoughtfully at me. "We've decided you must write our stories for all of us—we who are the survivors and those victims who can no longer speak of Bobby Joe Long's terror."

"Yes," I said, "I promise I will if you'll both help me."

They both nodded. "And we three will never stop fighting to make sure that he's never freed." Lisa said fervently.

Susan added, "It's a promise we'll all keep no matter what."

"I hope this time he gets the chair, but he's probably got more appeals. After his last death sentence he crowed he'd win on the next appeal."

"Maybe he will, but I'll be there!" Susan said definitively, slapping her hand on the table for emphasis.

"I will too," Lisa said and covered Susan's hand with her own.

"And I'll be there with you both," I promised, placing my hand on top of theirs.

Chapter 32

The Ungilded Truth

Six or seven weeks passed. I was busy putting our thoughts onto paper and kept in constant touch with my two fellow survivors. One sunny afternoon, I returned from the library to hear the lilt of happiness in Lisa's voice on my answering machine,

"Joy, please, please call me! I have great news. I love you."

I dialed immediately, wondering what had happened.

"I have to see you. What about five o'clock tomorrow?" she asked, maintaining her mysterious attitude. "And ask Susan to join us."

When I called Susan, she readily agreed, her curiosity tapped. "I'll be there. By the way, Joy, you must have some of our story written by now."

"I do," I said quietly.

"Well then with whatever Lisa has to tell, it will be a double celebration."

"I hope so," I said flatly. I was worried about how both

Susan and Lisa would feel reading about the traumas they'd
endured.

"What do you mean you hope so?"

"Well, your stories aren't pleasant. They're raw and
horrific."

"But unfortunately true."

"Yes, it's all true," I said heavily.

The next day, Susan came to my office a few minutes
early and sat silently, smoking the first cigarette I'd ever seen
her with. Lisa appeared at the appointed hour, radiant with
happiness.

"I'd like to introduce you both to my fiancé, Zack."

Zack offered his hand first to me and then to Susan. He
appeared to be a little older than Lisa and possibly a bit taller.
There was a calm, kindness about him as he looked into my
eyes when he wasn't admiring Lisa. Seeing them in love,
Susan and I smiled at each other and wished them much happiness.

Afterwards the room became pin-drop quiet. Susan
broke the silence.

"Well, so where are the chapters you told me about? I'd
like to take them home so I'll have time to read them and
reflect on them," Susan said.

"I have only fifty pages or so done. I don't want either
of you to read them alone or even with Zack, Lisa. Humor
me both of you, and read the first twenty pages right here."

I gave them each copies of the chapters and waited, feeling
more apprehensive as the minutes ticked by. Susan's body
began to twitch and tremble visibly. Tears ran down Lisa's
cheeks. Zack looked sadly at her and clasped her hand. Lisa
stopped reading and closed her eyes. "It's so terribly real, Joy."

"Hard to take," Susan murmured. She did not look at me, but stared at some invisible spot on the wall.

"My God, I just talked to my mother to tell her I've forgiven her," Lisa said.

"I'm glad you did. Remember, she was an abused child like you."

"I love my grandmother, too."

"If it makes you feel any better, she didn't realize how terrible it was for you to be with Marce. Some people believe young girls are Lolitas."

"I wish I'd had a normal childhood. I want to be like everyone else."

"Those experiences made you who you are, Lisa."

"I suppose that's true. Joy, I've accepted that my daughter will learn of my horrible encounter with Bobby Joe Long, but I'm worried about her learning about her grandmother and great grandmother," Lisa said.

"Lisa, it's for all the daughters in the world that we need to change the public's attitudes about rape. You were raped by Marce, and it was allowed by your grandmother. She looked away. You were raped by a mass murderer. The media and courts exploited and didn't protect you. But Lisa, I believe your ability to cope so much better than some other victims do occurred because you never thought you were responsible for what happened to you."

"I still believe that, but now I want to get married and put the past behind me. How do you feel Susan?"

"I want the story told, but I'm also concerned about how my family feels. Maybe I shouldn't use my real name."

"Susan, that would be a retreat. I know you both are apprehensive but after reading our book, no one will ever

mistake Bobby Joe Long's torture for romance. No one will believe the media's sympathetic portrait of him. We have to tell your stories and mine to the world! To get rid of the myths."

"Sometimes I think it's just too terrible for anyone to read," Lisa said.

"Do you ever watch programs on television or movies where people are shot with guns or blown up? Isn't that horrible and gross?" I asked.

"Yes, but that's different," Lisa replied.

"You mean people only get holes blown in them or their limbs torn off in explosions. They might feel terror, but it's okay because there's no sex?"

"We're used to that kind of thing. It's make believe — not shocking like reality," Zack said. "And if we don't want to watch, we don't."

"But this touches us so closely, we can't turn away," Susan said quietly.

"It's okay to use guns and knives, but if a penis is the weapon everything should be hidden, especially the victims," I said.

"You're tough, Joy. We'll need to take this home and try to digest it," Lisa said, putting the papers under her arm. She hugged her fiancé, and guided him toward the door.

"It's all the anger and pain I feel, but can't express," Susan said before she also left.

After they had gone, I searched my own motives wondering if I'd been completely honest about my reasons for persevering with the book. I had thought in the beginning I was doing all this work, not only for myself, but for Lisa and Susan. To explain how much their lives had been affected by

Bobby Joe Long. But was it my own pain and anger I wanted to express? Was I out of step, and women should keep silent about rape when it happened to them?

As if in answer, a few days later I won my quiet battle with the rape center. I learned the director had been transferred, and I was asked to be a counselor again. It was a small victory, but not policy making as I hoped our book would be. Still, I felt it was a sign.

Before even a week passed, Lisa called. "Joy, I'm sorry about my first reaction. Everything you write is so real. I lived the parts about my family, but it seems even worse seeing it written down. That stuff about Marce. It happened, but I hate to read it. And God! Seeing my grandmother so weak. The horror is, it was even more terrible."

"What have you decided?" I heard a sharp intake of breath.

"It's my life in those pages and it's horrible." She still sounded a bit ambivalent.

"It was horrible."

"You could soften it. It doesn't have to seem so raw and disgusting. You could change the words."

"You mean like some people like to say they 'sleep with someone.' It means they had sex. I think that's funny, because anyone who sleeps through sex has to be unconscious."

"You know that isn't what I mean. I hate the obscene parts."

"I think it's obscene that Bobby Joe Long believed you and his other victims enjoyed being tortured! You're alive because he had those misconceptions. We agreed we had to tell the real story so people won't romanticize criminals and blame victims."

"I think that's why I'm uncomfortable. Men and women judge victims and think they're responsible. My own twin didn't believe me. We are beginning to be friends, but we never talk about it."

"Thank God Susan, you and I never bought the myth we were responsible. The victims who do never recover."

"How does Susan feel?"

"She feels it hurts, but has decided it has to be said."

Her voice was firm now. "I've decided that too."

"I'm glad. I believe that I've conveyed, first, the horror of your experience and then your strength. Think of all the women who spiral downward after crimes such as you've endured have been committed against them. Neither you nor Susan has done that. You've fought back."

"And so have you."

I smiled. "Yes, at first I hid, but now I feel good about how far I've come, how far we've come. And think about Bobby Joe Long's reaction when he reads this."

"He thought he was shrewd, sly and powerful. Men could either be his enemies or friends, but the women he'd raped and killed were just objects to be used and tossed out as if they were trash. I wonder what he'll say when he finds out the ones who really brought him down and intend to see him get justice are three of the women he underestimated. You, Susan and me," Lisa said.

She paused for a moment, then added in an emotional voice, "I'm ready to let the truth be known."

Epilogue

Lofty Supreme Court Justices sit in their cool, remote chambers and set aside death sentences for condemned prisoners on death row based on technicalities. Their decisions are like lightning bolts cast down from on high which strike survivors and their families. Survivors of heinous crimes are the smoldering embers whose agony is ignited each time the appeals system gives a killer another chance. If I had never been a victim, I might never have been scorched; I might wear a blindfold like the lady who is our symbol of justice. She cannot see it, but her scales are no longer level. They tip in the direction of killers like Bobby Joe Long.

Long has been sitting on Death Row at Union Correctional Institution for thirteen years. His most recent death sentence was ruled by Judge Charles W. Cope on March 18, 1994. The automatic appeal against the death sentence filed by Assistant Public Defender William Eble has wound its way through the intricacies of the Florida court system. Another Public Defender, A. Anne Owens, prepared

Long's latest appeal for the Florida Supreme Court in April 1996, and oral arguments were heard in November 1996.

On March 6, 1997, the seven justices from on high dropped their pronouncement to the population below. The Florida Supreme Court directed Judge Cope to acquit Bobby Joe Long for the murder of Virginia Johnson almost three years to the day since Susan Replogle and I witnessed Judge Cope presenting Long his third death sentence for Virginia Johnson's murder. Mr. Long can't be tried again for her murder.

Bobby Joe Long has told his friends he wants to be the most expensive man on death row. The average cost to carry out a death sentence is three million dollars. So far, Long is ahead of most of his competition, even Ted Bundy. He brags about having played tennis in prison with Bundy. He has now served thirteen years of his twenty-five-years-to-life sentences (running concurrently) for murdering eight women. A sentence he plea bargained.

Assistant State Attorney G. Phillip Van Allen remains in that position. He has spent more than 1,275 hours in court prosecuting Bobby Joe Long for the murder of Virginia Johnson of Pasco County. If the Florida Supreme Court finds for the defendant and orders yet another trial, these numbers will rise. At this point, figuring $5,000 an hour, the trials for the murder of Virginia Johnson amount to over six million dollars. Not counted in that sum are Long's other public expenses: two trials for the murder of Michelle Denise Simms, a rape trial, innumerable police hours and the cost of public defenders. It has been learned that his crimes go back even further than the 1970s. It takes two shopping carts piled three feet high to hold the transcripts. William Eble asked

for a mistrial when a picture of the stockpile of transcripts was caught by a television camera.

Eble, Long's appointed attorney in his third murder trial for the death of Virginia Johnson, and Laura Chane, his assistant at that trial, have gone into private practice together.

Prosecutor Michael Benito is in private practice in Tampa, Florida.

Ellis Rubin remains in private practice in Miami and continues to defend high profile cases.

Major Polly Goethe Horn's professional life has changed more than any of the police officers involved in Bobby Joe Long's capture. She has been promoted from Detective to Major, which elevates her to equality with the head of the Sheriff's Task Force, Major Gary Terry, who was a captain thirteen years ago.

Larry Pinkerton is now a Lieutenant in the Tampa Police Department and remains a faithful supporter and friend of Lisa's.

Corporal Lee D. "Pops" Baker is close to retirement.

Distance has divided Lisa, Susan and me from the beginning. With Susan in Ocala, Lisa in Tampa and me in Indian Shores, I have had to be the mortar, the glue that has connected us. Though the three of us have diverse lifestyles, were born in three different decades and have varied interests, the intensity of our shared experiences has bound us together. Our joint desire is to make public the truth about Bobby Joe Long's serial rapes and murders. We want to tell the truth about the bloody trail he left and to help other victims see themselves as courageous survivors. Beyond our mission, the three of us have sought to rebuild our own lives.

Lisa McVey is a busy working mother, planning a future

career as an accountant. She still works with children at the Hillsborough Parks Department and is especially alert to signs of child abuse.

Although Lisa has made peace with her childhood traumas, her ordeal at the hands of Bobby Joe Long continues to haunt her. In January 1997, Lisa's grandmother died, and the family has drawn together. Through her renewed religious faith, she is carrying her message of hope to other survivors.

Susan Replogle has moved closer to self-actualization and has become a successful interior designer. She takes college courses at night. Because she still believes in this country's ability to correct the system, she has become a proactive lobbyist for sex crime victims.

I head a growing advertising firm, which handles public relations and publicity for business firms and individuals. I am an active speaker on the subject of rape survivors. However, as is the case with many other perpetrators of rape, my assailant has never been apprehended. Presently, I am at work on another true story tentatively entitled, *Huntington Women in Support of Our Men in Vietnam.* The Huntington Women's Group was responsible for the first memorial to servicemen killed in Vietnam.

According to the Florida Bureau Of Law Enforcement, Florida state statistics for murder for the past ten years have dropped slightly. However, forcible rape has gone up. Total rape statistics, including sodomy and forcible fondling, have quadrupled the numbers. These figures have an even greater impact when it is realized that half represent juvenile victims. If all convicted rapist/murderers receive the time, money and attention that Bobby Joe Long has for thirteen years, the effect on public funds would be awesome to contemplate.